CYBERSECURITY TECHNOLOGIES

Kruger Brentt

Publishers

CYBERSECURITY TECHNOLOGIES

Jessica Wendorf
Andra Siibak

Kruger Brentt
Publishers

2025

Kruger Brentt Publishers UK. LTD.
Company Number 9728962

Regd. Office: 68 St Margarets Road, Edgware, Middlesex HA8 9UU

© 2025 AUTHORS

ISBN: 978-1-78715-302-8

For information on all our publications visit our website at http://krugerbrentt.com/

PREFACE

"Cybersecurity Technologies" is a comprehensive exploration into the dynamic and evolving landscape of cybersecurity, offering insights into the technologies, strategies, and best practices essential for protecting digital assets in an increasingly interconnected world. This book serves as an indispensable resource for cybersecurity professionals, IT practitioners, policymakers, and anyone interested in safeguarding digital information and systems.

In today's digital age, cybersecurity has become a critical priority for organizations and individuals alike, as cyber threats continue to grow in scale, sophistication, and impact. From data breaches and ransomware attacks to phishing scams and identity theft, the threats to digital security are diverse and constantly evolving, requiring proactive measures to detect, prevent, and mitigate cyber risks.

As editors of this volume, we have endeavored to compile a diverse array of perspectives, methodologies, and case studies from leading experts and practitioners in the field of cybersecurity. Through a blend of theoretical insights, practical advice, and real-world examples, this book covers a wide range of topics, including network security, cryptography, threat intelligence, incident response, and emerging technologies such as artificial intelligence and blockchain.

Our overarching goal in presenting this book is to empower readers with the knowledge, tools, and strategies needed to navigate the complex and ever-changing landscape of cybersecurity. By providing practical guidance, actionable insights, and best practices from industry experts, we aim to help organizations and individuals strengthen their cyber defenses, mitigate risks, and safeguard their digital assets against cyber threats.

We extend our sincere gratitude to all the contributors who have generously shared their expertise, experiences, and insights in the field of cybersecurity. It is our hope that this book will serve as a valuable reference and guide for cybersecurity professionals, IT practitioners, educators, policymakers, and students, as they work together to protect the integrity, confidentiality, and availability of digital information and systems.

Jessica Wendorf
Andra Siibak

CONTENTS

CHAPTER-1

INTRODUCTION TO CYBERSECURITY

Cybersecurity encompasses the utilization of technologies, procedures, and safeguards to safeguard systems, networks, software, devices, and data against cyber assaults. Its primary objective is to mitigate the risk of cyber attacks and prevent unauthorized exploitation of systems, networks, and technologies.

In order to protect their sensitive information, maintain employee productivity, and instill confidence in their products and services, businesses typically employ cybersecurity professionals. The field of cybersecurity revolves around the industry standard of confidentiality, integrity, and availability (CIA).

Confidentiality ensures that data can only be accessed by authorized individuals, integrity ensures that information can only be added, altered, or removed by authorized users, and availability ensures that systems, functions, and data are readily accessible according to agreed-upon parameters. Authentication mechanisms play a crucial role in cybersecurity, with a user name identifying the account a user wishes to access and a password serving as a means to verify the user's identity.

EVOLUTION OF CYBER SECURITY

Early Days of Cybersecurity

The early stages of cyber security can be traced back to the initial days of computing. During the 1960s and 1970s, the primary focus of computer security revolved around physical measures, such as securing computer rooms and controlling access to them. However, as computers became more prevalent and powerful, the emphasis shifted towards safeguarding data from unauthorized access and hacking attempts.

The 1980s and 1990s

In the 1980s and 1990s, the emergence of computer viruses and worms caused substantial harm to computer systems. Notably, the Morris Worm inflicted an estimated $100,000 in damages and infected over 6000 computers. Consequently, this led to the development of antivirus software and the implementation of network security measures like firewalls and intrusion detection systems.

The 2000s

During the 2000s, cyber attacks became more sophisticated and targeted. This necessitated the creation of advanced security measures, including encryption, multi-factor authentication, and virtual private networks (VPNs). The advent of cloud computing and mobile devices introduced new security challenges, prompting the development of solutions like mobile device management (MDM) and cloud access security brokers (CASBs).

The Present Day

In the present day, cybersecurity has become more crucial than ever due to the increasing frequency and sophistication of cyber-attacks. The integration of artificial intelligence and machine learning has resulted in the creation of real-time security solutions capable of detecting and responding to cyber threats. Additionally, the proliferation of the Internet of Things (IoT) has introduced new security complexities as more devices connect to the internet.

Future Outlook

Looking ahead, cybersecurity is expected to continuously evolve and adapt to confront new threats and challenges. As artificial intelligence and machine learning advance further, they will assume a more significant role in detecting and countering cyber threats. Furthermore, the anticipated impact of quantum computing on cybersecurity is expected to be substantial.

IMPORTANCE OF CYBER SECURITY

In today's digital age, our reliance on the internet, computers, and electronic devices has become all-encompassing. Various sectors, including banking, healthcare, finance, government, and manufacturing, heavily rely on internet-connected devices and software applications to carry out their operations.

However, the information stored within these systems, such as intellectual property, financial data, and personal information, can be vulnerable to unauthorized access or exposure, leading to severe consequences. Intruders and threat actors can exploit this information for financial gain, extortion, political or social motives, or even engage in acts of vandalism.

The rise of cyber-attacks has become a global concern, as these attacks can compromise systems and pose a significant threat to the global economy. Therefore, it is crucial to establish a robust cybersecurity strategy to safeguard sensitive information and prevent high-profile security breaches.

With the increasing frequency of cyber-attacks, companies and organizations, particularly those dealing with national security, health, or financial records, must implement stringent cybersecurity measures and processes to protect their valuable business and personal data.

OVERVIEW OF CYBER SECURITY TECHNOLOGIES

Below, we describe some of the most popular cybersecurity technologies in the field. We cover how they work and their applications in cybersecurity.

Behavioral Analytics user-add icon

Behavioral analytics looks at data to understand how people behave on websites, mobile applications, systems, and networks. Cybersecurity professionals can use behavioral analytics platforms to find potential threats and vulnerabilities.

Analyzing patterns of behavior can lead to identifying unusual events and actions that may indicate cybersecurity threats.

For example, behavioral analytics may find that unusually large amounts of data are coming from one device. This may mean a cyberattack is looming or actively happening. Other indicators of malicious activity include odd timing of events and actions that happen in an unusual sequence.

Benefits of using behavioral analytics include early detection of potential attacks and the ability to predict future attacks. Organizations can automate detection and response using behavioral analytics.

Blockchain cube icon

Blockchain is a type of database that securely stores data in blocks. It connects the blocks through cryptography. Blockchain allows information to be collected, but not edited or deleted.

Cybersecurity professionals can use blockchain to secure systems or devices, create standard security protocols, and make it almost impossible for hackers to penetrate databases.

Benefits of blockchain include better user privacy, reduction of human error, greater transparency, and cost savings by removing the need for third-party verification.

Blockchain also eliminates the security problem of storing data in one place. Instead, data gets stored across networks, resulting in a decentralized system that is less vulnerable to hackers.

Challenges of using blockchain include the cost and inefficiency of the technology.

Cloud Encryption cloud icon

Cloud services improve efficiency, help organizations offer improved remote services, and save money. However, storing data remotely in the cloud can increase data vulnerabilities. Cloud encryption technology changes data from understandable information into an unreadable code before it goes into the cloud.

Cybersecurity professionals use a mathematical algorithm to complete cloud encryption. Only authorized users with an encryption key can unlock the code, making data readable again. This restricted access minimizes the chance of data breaches by unauthorized attackers.

Experts agree that cloud encryption is an excellent cybersecurity technology for securing data. Cloud encryption can prevent unauthorized users from gaining access to usable data. Cloud encryption can also foster customer trust in cloud services and make it easier for companies to comply with government regulations.

Context-Aware Security clock icon

Context-aware security is a type of cybersecurity technology that helps businesses make better security decisions in real time.

Traditional cybersecurity technologies assess whether or not to allow someone access to a system or data by asking yes/no questions. This simple process can cause some legitimate users to be denied, slowing productivity.

Context-aware security reduces the chance of denying entry to an authorized user. Instead of relying on answers to static yes/no questions, context-aware security uses various supportive information like time, location, and URL reputation to assess whether a user is legitimate or not.

Context-aware security streamlines data-accessing processes and makes it easier for legitimate users to do their work. However, end-user privacy concerns pose a challenge.

Defensive Artificial Intelligence (AI) shield-check icon

Cybersecurity professionals can use defensive artificial intelligence (AI) to detect or stop cyberattacks. Savvy cybercriminals use technologies like offensive AI and adversarial machine learning because they are more difficult for traditional cybersecurity tools to detect.

Offensive AI includes deep fakes, false images, personas, and videos that convincingly depict people or things that never happened or do not exist. Malicious actors can use adversarial machine learning to trick machines into malfunctioning by giving them incorrect data.

Cybersecurity professionals can use defensive AI to detect and stop offensive AI from measuring, testing, and learning how the system or network functions.

Defensive AI can strengthen algorithms, making them more difficult to break. Cybersecurity researchers can conduct harsher vulnerability tests on machine learning models.

Extended Detection and Response (XDR) arrows-expand icon

Extended detection and response (XDR) is a type of advanced cybersecurity technology that detects and responds to security threats and incidents. XDR responds across endpoints, the cloud, and networks. It evolved from the simpler traditional endpoint detection and response.

XDR provides a more holistic picture, making connections between data in different places. This technology allows cybersecurity professionals to detect and analyze threats from a higher, automated level. This can help prevent or minimize current and future data breaches across an organization's entire ecosystem of assets.

Cybersecurity professionals can use XDR to respond to and detect targeted attacks, automatically confirm and correlate alerts, and create comprehensive analytics. Benefits of XDR include automation of repetitive tasks, strong automated detection, and reducing the number of incidents that need investigation.

Manufacturer Usage Description (MUD) clipboard-list icon

Manufacturer usage description (MUD) is a standard created by the Internet Engineering Task Force to strengthen security for IoT devices in small business and home networks.

IoT devices are vulnerable to network-based attacks. These attacks can lead to loss of private data or cause a machine to stop working properly. IoT devices need to be secure without costing too much or being too complicated.

Benefits of using MUD include simply, affordable improved security for IoT devices. Cybersecurity professionals can use MUD to make devices more secure against distributed denial of service attacks. MUD can help reduce the amount of damage and data loss in the event of a successful attack.

Zero Trust exclamation icon

Traditional network security followed the motto "trust but verify," assuming that users within an organization's network perimeter were not malicious threats.

Zero Trust, on the other hand, aligns itself with the motto, "never trust, always verify."

A framework for approaching network security, Zero Trust makes all users authenticate themselves before they get access to an organization's data or applications.

Zero Trust does not assume that users inside the network are more trustworthy than anyone else. This stricter scrutiny on all users can result in greater overall information security for the organization.

Cybersecurity professionals can use Zero Trust to deal more safely with remote workers and challenges like ransomware threats. A Zero Trust framework may combine various tools, including multi-factor authentication, data encryption, and endpoint security.

Regulation adjustments icon

As the frequency of cyberattacks continues to grow significantly each year, governments are beginning to use and promote best practice regulations. In the past, the governments did not often get involved in cybersecurity issues.

Potential regulatory changes include executive orders regarding cybersecurity standards for government suppliers, penalties for companies that do not engage in best practices, increased demand for cyberinsurance, and ransomware disclosure laws. Greater regulation will likely lead to improved security standards.

CHAPTER-2

FUNDAMENTALS OF CYBERSECURITY

Cybersecurity encompasses the technology and procedures implemented to safeguard networks and devices against attacks, harm, or unauthorized entry. It holds utmost significance for various entities such as a nation's military, hospitals, large corporations, small businesses, and individuals, as data has become the foundation of any organization. If this data is exploited, numerous risks arise. Now that we have comprehended the essence of cybersecurity, let us delve into the CIA triad and its correlation with cyber security.

Device Protection

With the rise in cyber threats, individuals and companies should prioritize device protection. It is crucial to protect devices that connect to the internet using anti-virus software, enables the lock-and-erase options, activate two-factor authentication, and perform a regular automatic update of the system software, whether they are laptops, PCs, mobile phones, AI-based devices (Alexa, smart watches, etc.), iPads, tables, or any device that connects to the internet. Device protection will significantly reduce the risk of attacks on individuals and their devices regardless of their location.

Securing Online Connection

Once an individual device is connected online, information transmitted over the Internet requires more defenses. Furthermore, one should use VPNs: Virtual Private Networks as they automatically encrypt internet traffic. By using a VPN, all online transactions are secured, including the user's identity, location, browsing details, and any sensitive information such as passwords and bank details.

Securing Email Communication

Cybercriminals often use email to gather sensitive information about individuals or companies. It is highly recommended to encrypt emails to prevent sensitive data from being accessed by anyone other than the intended recipient since they mask the original information. In addition, email encryption often includes one-time password authentication.

Protecting and Performing Timely Backups of Files and Documents

Backups fall into two categories: Remote backups (offline) and cloud storage (online). Solutions differ in their advantages and disadvantages.

Remote backup services are convenient and inexpensive, but it is not easily accessible from anywhere. Alternatively, cloud solutions can be accessed from anywhere and are suitable for an organization that operates from different locations.

However, one must ensure that critical documents should have their own digital vault with encryption codes, as anything connected to the internet has a cyber threat risk.

Cyber threats can, however, affect anything connected to the internet. With a database and infrastructure security management system, the cloud computing solution is highly secure, with strong network security, application security, and cloud security. Additionally, strong mobile security enhances cloud computing security.

By implementing a BCDR plan, an organization can recover quickly from unforeseen cloud security situations such as natural disasters, power outages, team member negligence, hardware failure, and cyberattacks, allowing routine operations to resume in less time. Moreover, identity management frameworks provide endpoint security and data security at the highest level.

KEY CONCEPTS CONFIDENTIALITY INTEGRITY AND AVAILABILITY

The CIA Triad of confidentiality, integrity and availability is considered the core underpinning of information security. Every security control and every security vulnerability can be viewed in light of one or more of these key concepts. For a security program to be considered comprehensive and complete, it must adequately address the entire CIA Triad.

Confidentiality means that data, objects and resources are protected from unauthorized viewing and other access. Integrity means that data is protected from unauthorized changes to ensure that it is reliable and correct. Availability means that authorized users have access to the systems and the resources they need.

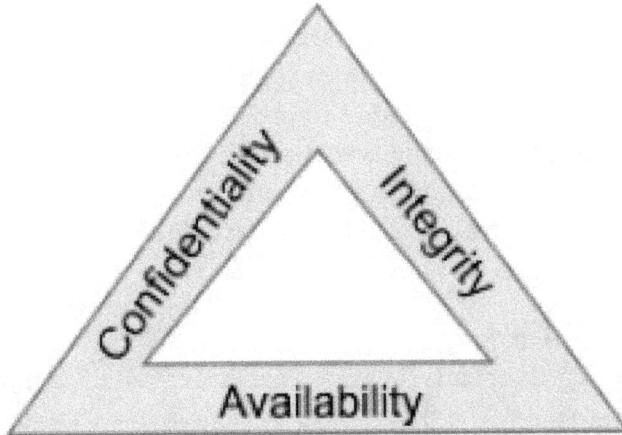

If you are preparing for the CISSP, Security+, CySA+, or another security certification exam, you will need to have an understanding of the importance of the CIA Triad, the definitions of each of the three elements, and how security controls address the elements to protect information systems.

Confidentiality

Confidentiality measures protect information from unauthorized access and misuse. Most information systems house information that has some degree of sensitivity. It might be proprietary business information that competitors could use to their advantage, or personal information regarding an organization's employees, customers or clients.

Confidential information often has value and systems are therefore under frequent attack as criminals hunt for vulnerabilities to exploit. Threat vectors include direct attacks such as stealing passwords and capturing network traffic, and more layered attacks such as social engineering and phishing. Not all confidentiality breaches are intentional. A few types of common accidental breaches include emailing sensitive information to the wrong recipient, publishing private data to public web servers, and leaving confidential information displayed on an unattended computer monitor.

Healthcare is an example of an industry where the obligation to protect client information is very high. Not only do patients expect and demand that healthcare providers protect their privacy, there are strict regulations governing how healthcare organizations manage security. The Health Insurance Portability and Accountability Act (HIPAA) addresses security, including privacy protection, in the the handling of personal health information by insurers, providers and claims processors. HIPAA rules mandate administrative, physical and technical safeguards, and require organizations to conduct risk analysis.

There are many countermeasures that organizations put in place to ensure confidentiality. Passwords, access control lists and authentication procedures use software to control access to resources. These access control methods are complemented by the use encryption to protect information that can be accessed despite the controls, such as emails that are in transit. Additional confidentiality countermeasures include administrative solutions such as policies and training, as well as physical controls that prevent people from accessing facilities and equipment.

Integrity

Upholding integrity means that measures are taken to ensure that data is kept accurate and up to date. The integrity of your data impacts how trustworthy and conscientious your organisation is. One of the eight Data Protection Principles (which are the foundations of the Data Protection Act 2018) is that data should be 'kept accurate and up to date'. Users must make sure that they comply with their legal duties and fulfil this requirement. It can be useful to assign individuals specific roles and responsibilities regarding data integrity. This way employees cannot shelve the responsibility and expect someone else to pick up the slack.

Availability

In order for an information system to be useful it must be available to authorized users. Availability measures protect timely and uninterrupted access to the system. Some of the most fundamental threats to availability are non-malicious in nature and include hardware failures, unscheduled software downtime and network bandwidth issues. Malicious attacks include various forms of sabotage intended to cause harm to an organization by denying users access to the information system.

The availability and responsiveness of a website is a high priority for many business. Disruption of website availability for even a short time can lead to loss of revenue, customer dissatisfaction and reputation damage. The Denial of Service (DoS) attack is a method frequently used by hackers to disrupt web service. In a DoS attack, hackers flood a server with superfluous requests, overwhelming the server and degrading service for legitimate users. Over the years, service providers have developed sophisticated countermeasures for detecting and protecting against DoS attacks, but hackers also continue to gain in sophistication and such attacks remain an ongoing concern.

Availability countermeasures to protect system availability are as far ranging as the threats to availability. Systems that have a high requirement for continuous uptime should have significant hardware redundancy with backup servers and data storage immediately available. For large, enterprise systems it is common to have redundant systems in separate physical locations. Software tools should be in place to monitor system performance and network traffic. Countermeasures to protect against DoS attacks include firewalls and routers.

Understanding the CIA Triad is an important component of your preparation for a variety of security certification programs. If you're interested in earning your next security certification, sign up for the free CertMike study groups for the CISSP, Security+, SSCP, or CySA+ exam.

VULNERABILITIES, THREATS, AND RISKS ASSESSMENT

These three fundamental cybersecurity concepts are related but have distinct meanings. Security experts define these three concepts in a variety of ways, and the terms threat and risk are sometimes used interchangeably. This article's definitions come from paraphrasing Computer Security: Principles and Practice by William Stallings and Lawrie Brown. Each term can be thought of in reference to an asset or "something that needs to be protected."

- ⊙ A vulnerability is a flaw or weakness in an asset's design, implementation, or operation and management that could be exploited by a threat.

- ⊙ A threat is a potential for a threat agent to exploit a vulnerability.

- ⊙ A risk is the potential for loss when the threat happens.

Identifying vulnerabilities is similar to addressing the query, "In what ways could harm be caused?" Occasionally, a vulnerability may arise solely from the implementation or deployment of an asset. For instance, leaving your car unlocked in a public parking lot is a vulnerability. Although leaving the doors unlocked does not guarantee harm will happen, it provides an opportunity for someone to access your car. Our office actively seeks out vulnerabilities in WashU systems to detect them before malicious individuals can take advantage of them.

A vulnerability is a weakness or flaw in an operating system, network, or application. A threat actor tries to exploit vulnerabilities to gain unauthorized access to data or systems. Security vulnerabilities can arise for many reasons, including misconfigurations, design flaws, or outdated software versions.

Common vulnerabilities include software vulnerabilities (that is, bad code), easily guessable passwords, unpatched systems, lack of encryption, insecure network configurations, and human error such as falling for phishing scams or sharing sensitive information unintentionally.

Threats

A threat refers to any potential danger or harmful event that can exploit a vulnerability and cause harm to a system, organization, or individual.

Threats can be intentional or unintentional in nature. Intentional threats are deliberate actions or attacks carried out by threat actors with malicious intent.

These can include cyberattacks, such as malware infections, malicious code or SQL injection attacks, ransomware, phishing attempts, and distributed denial-of-service (DDoS) attacks.

On the other hand, unintentional threats originate from human error or accidental actions that can lead to security breaches. These threats include accidental disclosure of sensitive information or falling victim to social engineering tactics.

Risk Assessment

Risk is the likelihood of a threat exploiting a vulnerability and causing harm. It represents the potential loss or damage associated with a specific threat.

Cyber risk encompasses the potential financial, operational, legal, or reputational consequences of a successful cyberattack or data breach. Risks can vary depending on the specific threat landscape, the value of the assets at risk, and the effectiveness of existing security controls.

Organizations employ risk management processes and methodologies to identify, evaluate, and prioritize security risks. Risk assessment is the systematic identification of potential cybersecurity threats, vulnerabilities and their associated impacts; and risk assessment is one of the most important parts of risk management. Risk assessment helps organizations to understand their security posture, prioritize resources, and make informed decisions regarding risk mitigation.

CYBERSECURITY FRAMEWORKS AND STANDARDS

A cybersecurity framework is a system of standards, guidelines, and best practices to manage risks that arise in the digital world. These frameworks typically match security objectives with controls. For instance, avoiding unauthorized system access by requiring a username and password.

Think of it this way: in the physical world, a framework is a beam system that holds up a building. In the ideal world, a framework is a structure that supportsa system or concept. It's a way of organizing information and, related tasks.

Cybersecurity frameworks take the framework approach to the work of securing digital assets. The framework is designed to give security managers a reliable, systematic way to mitigate cyber risk no matter how complex the environment might be.

Cybersecurity frameworks are often mandatory (or at least strongly encouraged) for companies that want to comply with state, industry, and international cybersecurity regulations. For example, to handle credit card transactions, a business must pass an audit attesting to its compliance with the Payment Card

Industry Data Security Standards (PCI DSS) framework. Cyber security frameworks are sets of documents describing guidelines, standards, and best practices designed for cyber security risk management. The frameworks exist to reduce an organization's exposure to weaknesses and vulnerabilities that hackers and other cyber criminals may exploit.

The word "framework" makes it sound like the term refers to hardware, but that's not the case. It doesn't help that the word "mainframe" exists, and its existence may imply that we're dealing with a tangible infrastructure of servers, data storage, etc.

But much like a framework in the "real world" consists of a structure that supports a building or other large object, the cyber security framework provides foundation, structure, and support to an organization's security methodologies and efforts.

Information security is a dynamic field that encompasses a wide range of technologies, frameworks, and best practices. Appropriate security frameworks and solutions will vary significantly across organizations depending on the industry, scale, and scope of the organization's operations. Here are some of the most widely used cybersecurity frameworks:

NIST

The National Institute of Standards and Technology (NIST) is a governmental agency responsible for advancing technology and security standards within the United States. NIST's Cybersecurity Framework provides guidelines for organizations to identify, protect, detect, respond to, and recover from cyber attacks. The framework was created in 2014 as guidance for federal agencies, but the principles apply to almost any organization seeking to build a secure digital environment.

Now in its second version, NIST's framework is a comprehensive set of best practices for organizations looking to improve their security posture. It includes detailed guidance on risk management, asset management, identity and access control, incident response planning, supply chain management, and more.

ISO 27001 and ISO 27002

ISO 27001 and ISO 27002 are two of the most common standards for information security management today. These standards provide a comprehensive framework for organizations looking to protect their data through robust policies and best practices.

Initially developed by the International Organization for Standardization (ISO), these standards lay out principles and practices that ensure organizations take appropriate measures to protect their data. From asset management and access control to incident response and business continuity, these standards provide detailed guidelines to help organizations secure their networks.

ISO 27001 is an international standard that provides a systematic approach to risk assessment, control selection, and implementation. It includes requirements for establishing an Information Security Management System (ISMS).

ISO 27002 is a code of practice that outlines more specific and detailed security controls. When implemented together, these two standards provide organizations with a comprehensive approach to information security management.

CIS Controls

The Center for Internet Security (CIS) Control Framework provides best practices for organizations seeking to protect their networks from cyber threats. This framework includes 20 controls, covering many security areas, such as access control, asset management, and incident response.

The CIS Controls are divided into three categories: Basic, Foundational, and Organizational.

- Basic Controls focus on the essential cybersecurity measures that all organizations should implement, such as regular patching and antivirus protection.

- Foundational Controls are more advanced measures that should be taken in addition to fundamental security protocols, incorporating two-factor authentication and regularly monitoring log files for suspicious activity.

- Organizational Controls are designed to provide additional protections specific to the needs of an organization's environment, such as user awareness and training.

SOC2

The Service Organization Control (SOC) framework is an auditing standard used by third-party auditors to assess the security, availability, processing integrity, confidentiality, and privacy of a company's systems and services. SOC2 is one of the most prevalent standards in this framework, specifically designed for cloud service providers.

The SOC standard requires organizations to provide detailed documentation on their internal processes and procedures related to security, availability, processing integrity, confidentiality, and privacy. SOC-compliant documents must include policies such as access control measures, data encryption protocols, incident response plans, and more.

Organizations must also provide evidence of the effectiveness of their controls, such as audit logs or penetration test results, helping to ensure that their security measures are functioning correctly and can protect their data from cyber threats.

PCI-DSS

A council of major payment processors developed the Payment Card Industry Data Security Standard (PCI-DSS) to protect customers' payment card data. This standard provides a comprehensive set of requirements designed to help organizations secure their systems and prevent unauthorized access to customer information.

The PCI-DSS framework includes 12 requirements organizations must meet to protect customer data. These requirements cover access control, network security, and data storage specific to the payment processing industry. It also includes measures for safeguarding customer payment card data, including encryption and tokenization technologies.

COBIT

Developed by the Information Systems Audit and Control Association (ISACA), Control Objectives for Information and related Technology (COBIT) is a comprehensive framework designed to help organizations manage their IT resources more effectively. This framework offers best practices for governance, risk management, and security.

The COBIT framework is divided into five categories: Plan & Organize, Acquire & Implement, Deliver & Support, Monitor & Evaluate, and Manage & Assess. Each category contains specific processes and activities to help organizations manage their IT resources effectively.

COBIT also includes detailed data security and protection guidelines, covering access control, user authentication, encryption, audit logging, and incident response areas. These guidelines provide organizations with a comprehensive set of measures that can be used to protect their systems from cyber threats.

HITRUST Common Security Framework

The Health Information Trust Alliance (HITRUST) Common Security Framework (CSF) is a comprehensive security framework designed for the healthcare industry. This standard includes best practices for protecting the security of patient data, covering areas such as access control, identity and access management, encryption, audit logging, and incident response.

The HITRUST CSF includes detailed cybersecurity governance, risk management, and compliance requirements, helping organizations meet relevant regulatory requirements while protecting their systems from potential cyber threats.

Cloud Control Matrix

The Cloud Security Alliance's (CSA) Cloud Control Matrix (CCM) is a comprehensive security framework for cloud-based systems and applications which covers access control, user authentication, encryption, audit logging, and incident response.

Similar to HITRUST, the CCM also includes detailed guidelines for security governance and risk management and is aimed at helping organizations meet relevant regulatory standards.

CMMC 2.0

CMMC 2.0 (Cybersecurity Maturity Model Certification) is the latest version of the US Department of Defense's (DOD) framework, announced in 2021. This was designed to protect national security information by creating a set of consistent cybersecurity standards for any organization working with the DOD.

Some of the major changes from 1.0 to 2.0 include:

- ⊙ Allowing self-assessment for some requirements to help ease compliance
- ⊙ Creating priorities to protect DoD information
- ⊙ Building better cooperation between organizations and the DoD as cyber threats evolve

Within CMMC 2.0., there are 3 separate levels based on the sensitivity of data an organization processes. Each level has an increased amount of required practices as well as the intensity of assessments. At the baseline level 1, there are 17 practices in place with an annual self-assessment. At level 3, over 110 practices are required, along with triennial government-led assessments.

Country-specific cybersecurity frameworks

Along with the list above, there are several more cybersecurity frameworks that are specifically designed for the compliance needs of certain countries and regions. While these may not apply to every MSP, it's still a good idea to have a basic awareness and understanding of them. Here are some key examples below:

Essential 8

The Essential 8 is the APAC region's baseline cybersecurity framework that all organizations are recommended to follow, similar to the NIST Framework in the U.S. Established by the ACSC (Australia Cyber Security Centre) in 2017, this serves as a baseline set of minimum best practices to avoid compromised systems. Note that unlike many other frameworks, it specifically focuses on Microsoft Windows-based networks.

The titular Essential 8 represents the following threat mitigation practices:

- Application control
- Patch applications
- Configuring Microsoft Office macro settings
- User application hardening
- Restricting administrative privileges
- Patching operating systems
- Multi-factor authentication
- Regular backups.

The ACSC also has implemented the Essential 8 Maturity Model, which adjusts recommendations for the framework based on the capabilities of both the organization and potential threat actors.

Check out our blog series for a deep dive into the Essential Eight framework, strategies and steps for implementing these critical controls.

Cyber Essentials

Cyber Essentials is the primary framework for the UK, established by the NCSC (National Cyber Security Centre) in 2014. The framework is built around five main technical controls designed to protect against the most common cyber attacks:

- Firewalls and routers
- Secure configuration
- Access control
- Malware protection
- Patch management/software updates

Along with providing a base set of standards to protect organizations, compliance with Cyber Essentials is required for some U.K. government contracts. There are two levels of certification available: a basic self-assessment as well as the Cyber Essentials Plus certification, which requires a technical check-in from a third party.

Need of cybersecurity frameworks and standards

Cybersecurity frameworks provide guidelines and best practices for organizations to follow to secure their systems, networks, and data. These frameworks provide a comprehensive approach to cybersecurity that includes policies, procedures, and technical controls.

Organizations need cybersecurity frameworks to:

- ◉ Establish a culture of security and protect their valuable assets from data breaches and cyber threats.
- ◉ Identify and manage risks, detect and respond to cyber threats, and recover from cybersecurity incidents.
- ◉ Build trust with their customers, partners, and stakeholders by demonstrating a commitment to cybersecurity and protecting sensitive information.
- ◉ Comply with relevant regulations and laws.

CHAPTER-3

NETWORK SECURITY TECHNOLOGIES

Network security is a combination of people, process, policy, and technology used in in a layered approach to create a network environment that allows for organizational productivity while simultaneously minimizing the ability for misuse by both external and internal threat actors.

The people, process, and policy previously mentioned are a key part of the implementation of network security. They work together to take the security goals and create various types of security controls that are used to help establish how network security technologies will be implemented.

The three most common types of network security controls are:

⊙ **Physical controls** – These controls are used to prevent someone from physically gaining access to any of your organization's network components. Your data center or server room likely has a keycard system to limit access. That's a great example of a physical control. Security guards, video surveillance, picture IDs, and biometrics are other types of physical controls.

⊙ **Data and access controls** – These controls are the process and policy that define how employees can and should act when working with sensitive data, applications, and systems. Password requirements, mobile device usage, and incident response are just a few examples of administrative controls.

⊙ **Technical controls** – Acting as a safeguard or countermeasure when interacting with critical parts of your network environment, these controls are typically implemented via network security technologies. The remainder of this article will focus on these technologies.

PRIMARY NETWORK SECURITY TECHNOLOGIES

A successful layered approach to network security requires a number of technologies be put in place that each attempt to address the problem of malicious attacks from a different perspective. Some of the more common network security technologies include:

- **Secure remote access** – Access is the one thing every cybercriminal must have to successfully attack your organization. Access controls limit which users and devices are able to access specific internal or cloud-based resources. Modern implementations of access controls include zero trust network access (which facilitates access to internal and cloud-based resources without logically placing the user or their device on the corporate network), and secure remote access (a mix of technologies that can address endpoint security, authentication, secure remote connections, and elevation of privileges).

- **Firewall** – Firewalls sit at the logical perimeter of your organization's network acting as a network security guard, inspecting inbound and outbound traffic and determining whether to allow or deny it in real-time.

- **Virtual Private Network (VPN)** – VPNs encrypt the connection between a remote endpoint (e.g., your user working from home) and the internal corporate network.

- **DDoS prevention / mitigation** – Distributed denial of service (DDoS) attacks are designed to overwhelm firewalls, web application servers and other Internet-facing systems by saturating the network connection or consuming system resources with requests. DDoS prevention/mitigation technologies seek to block these types of attacks while allowing legitimate traffic to continue to flow to their intended application or system.

- **Application security** – Many applications and the hardware and OS they run on have vulnerabilities that need to be secured. Application security technologies seek to identify and remediate those vulnerabilities. While application security can encompass many technologies, here we're referencing those that are considered true network security technologies, such as web application firewalls.

- **Cloud access security broker (CASB)** – Worthy of an article of its' own, CASB is comprised of a number of technologies designed to protect online services, applications, and environments from threats that take advantage of the anytime, from anywhere, from any device nature of the cloud.

- **Intrusion Prevention System (IPS)** – Unlike a firewall that uses simple protocol rules to allow and deny traffic, IPS scans network traffic and leverages threat intelligence to identify and block potentially malicious traffic.

- **Web security** – Outbound use of the Internet by your employees can equally result in malicious access. Web security technologies focus on blocking malicious websites and threats found on the Internet.

FIREWALLS AND INTRUSION DETECTION SYSTEMS (IDS)

Firewall

Firewall is a computer network security system designed to prevent unauthorized access to or from a private network. It can be implemented as hardware, software, or a combination of both. Firewalls are used to prevent unauthorized Internet users from accessing private networks connected to the Internet. All messages are entering or leaving the intranet pass through the firewall. The firewall examines each message and blocks those that do not meet the specified security criteria.

Categories of Firewalls: Firewall can be categorised into the following types-

Processing mode

The five processing modes that firewalls can be categorised are-

Packet filtering
Application gateways
Circuit gateways
MAC layer firewalls
Hybrid firewalls

Processing mode

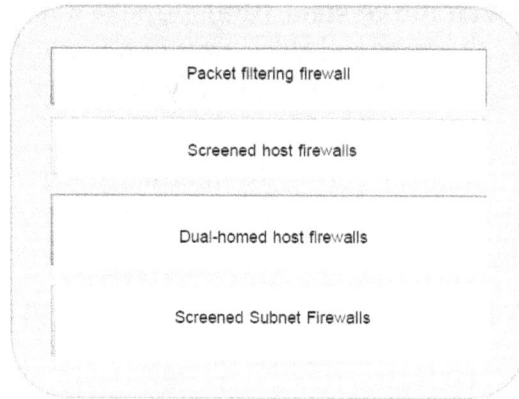

| Packet filtering firewall |
| Screened host firewalls |
| Dual-homed host firewalls |
| Screened Subnet Firewalls |

Packet filtering

Packet filtering firewalls examine header information of a data packets that come into a network. This firewall installed on TCP/IP network and determine whether to forward it to the next network connection or drop a packet based on the rules programmed in the firewall. It scans network data packets looking for a violation of the rules of the firewalls database. Most firewall often based on a combination of:

⊙ Internet Protocol (IP) source and destination address.

⊙ Direction (inbound or outbound).

⊙ Transmission Control Protocol (TCP) or User Datagram Protocol (UDP) source and destination port requests.

Packet filtering firewalls can be categorized into three types-

⊙ **Static filtering:** The system administrator set a rule for the firewall. These filtering rules governing how the firewall decides which packets are allowed and which are denied are developed and installed.

⊙ **Dynamic filtering:** It allows the firewall to set some rules for itself, such as dropping packets from an address that is sending many bad packets.

⊙ **Stateful inspection:** A stateful firewalls keep track of each network connection between internal and external systems using a state table.

Application gateways

It is a firewall proxy which frequently installed on a dedicated computer to provides network security. This proxy firewall acts as an intermediary between the requester and the protected device. This firewall proxy filters incoming node traffic to certain specifications that mean only transmitted network application data is filtered. Such network applications include FTP, Telnet, Real Time Streaming Protocol (RTSP), BitTorrent, etc.

Circuit gateways

A circuit-level gateway is a firewall that operates at the transport layer. It provides UDP and TCP connection security which means it can reassemble, examine or block all the packets in a TCP or UDP connection. It works between a transport layer and an application layers such as the session layer. Unlike application gateways, it monitors TCP data packet handshaking and session fulfilment of firewall rules and policies. It can also act as a Virtual Private Network (VPN) over the Internet by doing encryption from firewall to firewall.

MAC layer firewalls

This firewall is designed to operate at the media access control layer of the OSI network model. It is able to consider a specific host computer's identity in its filtering decisions. MAC addresses of specific host computers are linked to the access control list (ACL) entries. This entry identifies specific types of packets that can be sent to each host and all other traffic is blocked. It will also check the MAC address of a requester to determine whether the device being used are able to make the connection is authorized to access the data or not.

Hybrid firewalls

It is a type of firewalls which combine features of other four types of firewalls. These are elements of packet filtering and proxy services, or of packet filtering and circuit gateways.

Development Era

Firewall can be categorised on the basis of the generation type. These are-

- ⊙ First Generation
- ⊙ Second Generation
- ⊙ Third Generation
- ⊙ Fourth Generation
- ⊙ Fifth Generation

First Generation

he first generation firewall comes with static packet filtering firewall. A static packet filter is the simplest and least expensive forms of firewall protection. In this generation, each packet entering and leaving the network is checked and will be either passed or rejected depends on the user-defined rules. We can compare this security with the bouncer of the club who only allows people over 21 to enter and below 21 will be disallowed.

Second Generation

Second generation firewall comes with Application level or proxy servers. This generation of firewall increases the security level between trusted and untrusted networks. An Application level firewall uses software to intercept connections for each IP and to perform security inspection. It involves proxy services which act as an interface between the user on the internal trusted network and the Internet. Each computer communicates with each other by passing network traffic through the proxy program. This program evaluates data sent from the client and decides which to move on and which to drop.

Third Generation

The third generation firewall comes with the stateful inspection firewalls. This generation of the firewall has evolved to meet the major requirements demanded by corporate networks of increased security while minimizing the impact on network performance. The needs of the third generation firewalls will be even more demanding due to the growing support for VPNs, wireless communication, and enhanced virus protection. The most challenging element of this evolution is maintaining the firewall's simplicity (and hence its maintainability and security) without compromising flexibility.

Fourth Generation

The fourth generation firewall comes with dynamic packet filtering firewall. This firewall monitors the state of active connections, and on the basis of this information, it determines which network packets are allowed to pass through the firewall. By recording session information such as IP addresses and port numbers, a dynamic packet filter can implement a much tighter security posture than a static packet filter.

Fifth Generation

The fifth generation firewall comes with kernel proxy firewall. This firewall works under the kernel of Windows NT Executive. This firewall proxy operates at the application layer. In this, when a packet arrives, a new virtual stack table is created which contains only the protocol proxies needed to examine the specific packet. These packets investigated at each layer of the stack, which involves evaluating the data link header along with the network header, transport header, session layer information, and application layer data. This firewall works faster than all the application-level firewalls because all evaluation takes place at the kernel layer and not at the higher layers of the operating system.

Intended deployment structure

Firewall can also be categorized based on the structure. These are:

Commercial Appliances

It runs on a custom operating system. This firewall system consists of firewall application software running on a general-purpose computer. It is designed to provide protection for a medium-to-large business network. Most of the commercial firewalls are quite complex and often require specialized training and certification to take full advantage of their features.

Small Office Home Office

The SOHO firewall is designed for small office or home office networks who need protection from Internet security threats. A firewall for a SOHO (Small Office Home Office) is the first line of defence and plays an essential role in an overall security strategy. SOHO firewall has limited resources so that the firewall product they implement must be relatively easy to use and maintain, and be cost-effective. This firewall connects a user's local area network or a specific computer system to the Internetworking device.

Residential Software

Residential-grade firewall software is installed directly on a user's system. Some of these applications combine firewall services with other protections such as antivirus or intrusion detection. There are a limit to the level of configurability and protection that software firewalls can provide.

Architectural Implementation

The firewall configuration that works best for a particular organization depends on three factors: the objectives of the network, the organization's ability to develop and implement the architectures, and the budget available for the function.

There are four common architectural implementations of firewalls:

Packet filtering firewall

Packet filtering firewall is used to control the network access by monitoring the outgoing and incoming packets. It allows them to pass or halt based on the source and destination IP addresses, protocols and ports. During communication, a node transmits a packet; this packet is filtered and matched with the predefined rules and policies. Once it is matched, a packet is considered secure and verified and are able to be accepted otherwise blocked them.

Screened host firewalls

This firewall architecture combines the packet-filtering router with a separate and dedicated firewall. The application gateway needs only one network interface. It is allowing the router to pre-screen packets to minimize the network traffic and load on the internal proxy. The packet-filtering router filters dangerous protocols from reaching the application gateway and site systems.

Dual-homed host firewalls

The network architecture for the dual-homed host firewall is simple. Its architecture is built around the dual-homed host computer, a computer that has at least two NICs. One NIC is to be connected with the external network, and other is connected to the internal network which provides an additional layer of protection. With these NICs, all traffic must go through the firewall in order to move between the internal and external networks.

The Implementation of this architecture often makes use of NAT. NAT is a method of mapping assigned IP addresses to special ranges of no routable internal IP addresses, thereby creating another barrier to intrusion from external attackers.

Screened Subnet Firewalls

This architecture adds an extra layer (perimeter network) of security to the screened host architecture by adding a perimeter network that further isolates the internal network from the Internet. In this architecture, there are two screening routers and both connected to the perimeter net. One router sits between the perimeter net and the internal network, and the other router sits between the perimeter net and the external network. To break into the internal network, an attacker would have to get past both routers. There is no single vulnerable point that will compromise the internal network.

VPNs

A VPN stands for virtual private network. It is a technology which creates a safe and an encrypted connection on the Internet from a device to a network. This type of connection helps to ensure our sensitive data is transmitted safely. It prevents our connection from eavesdropping on the network traffic and allows the user to access a private network securely. This technology is widely used in the corporate environments.

A VPN works same as firewall like firewall protects data local to a device wherever VPNs protects data online. To ensure safe communication on the internet, data travel through secure tunnels, and VPNs user used an authentication method to gain access over the VPNs server. VPNs are used by remote users who need to access corporate resources, consumers who want to download files and business travellers want to access a site that is geographically restricted.

Intrusion Detection System (IDS)

An IDS is a security system which monitors the computer systems and network traffic. It analyses that traffic for possible hostile attacks originating from the outsider and also for system misuse or attacks originating from the insider. A firewall does a job of filtering the incoming traffic from the internet, the IDS in a similar way compliments the firewall security. Like, the firewall protects an organization sensitive data from malicious attacks over the Internet, the Intrusion detection system alerts the system administrator in the case when someone tries to break in the firewall security and tries to have access on any network in the trusted side.

Intrusion Detection System have different types:

NIDS

It is a Network Intrusion Detection System which monitors the inbound and outbound traffic to and from all the devices over the network.

HIDS

It is a Host Intrusion Detection System which runs on all devices in the network with direct access to both internet and enterprise internal network. It can detect anomalous network packets that originate from inside the organization or malicious traffic that a NIDS has failed to catch. HIDS may also identify malicious traffic that arises from the host itself.

Signature-based Intrusion Detection System

It is a detection system which refers to the detection of an attack by looking for the specific patterns, such as byte sequences in network traffic, or known malicious instruction sequences used by malware. This IDS originates from anti-virus software which can easily detect known attacks. In this terminology, it is impossible to detect new attacks, for which no pattern is available.

Anomaly-based Intrusion Detection System-

This detection system primarily introduced to detect unknown attacks due to the rapid development of malware. It alerts administrators against the potentially malicious activity. It monitors the network traffic and compares it against an established baseline. It determines what is considered to be normal for the network with concern to bandwidth, protocols, ports and other devices.

VIRTUAL PRIVATE NETWORKS (VPNS)

VPN stands for the **Virtual Private Network**. A virtual private network (VPN) is a technology that creates a safe and encrypted connection over a less secure network, such as the Internet. A Virtual Private Network is a way to extend a private network using a public network such as the Internet. The name only suggests that it is a "Virtual Private Network", i.e. user can be part of a local network sitting at a remote location. It makes use of tunnelling protocols to establish a secure connection.

Benefits of a VPN connection

A VPN connection disguises your data traffic online and protects it from external access. Unencrypted data can be viewed by anyone who has network access and wants to see it. With a VPN, hackers and cyber criminals can't decipher this data.

- **Secure encryption:** To read the data, you need an *encryption key* . Without one, it would take millions of years for a computer to decipher the code in the event of a brute force attack . With the help of a VPN, your online activities are hidden even on public networks.

- **Disguising your whereabouts** : VPN servers essentially act as your proxies on the internet. Because the demographic location data comes from a server in another country, your actual location cannot be determined. In addition, most VPN services do not store logs of your activities. Some providers, on the other hand, record your behavior, but do not pass this information on to third parties. This means that any potential record of your user behavior remains permanently hidden.

- **Access to regional content:** Regional web content is not always accessible from everywhere. Services and websites often contain content that can only be accessed from certain parts of the world. Standard connections use local servers in the country to determine your location. This means that you cannot access content at home while traveling, and you cannot access international content from home. With **VPN location spoofing** , you can switch to a server to another country and effectively "change" your location.

- **Secure data transfer:** If you work remotely, you may need to access important files on your company's network. For security reasons, this kind of information requires a secure connection. To gain access to the network, a VPN connection is often required. VPN services connect to private servers and use encryption methods to reduce the risk of data leakage.

Types of VPNs

VPNs are designed to provide a private, encrypted connection between two points – but does not specify what these points should be. This makes it possible to use VPNs in a few different contexts:

- **Site-to-Site VPN:** A site-to-site VPN is designed to securely connect two geographically-distributed sites. VPN functionality is included in most security gateways today. For instance a next-generation firewall (NGFW) deployed at the perimeter of a network protects the corporate network and also serves as a VPN gateway. All traffic flowing from one site to the other passes through this gateway, which encrypts the traffic sent to the gateway at the other site. This gateway decrypts the data and forwards it on to its destination.

- ⊙ **Remote Access VPN:** A remote access VPN is designed to link remote users securely to a corporate network. For instance when the COVID-19 pandemic emerged in 2020, many organizations transitioned to a remote workforce, and set up secure remote access VPNs from the remote clients to connect to critical business operations at the corporate site.

- ⊙ **VPN as a Service:** VPN as a Service or a cloud VPN is a VPN hosted in cloud-based infrastructure where packets from the client enter the Internet from that cloud infrastructure instead of the client's local address. Consumer VPNs commonly use this model, enabling users to protect themselves while connecting to the Internet via insecure public Wi-Fi and provide some anonymity while accessing the Internet.

Limitations and Security Risks of VPNs

While VPNs are designed to fill a vital role for the modern business, they are not a perfect solution. VPNs have several limitations that impact their usability and corporate cybersecurity, including:

- ⊙ **Fragmented Visibility:** VPNs are designed to provide secure point to point connectivity with every VPN user on their own link. This makes it difficult for an organization's security team to maintain the full network visibility required for effective threat detection and response.

- ⊙ **No Integrated Security:** An organization must deploy additional security solutions behind the VPN to identify and block malicious content and to implement additional access controls.

- ⊙ **Inefficient Routing:** VPNs can be used in a "hub and spoke" model to ensure that all traffic flows through the organization's centralized security stack for inspection. As remote work and cloud applications become more common, this detour may not be the optimal path between the client and the cloud application or the Internet. Learn more about the SD-WAN vs VPN debate.

- ⊙ **Poor Scalability:** As a point-to-point security solution, VPNs scale poorly. For example, the number of site-to-site VPN connections in a fully-connected network grows exponentially with the number of sites. This creates a complex network infrastructure that is difficult to deploy, monitor and secure.

◉ **Endpoint Vulnerabilities:** Endpoints who have legitimate access to the VPN can sometimes be compromised via phishing and other cyber attacks. Since the endpoint has full access to the VPN resources, so does the threat actor who has compromised the endpoint.

NETWORK ACCESS CONTROL (NAC)

Network access control (NAC) is a security solution that helps prevent unauthorized users and devices from accessing a private network. It uses a set of protocols, rules, and processes to control access to network-connected resources. NAC also helps to unify endpoint security technology, such as vulnerability assessment, host intrusion prevention, and antivirus.

As endpoints proliferate across an organization—typically driven by bring-your-own-device (BYOD) policies and an expansion in the use of Internet-of-Things (IoT) devices—more control is needed. Even the largest IT organizations do not have the resources to manually configure all the devices in use. The automated features of a NAC solution are a sizable benefit, reducing the time and associated costs with authenticating and authorizing users and determining that their devices are compliant.

Further, cyber criminals are well aware of this increase in endpoint usage and continue to design and launch sophisticated campaigns that exploit any vulnerabilities in corporate networks. With more endpoints, the attack surface increases, which means more opportunities for fraudsters to gain access. NAC solutions can be configured to detect any unusual or suspicious network activity and respond with immediate action, such as isolating the device from the network to prevent the potential spread of the attack.

Although IoT and BYOD have changed NAC solutions, NAC also serves as a perpetual inventory of users, devices, and their level of access. It serves as an active discovery tool to uncover previously unknown devices that may have gained access to all or parts of the network, requiring IT administrators to adjust security policies.

Further, organizations can choose how NAC will authenticate users who attempt to gain access to the network. IT admins can choose multi-factor authentication (MFA), which provides an additional layer of security to username and password combinations.

Restricting network access also means control of the applications and data within the network, which is normally the target of cyber criminals. The stronger the network controls, the more difficult it will be for any cyberattack to infiltrate the network.

Components of Network Access Control Scheme:

- **Restricted Access:** It restricts access to the network by user authentication and authorization control. For example, the user can't access a protected network resource without permission to access it.

- **Network Boundary Protection:** It monitors and controls the connectivity of networks with external networks. It includes tools such as controlled interfaces, intrusion detection, and anti-virus tools. It is also called perimeter defense. For example, the firewall can be used to prevent unauthorized access to network resources from outside of the network.

Types of Network Access Control:

- **Pre-admission:** It happens before access to the network is granted on initialization of request by user or device to access the network. It evaluates the access attempt and only allows the access if the user or device is compliant with organization security policies and authorized to access the network.

- **Post-admission:** It happens within the network when the user or device attempts to access the different parts of the network. It restricts the lateral movement of the device within the network by asking for re-authentication for each request to access a different part of the network.

Implement NAC Solutions

- **Gather Data:** Perform an exhaustive survey and collect information about every device, user, and server that has to interface with the network resources.

- **Manage Identities:** Verify user identities within the organization by authentication and authorization.

- **Determine Permissions:** Create permission policies stating different access levels for identified user groups.

- **Apply for Permissions:** Apply permission policies on identified user groups and register each user in the NAC system to trace their access level and activity within the network.

- **Update:** Monitor security operations and make adjustments to permission policies based on changing requirements of the organization with time.

Importance of Network Access Control:

There has been exponential growth in the number of mobile devices accessing private networks of organizations in the past few years. This has led to an increase in security risks for the organization's resources and therefore, some tools are required that can provide the visibility, access control, and compliance capabilities to strengthen the network security infrastructure.

A NAC system can deny network access to non-compliant devices or give them only restricted access to computing resources, thus preventing insecure nodes from infecting the network. Also, NAC products can handle large enterprise networks that have a large range of different device types connected to the network.

SECURING WIRELESS NETWORKS

Wireless network security is crucial and cannot be overstated. Data breaches and other Cybersecurity dangers are becoming much more likely due to the widespread use of mobile devices and the popularity of public Wi-Fi hotspots.

These best practices are crucial for making sure that your data and devices are protected from malicious actors, even though there are many alternative ways to secure a wireless network.

Enabling Two-Factor Authentication (2FA)

The login process has an additional layer of protection thanks to two-factor authentication. Users must provide their username, password, and a code produced by an authenticator app, among other things. This makes it more challenging for someone to enter the network without authorization.

Go to the wireless router's configuration page and enable two-factor authentication there. Make sure you download and have on hand an authenticator app before logging in, such as Google Authenticator or Authy.

For even stronger security, you may also think about implementing passwordless authentication, such as cloud radius. This is a crucial best practice since it prevents unauthorized users from accessing your network in the event that they do manage to obtain your password. You can be almost 100% sure that only authorized users will have access to your network by employing a cloud-based solution.

Encrypting Data

Another crucial best practice for wireless network security is data encryption. Data is encrypted so that only authorized users may decrypt it and read it. This helps prevent unauthorized parties from accessing critical information.

There are many ways to implement encryption, including by using encryption software, hardware, or services. Ensure that staff members understand the significance of protecting sensitive data with encryption and how to do so effectively.

Using A Strong Password

One of the most crucial best practices for wireless network security is using a strong password. The main characteristics of a strong password include length (the longer the better), a combination of letters (in both capital and lower case), digits, and symbols, the absence of any associations with your personal information, and the avoidance of dictionary words. The good news is that you may include all of these elements in your passwords without having to memorize horrible sequences of random letters, numbers, and symbols.

Disabling SSID Broadcast

Broadcasting a WLAN's SSID will make it visible to all wireless enabled devices within range. This has the benefit of making the WLAN easy to join. It does, on the other hand, make the WLAN more of a target for attacks.

This broadcast can be disabled, essentially hiding the WLAN. Devices can still connect to it, but the user must know the SSID.

This does not make the network itself more secure, but does make it less likely to be attacked.

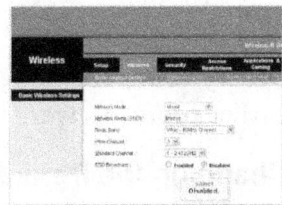

Using MAC Filtering

The use of MAC filtering is also a popular best practice in wireless security. A network's physical devices are given specific identifiers called MAC addresses.

You can aid in preventing unauthorized access by limiting the devices that are permitted to connect to the network to those with certain MAC addresses. By going to the wireless router's configuration page and inputting the MAC addresses of devices that are permitted to join to the network, MAC filtering can be put into place.

MAC : 06-00-00-00-00-00

MAC Filtering

Internet

MAC : 06-00-00-00-20-9D

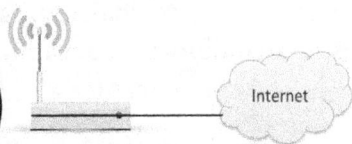

Disabling SSID Broadcast

Another best practice for wireless network security is to turn off SSID broadcast. Anyone within the wireless network's range can see the network name when SSID broadcast is enabled. By going to the wireless router's setup page and turning off the SSID broadcast capability, you can disable SSID broadcast.

Making it more challenging for unauthorized users to connect to the network is the aim. If someone is within the network's range and uses a wireless network scanner, they can still see the SSID, but it won't be as simple to access.

Using A VPN

Another excellent practice for wireless network security is using a VPN. A VPN makes it more difficult for someone to eavesdrop on the connection by encrypting all traffic between a device and the VPN server. Given that public Wi-Fi networks are frequently less secure than private ones, this is especially crucial while utilizing them. Use only VPNs from reputable providers, and emphasize to staff how crucial it is to use a VPN when working remotely.

Enabling WPA3 Security

Password encryption is included in best practices for securing a wireless network. The most up-to-date and secure wireless security standard is WPA3. When possible, it ought to be utilized because it offers higher security than WPA2.

Ensure that you check for routers that offer this most modern security protocol when you are shopping about. It's crucial to ensure sure WPA3 is enabled because earlier protocols were simpler to hack.

Changing the Default Password

A further best practice for wireless network security is changing the default password. A default password that is simple to guess comes with many routers. This is a security risk because it gives potential access to the network for unauthorized users.

Enter the wireless router's setup page to change the default password to something more challenging to decipher. Make sure your password is strong by using a combination of capital and lowercase letters, numbers, and symbols that is at least 8 characters long.

Disabling Remote Administration

An additional recommended practice for wireless network security is to disable remote administration. Anyone with the right credentials can visit the router's configuration page and modify the network when remote administration is enabled. This is a security risk because it gives potential access to the network for unauthorized users.

Go to the wireless router's configuration page and turn off remote administration there. This will assist in limiting illegal network access.

Disabling UPnP

A system called Universal Plug and Play (UPnP) enables devices to automatically find and connect to one another. This is a security risk since it gives unauthorized devices a chance to connect to the network. You can turn off UPnP by going to the wireless router's configuration page. By going to the settings menu on specific devices, you may also turn off UpnP.

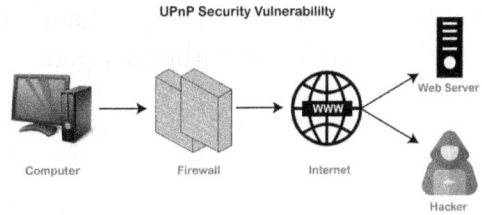

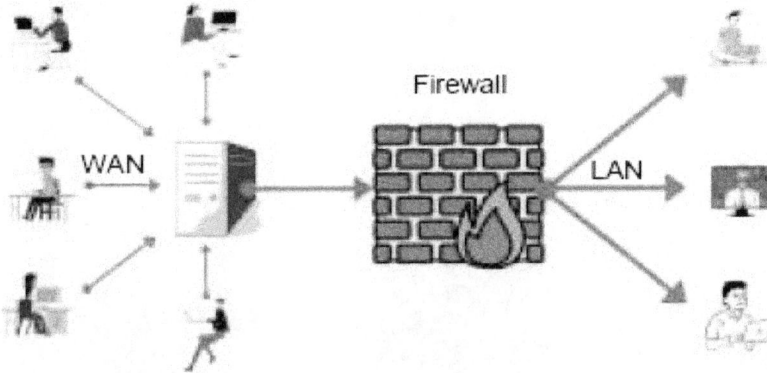

Using A Firewall

Enabling a firewall is yet another way to secure a wireless network. A firewall assists in network security by preventing unauthorized incoming traffic. In preventing attacks from malware and other harmful software, this can be very crucial.

Access the wireless router's configuration page and turn on the feature to utilize a firewall. Network-based and host-based firewalls are the two main categories of firewalls. Host-based firewalls can be deployed on individual devices, whereas network-based firewalls are frequently employed in business settings.

Disabling Unnecessary Services

Frequently, routers are sold with a lot of unused services activated. These pose a security risk since they could give potential attackers knowledge of the network. Access the configuration page of the wireless router and turn off any superfluous services there. This will assist in lowering the network's attack surface. Commonly used yet pointless services include telnet, SSH, and HTTP.

Conclusion

To safeguard a network against potential assaults, it is crucial to put the previously mentioned best practices for wireless network security into effect. This will definitely make it more challenging for unauthorized users to access the network by turning off superfluous services, altering the default password, and enabling two-factor authentication.

CHAPTER-4

ENDPOINT SECURITY

Endpoint security is the practice of securing endpoints or entry points of end-user devices such as desktops, laptops, and mobile devices from being exploited by malicious actors and campaigns. Endpoint security systems protect these endpoints on a network or in the cloud from cybersecurity threats. Endpoint security has evolved from traditional antivirus software to providing comprehensive protection from sophisticated malware and evolving zero-day threats.

Organizations of all sizes are at risk from nation-states, hacktivists, organized crime, and malicious and accidental insider threats. Endpoint security is often seen as cybersecurity's frontline, and represents one of the first places organizations look to secure their enterprise networks.

As the volume and sophistication of cybersecurity threats have steadily grown, so has the need for more advanced endpoint security solutions. Today's endpoint protection systems are designed to quickly detect, analyze, block, and contain attacks in progress. To do this, they need to collaborate with each other and with other security technologies to give administrators visibility into advanced threats to speed detection and remediation response times.

Endpoint Definition

An endpoint can be considered as a device that enables an employee to connect to a corporate network. The growth in BYOD and other connected systems such as the Internet of Things (IoT) is seeing the number of devices that could potentially connect to a network increase exponentially.

Some of the more common devices that can be considered an endpoint include:

⦿ ATM machines

⦿ IoT-enabled smart devices

⦿ Industrial machines

- ⊙ Laptop computers
- ⊙ Medical devices
- ⊙ Mobile phones
- ⊙ Printers
- ⊙ Servers
- ⊙ Tablets
- ⊙ Wearables, such as smartwatches

Endpoints now extend beyond the laptops and mobile phones that employees use to get their work done. They encompass any machine or connected device that could conceivably connect to a corporate network. And these endpoints are particularly lucrative entry points to business networks and systems for hackers.

It is therefore vital for organizations to consider every device that is or could be connected to their network and ensure it is protected. Furthermore, as the endpoints evolve and increase in sophistication, so too do the security solutions that protect them from being exploited.

Benefits of An Endpoint Security

Endpoint security technology plays a vital role in protecting organizations from the increasingly dangerous threat landscape. Some of the key benefits of an endpoint security approach include:

- ⊙ **Protecting all endpoints:** As employees now connect via not only a growing number of endpoints but also different types of devices, it is vital for organizations to ensure they do so securely. They also need to ensure that the data on those devices is secure and cannot be lost or stolen.

- ⊙ **Securing remote working:** The rise in device usage is linked to new ways of getting work done, such as bring your own device (BYOD) and remote working policies. These policies enable employees to be as effective as possible wherever they are and on any device. However, they also make it more difficult to ensure users are working securely, thus creating vulnerabilities for hackers to exploit. Protecting the device with an endpoint security platform is crucial.

- ⊙ **Sophisticated threat protection:** Hackers are deploying more sophisticated attack methods that see them come up with new ways of gaining access to corporate networks, stealing data, and manipulating employees into giving up sensitive information. Endpoint protection is critical to securing the modern enterprise and preventing cyber criminals from gaining access to their networks.

⊙ **Protecting identity:** As employees connect to business systems via various devices and from different networks and locations, the traditional process of protecting the business perimeter is no longer viable. Endpoint security ensures that the business puts security on employees' devices, enabling them to work safely regardless of how and where they connect to corporate data and resources.

ANTIVIRUS AND ANTI-MALWARE SOLUTIONS

Antivirus

Computer virus

To understand what antivirus software does, you need to know what a computer virus is. "Virus" in this context has a broad definition, but to put it simply, it's a program that gets installed on your computer, then automatically spreads itself to other computers across a network or the internet, mimicking the spread of a biological virus spreading through an organism's cells.

What precisely a virus does depends on the specific virus, but it's never good. In the early days of personal computers, a lot of viruses were designed merely to damage your computer for the sake of pure mischief. The famous "ILOVEYOU" virus spread through email downloads and merely overwrote files on the hard drive with junk data, until the computer became unstable and had to be completely wiped.

But the most insidious and personally dangerous type of virus, and the more common one in the modern world, is designed to steal from users themselves. This can be done several ways. A "spyware" or "spybot" program searches the files on your computer for your personal information like login passwords or bank accounts, while "ransomware" locks down your files and instructs you to send money to criminals to get them back. Often these will be sent as emails or websites pretending to be something they're not, like a crucial software update you need to click on, a process called "phishing."

In these cases, the self-replicating viral factor might not even be present, so the software isn't even technically a virus. Other terms, like "worm," "trojan" (as in the Trojan Horse) or the more all-encompassing "malware" might be more accurate.

Definition

Software that is created specifically to help detect, prevent and remove malware (malicious software) such as viruses.

Antivirus is a kind of software used to prevent, scan, detect and delete viruses from a computer. Once installed, most antivirus software runs automatically in the background to provide real-time protection against virus attacks.

Comprehensive virus protection programs help protect your files and hardware from malware such as worms, Trojan horses and spyware, and may also offer additional protection such as customizable firewalls and website blocking.

Common types of cyber threats

As the Internet of Things (IoT) grows, so does the risk of cybercrime for mobile phones and other internet-connected devices, not just your personal computer. According to Verizon's 2022 Data Breach Investigations Report, 45% of organizations had recently experienced a mobile-related compromise. You need to protect yourself against malware.

Malware

Malware, short for "malicious software," is a blanket term that refers to a wide variety of software programs designed to do damage or do other unwanted actions to a computer, server or computer network Common examples include viruses, spyware and trojan horses. Malware can slow down or crash your device or delete files. Criminals often use malware to send spam, obtain personal and financial information and even steal your identity.

What is spyware?

Spyware is a type of malware that attaches itself and hides on a computer's operating system without your permission to make unwanted changes to your user experience. It can be used to spy on your online activity and may generate unwanted advertisements or make your browser display certain website sites or search results.

What is phishing?

Phishing attacks use email or fraudulent websites to try to trick you into providing personal or financial information to compromise an account or steal money by posing as a trustworthy entity. They may claim there's a problem with payment information or that they've noticed activity on an account and ask you to click on a link or attachment and provide personal information.

Antivirus programs and computer protection software.

Antivirus programs and computer protection software are designed to evaluate data such as web pages, files, software and applications to help find and eradicate malware as quickly as possible. Most provide real-time protection, which can protect your devices from incoming threats; scan your entire computer regularly for known threats and provide automatic updates; and identify, block and delete malicious codes and software.

Because so many activities are now conducted online and new threats emerge continuously, it's more important than ever to install a protective antivirus program. Fortunately, there are a number of excellent products on the market today to choose from.

How does antivirus work?

Antivirus software begins operating by checking your computer programs and files against a database of known types of malware. Since new viruses are constantly created and distributed by hackers, it will also scan computers for the possibility of new or unknown types of malware threats.

Typically, most programs will use three different detection devices: specific detection, which identifies known malware; generic detection, which looks for known parts or types of malware or patterns that are related by a common codebase; and heuristic detection, which scans for unknown viruses by identifying known suspicious file structures. When the program finds a file that contains a virus, it will usually quarantine it and/or mark it for deletion, making it inaccessible and removing the risk to your device.

Comprehensive protection for your computer and devices

With so many internet-connected devices in the home today, technology has made everyday living more convenient—but also riskier. To help protect your devices, Verizon offers protection services, which includes a combination of anti-virus software, 24/7 tech support for Verizon services and hardware; identity theft protection, password management; and repair insurance for damaged and broken devices.

Antivirus software

The types of threat are wide and varied, but antivirus software is designed to detect and stop them all. These security packages might be called simply "antivirus," but also a "protection suite," or just "defender." Regardless, they all use a few straightforward methods to identify, contain, and neutralize viruses and other kinds of malware before it can infect your system. Antivirus software also continuously scans both your computer and your network traffic to identify threats.

What does antivirus software do?

The most straightforward way an antivirus program can protect against viruses is by scanning your files. The antivirus software taps into a huge database of known viruses, trojans, and other kinds of malware—thousands and thousands of different kinds, constantly being updated—and searches for them on the files in your computer. The antivirus program even scans new files that you download immediately, including installable programs that might hide viruses behind other programs like games or tools.

When the antivirus program finds a file that it's identified as malware, it immediately isolates the file from the rest of your computer and prevents it from running any operations that might affect other files or programs. With the threat isolated, it then thoroughly deletes the dangerous files. Usually it will display some kind of alert letting you know that it's found and neutralized the danger.

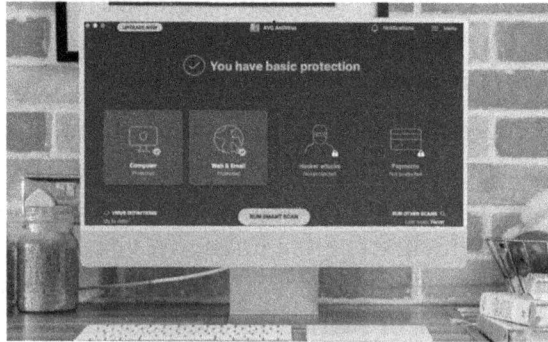

This method of protection has proven to be extremely effective, but it's not perfect. A virus or a piece of malware has to be identified before it can be added to the detection database... which means that for at least some amount of time, it has to be active "in the wild" of the internet before the database gets updated. That's a good reason to practice basic computer security at all times, for example, not downloading unknown programs or opening email attachments from untrusted sources.

What does antivirus software do?

Functionality varies depending on what kind of software you choose to use. However, features often include:

- **Scanning**: Users can perform scans of their devices manually, or set up a schedule for system checks to launch automatically. Alternatively, AV products often offer real-time background scanning capabilities that will check new files, archives, and browser activities for potential threats. Users can select individual files, drives, or full systems that need to be scanned, as well as perform quick scans — which normally take no more than a few minutes — for general 'health' checks.

- **Web browsing**: Real-time monitoring for internet-based threats can be enabled to protect users from phishing attempts, malicious websites, suspicious executable file downloads or execution, unintentional drive-by downloads, and more.

- **Firewalls**: Modern operating systems will include a firewall, which is a network monitoring system that will block traffic — incoming and outgoing — based on set rules. Unauthorized or suspicious connections can be stopped to prevent intrusion.

- **Virtual Private Network (VPN) connections**: Some AV products now offer an optional, inbuilt VPN connection. A VPN is not a replacement for an AV product, but rather should be considered a useful addition to hide your IP address, encrypt the communication between you and online services, and prevent both monitoring and tracking by third parties.

- **Password managers**: Password managers lock up, manage, and generate the passwords used to access online services, and may also auto-fill forms on a user's behalf. Some AV products now even include a password manager.

- **Parental controls**: These may include website blocks on adult content and keyword monitoring.

- **Junk clean-up, system optimization**: Bolt-on AV software features can include cleaning up junk and unnecessary files, therefore freeing up space on your PC or mobile device.

- **Payment protection**: AV products may include a feature to monitor visits to suspected fake banking or payment provider websites and warn you if you may be about to input your details on a malicious website. In addition, AV products may provide a custom browser window that is isolated and hardened, providing a more secure environment to make online purchases.

- **Automatic updates**: AV software will automatically upgrade to new versions, and these updates will include changes to signature databases.

- **Multiple device protection**: Depending on the terms of an AV software license, you may be able to use the same subscription to protect more than one PC or mobile device. This is usually a paid-only option for users.

- **Wi-Fi monitoring**: An AV product may also watch what Wi-Fi access point your device connects to in order to warn you if it is not secure, such as an open hotspot in public areas or in hotels.

Anti-malware Solutions

Antimalware is a type of software program created to protect information technology (IT) systems and individual computers from malicious software, or malware. Antimalware programs scan a computer system to prevent, detect and remove malware.

What is malware?

Malware is short for malicious software, which is software specifically designed to damage data or a computer system. It's a broad term for software used to disrupt computer operation, gather sensitive information or gain access to private computer systems. Malware typically comes in the form of malicious code hidden in computer systems and is often installed without the knowledge or consent of the computer's owner. Malware spreads by email, operating systems (OSes), removable media or the internet. Common examples of malware include viruses, spyware, worms, rootkits and Trojan horses.

The three most common types of malware mentioned above are viruses, worms and Trojan horses. A virus is a piece of software that duplicates itself and spreads from one computer to another. A worm is similar to a virus, except that it doesn't need to infect other programs on a computer to spread. A worm can spread on its own. A Trojan horse appears to be something benign, such as a game or a screen saver, but it actually contains code that causes damage to the computer or enables the author to access the user's data.

How antimalware works?

Antimalware software uses three strategies to protect systems from malicious software: signature-based detection, behavior-based detection and sandboxing.

Signature-based malware detection

Signature-based malware detection uses a set of known software components and their digital signatures to identify new malicious software. Software vendors develop signatures to detect specific malicious software. The signatures are used to identify previously identified malicious software of the same type and to flag the new software as malware. This approach is useful for common types of malware, such as keyloggers and adware, which share many of the same characteristics.

Behavior-based malware detection

Behavior-based malware detection helps computer security professionals more quickly identify, block and eradicate malware by using an active approach to malware analysis. Behavior-based malware detection works by identifying malicious software by examining how it behaves rather than what it looks like. Behavior-based malware detection is designed to replace signature-based malware detection. It is sometimes powered by machine learning algorithms.

Sandboxing

Sandboxing is a security feature that can be used in antimalware to isolate potentially malicious files from the rest of the system. Sandboxing is often used as a method to filter out potentially malicious files and remove them before they have had a chance to do damage.

For example, when opening a file from an unknown email attachment, the sandbox will run the file in a virtual environment and only grant it access to a limited set of resources, such as a temporary folder, the internet and a virtual keyboard. If the file tries to access other programs or settings, it will be blocked, and the sandbox has the ability to terminate it.

Common Types of Malware

Here are some of the most common types of malware:

- **Ransomware**—malware which is designed to infiltrate computers and encrypt key files. After these files have been encrypted, the individual behind the ransomware demands payment for access to the secret key required to decrypt the encrypted files.

- **Viruses**—malware that functions by infecting different computer programs. For instance, a virus could overwrite the code of an affected program with its own code or make the program import and use a malicious code.

- **Worms**—malware that is created to sprawl out to additional infected systems. This could include malware that spreads by releasing phishing emails or that scans for different vulnerable computers.

- **Rootkits**—malware that is created to be secretive and can watch a computer user. Once it has been installed, the rootkit attempts to hide itself so as to avoid detection by antivirus and other security programs, while exfiltrating and collecting data for the operator.

- **Cryptomining malware**—cryptocurrency mining programs are created to exploit cryptocurrencies awards by solving Proof of Work computational puzzles. Cryptomining malware makes use of the CPU tools of an infected computer to find solutions to these problems. This enables criminals to win award money.

- **Botnet**—a network of infected computers. Cybercriminals use and control botnets in order to carry out large-scale, automated attacks, such as Distributed Denial of Service (DDoS) and credential stuffing. Botnet malware is intended to infect computers with a place a control and command structure that lets attackers send commands to the malware so that it carries out the attacker's intention.

- **Trojans**—malware created to impersonate something. Trojans try to steal the credentials of online accounts that may offer access to various streams of income like online bank accounts.

- **Fileless**—a form of malware that avoids detection by traditional antivirus applications, which scan a computer's files for indications of malware. This is achieved by removing custom malicution code and using functionality built into the system being targeted. This makes fileless malware difficult to detect, because it doesn't have the file that matches signatures previously retained by antivirus applications.

⦿ **Adware**—malware that is created to serve malicious ads to computer users. Malware developers gain revenue from the advertisers whose ads the author serves.

How to Prevent Malware Infections in Your Organization

You can prevent malware with a variety of techniques:

⦿ Install anti-malware software on your devices

⦿ Ensure safe user behavior on devices (i.e. avoiding opening attachments from untrusted sources)

⦿ Keep your anti-malware software updated, so you can benefit from the latest patches

⦿ Implement a dual approval process for transactions between different organizations

⦿ Implement second-channel verification processes for transactions with customers

⦿ Apply threat detection and response procedures to identify malware and prevent it from spreading

⦿ Implement robust security policies such as whitelists or allow lists

⦿ Deploy advanced threat protection solutions for email security

⦿ Ensure that files uploaded via collaboration channels and cloud storage are properly scanned

⦿ Implement security at the web browser level

Uses of antimalware

The value of antimalware applications is recognized beyond simply scanning files for viruses. Antimalware can help prevent malware attacks by scanning all incoming data to prevent malware from being installed and infecting a computer. Antimalware programs can also detect advanced forms of malware and offer protection against ransomware attacks.

Antimalware programs can help in the following ways:

⦿ prevent users of from visiting websites known for containing malware;

⦿ prevent malware from spreading to other computers in a computer system;

⦿ provide insight into the number of infections and the time required for their removal; and

⦿ provide insight into how the malware compromised the device or network.

Antimalware is helpful to keep a computer malware-free, and running an anti-malware program regularly can help keep a personal computer (PC) running smoothly and safely. The best type of antimalware software catches the most threats and requires the fewest updates, meaning it can run in the background without slowing the computer down. There are many free antimalware programs that can protect a computer from becoming infected with malware.

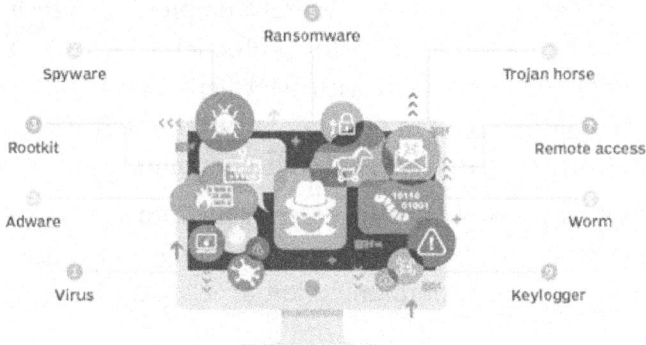

Types of malware

Differences between antimalware and antivirus

While the terms malware and virus are often used interchangeably, historically, they did not always refer to the same thing. A virus is a type of malware, but not all forms of malware are viruses. Viruses are the most common type of malware; they are a type of malicious code used to gain access to a computer or data network in order to cause damage. Viruses were regarded as older, more well-known threats, such as Trojan horses, viruses, keyloggers and worms. A virus is a program that can replicate itself, whereas malware is a program that attempts to accomplish a given goal but is not self-replicating. Malware became a term used to describe newer, increasingly dangerous threats spread by malicious advertising (malvertising) and zero-day exploits.

Similarly, the terms antivirus and antimalware are often used interchangeably, but the terms initially referred to different types of security software. Although both were designed to combat viruses, they originated to serve different functions and target different threats. Today, both antimalware and antivirus software perform the same or similar functions.

Malware Protection Best Practices

Here are several best practices to consider when implementing malware protection:

- ◉ **Strong passwords and software updates**—ensure all users create strone, unique passwords, and regularly change passwords. Use a password manager to make it easier for users to use and remember secure passwords. Update your systems as quickly, as security flaws become known and patches are released.

⊙ **Back up your data and your test restore procedures**—backup is a critical practice that can help to protect against data loss. It can help ensure that normal operations can be maintained even if the organization is attacked by network-based ransomware worms or other destructive cyber attacks.

⊙ **Protect against malware**—you should employ a layered approach that employs a combination of endpoint protection tools. For example, you can combine endpoint protection with next-generation firewalls (NGFW), and also implement an intrusion prevention system (IPS). This combination can help you ensure security is covered from endpoints to emails to the DNS layer.

⊙ **Educate users on malware threats**—train your users on techniques that can help them avoid social engineering schemes, such as phishing attacks, and report suspicious communication or system behavior to the security team.

⊙ **Partition your network**—you should use network segmentation to isolate important parts of your network from each other. This can significantly reduce the "blast radius" of successful attacks, because attackers will be limited to a specific network segment, and cannot move laterally to other parts of the network.

⊙ **Deploy advanced email security**—the majority of ransomware infections are spread via malicious downloads or email attachments. You should implement a layered security approach; one that can prevent advanced threats from reaching your end users as well as a company-sanctioned file-sharing solution that is scanned, and endpoint protection on user devices.

⊙ **Use security analytics**—continuously monitor network traffic, and use real-time threat intelligence feeds to add context to security alerts. This can help you gain extended visibility into threats affecting your network, understand their severity and how to respond effectively.

⊙ **Create instructions for your IT staff**—develop an incident response plan, which tells security staff and other stakeholders what they should do to detect, contain, and eradicate a cyber attack.

⊙ **Deploy a zero-trust security framework**—in this security approach, all access requests, whether coming from outside or inside the network, must be verified for trustworthiness before they can gain access to a system. The goal is to secure access by end-user devices, users, APIs, microservices, IoT, and containers, all of which may be compromised by attackers.

Malware Protection with Perception Point

Perception Point delivers one platform that prevents malware, ransomware, APTs and zero-days from reaching your end users.

Advanced email security is an integrated cloud email security solution (ICES) that can replace SEGs. The solution cloud-native SaaS solution protects your organization against all threats using 7 layers of advanced threat detection layers to prevent malicious files, URLs, and social-engineering based techniques.

Advanced Browser Security adds enterprise-grade security to your organizations native browsers. The managed solution fuses browser protection technology with multi-layer advanced threat prevention engines which delivers the unprecedented ability to detect and remediate all malicious threats from the web, including phishing, ransomware, malware, APTs, and more. Multi-layered static and dynamic detection capabilities instantly detect and block access to malicious/phishing websites and prevent malicious file downloads of ransomware, malware, and APTs.

Advanced Threat Protection for Cloud Collaboration, File Sharing and Storage Applications, such as Microsoft 365 applications (OneDrive, SharePoint, Teams), Google Drive Box, AWS S3 buckets, Zendesk, Salesforce, and any of the other hundreds of apps out there, protects your organization with near real-time dynamic scanning. It does not tamper with files and does not impede on productivity.

An all-included managed Incident Response service is available for all customers 24/7 with no added charge. Perception Point's team of cybersecurity experts will manage incidents, provide analysis and reporting, and optimize detection on-the-fly. The service drastically minimizes the need for internal IT or SOC team resources, reducing the time required to react and mitigate web-borne attacks by up to 75%.

HOST-BASED INTRUSION PREVENTION SYSTEMS (HIPS)

An abbreviation for Host-based Intrusion Prevention System, HIPS is an Intrusion Prevention System (IPS) used to keep safe crucial computer systems holding important information against intrusions, infections, and other Internet malware.

HIPS surveil a single host for dubious activity by examining incidents happening within that specific host. To put it differently, a Host Intrusion Prevention System (HIPS) seeks to halt malware by monitoring the code's way of behaving.

This helps to keep your system secure without having to rely on a specific threat to be added to a detection update. If a threat actor or virus tries to change the operating system, the host intrusion prevention system blocks the activity and notifies the potential victims so they can take proper action.

Some of the changes that HIPS might consider to be important are assuming command of other programs, attempting to change major registry keys, ending other programs, or installing devices.

Besides the action of sending notifications to the device user when it detects malicious movement, HIPS can also log the malicious activity for future investigation, reset the connection, and stop future traffic from the dubious IP address.

Host Intrusion Prevention System (HIPS) successfully fights against:

- ⊙ Private information theft;
- ⊙ Dubious applications while it stops harmful actions;
- ⊙ Familiar threats, as it averts them from being initiated;
- ⊙ The latest threats before antivirus databases are updated while diminishes the probability of invasion and contamination being scattered.

Different types of devices such as servers, workstations, and computers can have the host intrusion prevention system implemented.

As studies have recently shown that unprotected systems can be compromised within minutes, the benefit of intrusion prevention is that there's no more waiting for a security administrator to answer before prophylactic steps are taken to maintain host integrity. This approach can be very helpful when in need.

Usually, a host intrusion prevention system is both signature and anomaly-based.

An anomaly-based HIPS tries to differentiate normal from atypical behavior, unlike signature based-systems that have the capability to protect against only familiar bad signatures.

Host Intrusion Prevention System (HIPS) Operation Mode

A host intrusion prevention system utilizes a database of systems items supervised to discover intrusions by investigating system calls, application logs, and file-system changes.

HIPS recalls every item's features and generates a numerical value calculated from a series of bits of digital data used to test whether the data has changed during storage or transmission for the contents.

The system also verifies if suitable parts of memory have not been altered. A program that ignores its permissions is blocked from performing unauthorized actions.

A HIPS has many advantages, the most important one being that business and home users have intensified defense from hidden malicious cyber assaults.

Host Intrusion Prevention HIPS utilizes an unusual prevention system that has a better chance of halting such attacks in contrast to conventional protective actions.

One more advantage of using HIPS is the necessity to manage numerous security applications to secure computers, including antivirus, anti-spyware, firewalls, and patch management.

Now that we talked about the benefits, let's take a quick look at the disadvantage of HIPS. A drawback would be that the response taken may leave the host ineffective or even affect the availability of a vital resource. Incorrect user decisions and false positives are also menaces linked to host intrusion prevention systems.

Host Intrusion Prevention Systems (HIPS) can be an extremely important component of stratified protection if combined with a minimum of one detection-based security solution. Users and organizations should definitely benefit from HIPS, but it is essential to have some knowledge of how to use it successfully.

Advantages of the Host Intrusion Prevention System (HIPS)?

Let's examine the usability and advantages of a host-based intrusion prevention system (HIPS):

- For enterprise and home users, zero-day vulnerabilities are too dangerous. Because HIPS uses anomaly detection, it has a greater possibility of detecting and stopping a zero-day attack.

- There is no need to wait for a security officer to respond before preventive steps are implemented to preserve host integrity using intrusion prevention. This strategy may be useful, especially in light of recent research indicating that susceptible systems may be corrupted within minutes.

- HIPS employs a unique preventative technique that can prevent such attacks more than conventional safeguards.

- Multiple PC-protecting security solutions, such as anti-virus, anti-spyware, and software firewall, can be merged into one.

- TCO is another advantage of HIPS. HIPS is a single security solution that may be purchased as opposed to three.

The Host Intrusion Prevention System (HIPS) effectively combats:

- Theft of private information

- Questionable uses while preventing hazardous activities

- Familiar dangers, as it prevents their initiation

- The prevalence of the most recent threats before antivirus databases are updated

| Theft of private information | Questionable uses while preventing hazardous activities | Familiar dangers, as it prevents their initiation | The prevalence of the most recent threats before antivirus data-bases are updated |

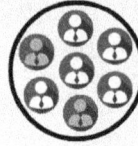

Host Intrusion Prevention System

The Host-based Intrusion Prevention System (HIPS) protects your system against malicious software and unwanted activities that attempt to harm your computer. HIPS employs advanced behavioral analysis in conjunction with network filtering's detection capabilities to monitor running programs, files, and registry keys. HIPS is distinct from real-time file system protection and is not a firewall: it monitors just operating system operations.

Advantages of HIPS

What are the Disadvantages of the Host Intrusion Prevention System (HIPS)?

The HIPS is that the reaction may render the host ineffective or affect the accessibility of a vital resource. It is one thing for an IDS to generate a false positive, but a false positive that triggers a reflexive action might be worse.

Existing HIPS that incorporate firewall, system-level action control, and sandboxing into a unified detection net, in addition to a typical AV product, may have a high system resource need.

ENDPOINT DETECTION AND RESPONSE (EDR)

Endpoint detection and response (EDR) is a system to gather and analyze security threat-related information from computer workstations and other endpoints, with the goal of finding security breaches as they happen and facilitating a quick response to discovered or potential threats. The term "endpoint detection and response" only describes the overall capabilities of a tool set. Therefore, the details and capabilities of an EDR system can vary greatly depending on the implementation.

An EDR implementation may be:

⊙ A specific purpose-built tool;

⊙ A small portion of a larger security monitoring tool; or

⊙ A loose collection of tools used together to accomplish the task.

As attackers continuously update their methods and capabilities, traditional protection systems may fall short. EDR combines data and behavioral analysis, which makes them effective against emerging threats and active attacks, such as:

⊙ Novel malware;

- Emerging exploit chains;

- Ransomware; and

- Advanced persistent threats (APT).

The historical data collected by endpoint detection and response tools can provide peace of mind and remediation for actively exploited zero-day attacks, even when a mitigation isn't available. The IT security industry considers EDR a form of advanced threat protection.

Importance of EDR

Evolving threat landscape

Cyber threats are constantly evolving, with attackers using increasingly sophisticated tactics to bypass traditional security measures. EDR helps organizations stay ahead of these threats by providing continuous monitoring, detection, and response capabilities.

Growing remote workforce

The rise of remote work has expanded the attack surface, as employees connect to corporate networks from various locations and devices. EDR helps secure these dispersed endpoints by providing centralized monitoring and management, ensuring consistent security across all devices.

Faster incident response

EDR accelerates incident response by automating threat containment and remediation actions, reducing the time it takes to address security incidents. This minimizes potential damage and business disruption caused by cyberattacks.

Reducing dwell time

EDR reduces the amount of time attackers can remain undetected within a network (dwell time) by promptly identifying and addressing security incidents. Minimizing dwell time is crucial in limiting the potential damage caused by a cyberattack.

Proactive security

EDR helps organizations shift from a reactive security approach to a more proactive one, where potential threats are detected and mitigated before they can cause significant harm. This proactive approach can significantly reduce the risk of data breaches and other security incidents.

Endpoint detection and response use and capabilities

EDR is primarily concerned with endpoints, which can be any computer system in a network, such as end-user workstations or servers. They can protect most operating systems (i.e., Windows, macOS, Linux, BSD, etc.) but do not include network monitoring.

A system that gathers information from many sources, such as endpoints, firewalls, network scans and internets logs, is considered security information and event management (SIEM). Security vendors may offer EDR as part of a SIEM package, however, for use by a security operations center (SOC) to investigate and respond to threats.

EDR is an integral part of a complete information security posture. It is not antivirus software, but it may have antivirus capabilities or use data from another antivirus product. Antivirus software is primarily responsible for protecting against known malicious software, while a well-executed endpoint protection and response program finds new exploits as they are running and detect malicious activity by an attacker during an active incident. This allows EDR to detect Fileless malware attacks and attackers using stolen credentials, which traditional antivirus alone will not stop. Many EDR systems are part of next-generation antivirus products, however.

The role of an EDR system falls broadly into two categories:

- information collection and analysis; and
- threat response.

Because EDR capabilities can vary greatly from vendor to vendor, an organization researching EDR systems should carefully investigate the capabilities of any proposed system. They should also take into consideration how well it can integrate with their current overall security capabilities.

The information collection and analysis capabilities of EDR gathers and organizes data from endpoints, and then uses that information to identify irregularities or trends. It uses many data sources from an endpoint, which can include:

- logs;
- performance monitoring;
- file details;
- running processes; and
- configuration data or other information.

A dedicated agent installed on the endpoint can collect this data, or the system may use built-in OS capabilities and other helper programs.

EDR systems organize and analyze the collected data. A client device may perform portions of this, but, generally, a central system — hardware device, a virtual server or a cloud service — performs these functions.

Simple EDR systems may only collect and display this data or aggregate it and show trends. Operators may find following and making decisions based on this type of data difficult.

Advanced EDR systems can include machine learning or AI to automatically identify and alert on new and emerging threats. They may also use aggregate information from the product vendor to better flag threats. Some systems allow mapping of observed suspicious behavior to the MITRE ATT&CK framework to help detect patterns.

Threat response capabilities of EDR help the operator take corrective action, diagnose further issues and perform forensic analysis, which may allow for issue tracking and can help surface similar activity or otherwise aid an investigation. Forensic capabilities help establish timelines, identify affected systems post breach and may be able to gather artifacts or investigate live system memory in suspect endpoints. Combining historical and current situational data help to provide a fuller picture during an incident.

Some endpoint detection and response systems can perform automated remediation activities, such as disconnecting or stopping compromised processes or alerting the user or information security group. They also may be able to actively isolate or disable suspect endpoints or accounts. A good incident response system will also help coordinate teams during an active incident, helping to reduce its impact.

CHAPTER- 5

CRYPTOGRAPHY AND ENCRYPTION

CRYPTOGRAPHY

Cryptography is the study of securing communications from outside observers. Encryption algorithms take the original message, or plaintext, and converts it into ciphertext, which is not understandable. The key allows the user to decrypt the message, thus ensuring on they can read the message. The strength of the randomness of an encryption is also studied, which makes it harder for anyone to guess the key or input of the algorithm. Cryptography is how we can achieve more secure and robust connections to elevate our privacy. Advancements in cryptography makes it harder to break encryptions so that encrypted files, folders, or network connections are only accessible to authorized users.

Cryptography focuses on four different objectives:

Confidentiality

Confidentiality ensures that only the intended recipient can decrypt the message and read its contents.

Non-repudiation

Non-repudiation means the sender of the message cannot backtrack in the future and deny their reasons for sending or creating the message.

Integrity

Integrity focuses on the ability to be certain that the information contained within the message cannot be modified while in storage or transit.

Authenticity

Authenticity ensures the sender and recipient can verify each other's identities and the destination of the message.

These objectives help ensure a secure and authentic transfer of information.

History of Cryptography

Cryptography began with ciphers, the first of which was the Caesar Cipher. Ciphers were a lot easier to unravel compared to modern cryptographic algorithms, but they both used keys and plaintext. Though simple, ciphers from the past were the earliest forms of encryption. Today's algorithms and cryptosystems are much more advanced. They use multiple rounds of ciphers and encrypting the ciphertext of messages to ensure the most secure transit and storage of data. There are also methods of cryptography used now that are irreversible, maintaining the security of the message forever.

The reason for more advanced cryptography methods is due to the need for data to be protected more and more securely. Most of the ciphers and algorithms used in the early days of cryptography have been deciphered, making them useless for data protection. Today's algorithms can be deciphered, but it would require years and sometimes decades to decipher the meaning of just one message. Thus, the race to create newer and more advanced cryptography techniques continues.

Types of Cryptography

Cryptography can be broken down into three different types:

- Secret Key Cryptography
- Public Key Cryptography
- Hash Functions

Secret Key Cryptography, or symmetric cryptography, uses a single key to encrypt data. Both encryption and decryption in symmetric cryptography use the same key, making this the easiest form of cryptography. The cryptographic algorithm utilizes the key in a cipher to encrypt the data, and when the data must be accessed again, a person entrusted with the secret key can decrypt the data. Secret Key Cryptography can be used on both in-transit and at-rest data, but is commonly only used on at-rest data, as sending the secret to the recipient of the message can lead to compromise.

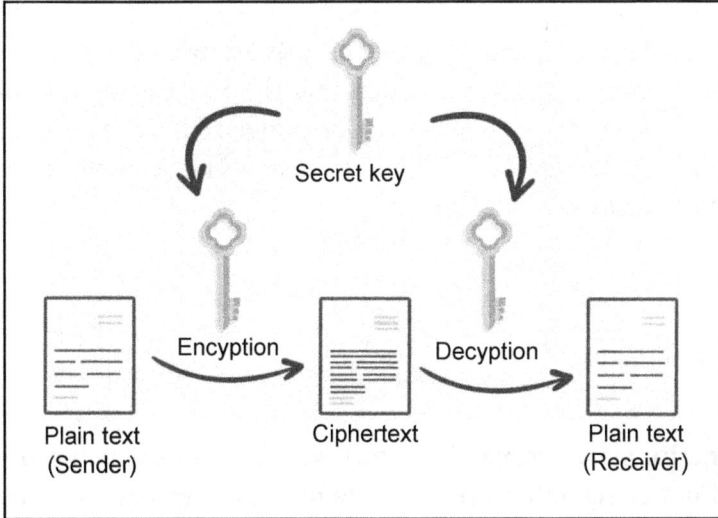

Symmetric Encyption

Examples:

- ⦿ AES
- ⦿ DES
- ⦿ Caesar Cipher

Public Key Cryptography, or asymmetric cryptography, uses two keys to encrypt data. One is used for encryption, while the other key can decrypts the message. Unlike symmetric cryptography, if one key is used to encrypt, that same key cannot decrypt the message, rather the other key shall be used.

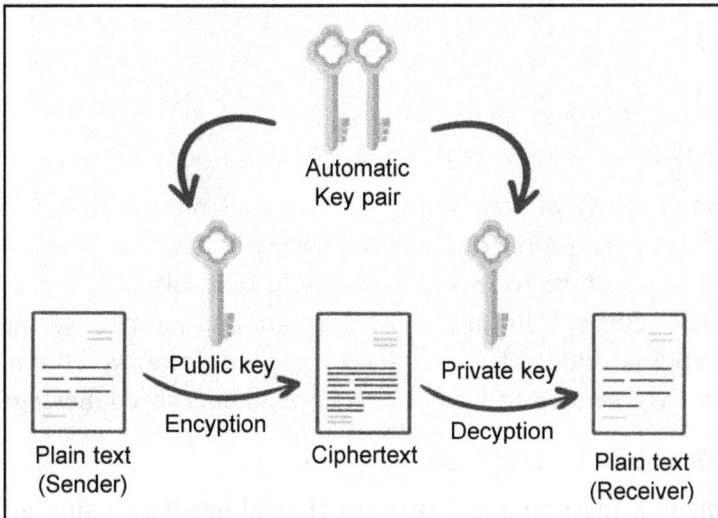

Asymmetric Encryption

One key is kept private, and is called the "private key", while the other is shared publicly and can be used by anyone, hence it is known as the "public key". The mathematical relation of the keys is such that the private key cannot be derived from the public key, but the public key can be derived from the private. The private key should not be distributed and should remain with the owner only. The public key can be given to any other entity.

Examples:

- ECC
- Diffie-Hellman
- DSS

Hash functions are irreversible, one-way functions which protect the data, at the cost of not being able to recover the original message. Hashing is a way to transform a given string into a fixed length string. A good hashing algorithm will produce unique outputs for each input given. The only way to crack a hash is by trying every input possible, until you get the exact same hash. A hash can be used for hashing data (such as passwords) and in certificates.

Some of the most famous hashing algorithms are:

- MD5
- SHA-1
- SHA-2 family which includes SHA-224, SHA-256, SHA-384, and SHA-512
- SHA-3
- Whirlpool
- Blake 2
- Blake 3

ENCRYPTION

Encryption is a way of scrambling data so that only authorized parties can understand the information. In technical terms, it is the process of converting human-readable plaintext to incomprehensible text, also known as ciphertext. In simpler terms, encryption takes readable data and alters it so that it appears random. Encryption requires the use of a cryptographic key: a set of mathematical values that both the sender and the recipient of an encrypted message agree on.

Working Process of Encryption

Encryption is a mathematical process that alters data using an encryption algorithm and a key. Imagine if Alice sends the message "Hello" to Bob, but she replaces each letter in her message with the letter that comes two places later in the alphabet. Instead of "Hello," her message now reads "Jgnnq." Fortunately, Bob knows that the key is "2" and can decrypt her message back to "Hello."

Alice used an extremely simple encryption algorithm to encode her message to Bob. More complicated encryption algorithms can further scramble the message:

Although encrypted data appears random, encryption proceeds in a logical, predictable way, allowing a party that receives the encrypted data and possesses the right key to decrypt the data, turning it back into plaintext. Truly secure encryption will use keys complex enough that a third party is highly unlikely to decrypt or break the ciphertext by brute force — in other words, by guessing the key. (Alice's first encryption method would be broken very quickly.)

Data can be encrypted "at rest," when it is stored, or "in transit," while it is being transmitted somewhere else.

Cryptographic key

A cryptographic key is a string of characters used within an encryption algorithm for altering data so that it appears random. Like a physical key, it locks (encrypts) data so that only someone with the right key can unlock (decrypt) it.

Types of encryption

The two main kinds of encryption are symmetric encryption and asymmetric encryption. Asymmetric encryption is also known as public key encryption.

In symmetric encryption, there is only one key, and all communicating parties use the same (secret) key for both encryption and decryption. In asymmetric, or public key, encryption, there are two keys: one key is used for encryption, and a different key is used for decryption. The decryption key is kept private (hence the "private key" name), while the encryption key is shared publicly, for anyone to use (hence the "public key" name). Asymmetric encryption is a foundational technology for TLS (often called SSL).

Importance of Encryption

- ⊙ **Privacy:** Encryption ensures that no one can read communications or data at rest except the intended recipient or the rightful data owner. This prevents attackers, ad networks, Internet service providers, and in some cases governments from intercepting and reading sensitive data, protecting user privacy.

- ⊙ **Security:** Encryption helps prevent data breaches, whether the data is in transit or at rest. If a corporate device is lost or stolen and its hard drive is properly encrypted, the data on that device will still be secure. Similarly, encrypted communications enable the communicating parties to exchange sensitive data without leaking the data.

⦿ **Data integrity:** Encryption also helps prevent malicious behavior such as on-path attacks. When data is transmitted across the Internet, encryption ensures that what the recipient receives has not been viewed or tampered with on the way.

⦿ **Regulations:** For all these reasons, many industry and government regulations require companies that handle user data to keep that data encrypted. Examples of regulatory and compliance standards that require encryption include HIPAA, PCI-DSS, and the GDPR.

Encryption Algorithm

An encryption algorithm is the method used to transform data into ciphertext. An algorithm will use the encryption key in order to alter the data in a predictable way, so that even though the encrypted data will appear random, it can be turned back into plaintext by using the decryption key.

Some common encryption algorithms

Commonly used symmetric encryption algorithms include:

⦿ AES

⦿ 3-DES

⦿ SNOW

Commonly used asymmetric encryption algorithms include:

⦿ RSA

⦿ Elliptic curve cryptography

BASICS OF CRYPTOGRAPHY

Encryption

In a simplest form, encryption is to convert the data in some unreadable form. This helps in protecting the privacy while sending the data from sender to receiver. On the receiver side, the data can be decrypted and can be brought back to its original form. The reverse of encryption is called as decryption. The concept of encryption and decryption requires some extra information for encrypting and decrypting the data. This information is known as key. There may be cases when same key can be used for both encryption and decryption while in certain cases, encryption and decryption may require different keys.

Authentication

This is another important principle of cryptography. In a layman's term, authentication ensures that the message was originated from the originator claimed in the message. Now, one may think how to make it possible? Suppose,

Alice sends a message to Bob and now Bob wants proof that the message has been indeed sent by Alice. This can be made possible if Alice performs some action on message that Bob knows only Alice can do. Well, this forms the basic fundamental of Authentication.

Integrity

Now, one problem that a communication system can face is the loss of integrity of messages being sent from sender to receiver. This means that Cryptography should ensure that the messages that are received by the receiver are not altered anywhere on the communication path. This can be achieved by using the concept of cryptographic hash.

Non Repudiation

What happens if Alice sends a message to Bob but denies that she has actually sent the message? Cases like these may happen and cryptography should prevent the originator or sender to act this way. One popular way to achieve this is through the use of digital signatures.

PUBLIC KEY INFRASTRUCTURE (PKI)

This type of cryptography technique involves two key crypto system in which a secure communication can take place between receiver and sender over insecure communication channel. Since a pair of keys is applied here so this technique is also known as asymmetric encryption.

In this method, each party has a private key and a public key. The private is secret and is not revealed while the public key is shared with all those whom you want to communicate with. If Alice wants to send a message to bob, then Alice will encrypt it with Bob's public key and Bob can decrypt the message with its private key.

Elements of PKI

A typical PKI includes the following key elements:

⊙ **Certificate authority.** A trusted party provides the root of trust for all PKI certificates and provides services that can be used to authenticate the identity of individuals, computers and other entities. Usually known as certificate authorities (CAs), these entities provide assurance about the parties identified in a PKI certificate. Each CA maintains its own root CA, for use only by the CA.

⊙ Registration authority. This is often called a subordinate CA and issues PKI certificates. The registration authority (RA) is certified by a root CA and is authorized to issue certificates for specific uses permitted by the root.

⊙ Certificate store. This is usually permanently stored on a computer but can also be maintained in memory for applications that do not require that certificates be stored permanently. The certificate store enables programs running on the system to access stored certificates, certificate revocation lists (CRLs) and certificate trust lists (CTLs).

⊙ Certificate database. This database stores information about issued certificates. In addition to the certificate itself, the database includes the validity period and status of each PKI certificate. Certificate revocation is done by updating this database, which must be queried to authenticate any data digitally signed or encrypted with the secret key of the certificate holder.

The Role of Certificate Authorities (CAs)

In order to bind public keys with their associated user (owner of the private key), PKIs use digital certificates. Digital certificates are the credentials that facilitate the verification of identities between users in a transaction. Much as a passport certifies one's identity as a citizen of a country, the digital certificate establishes the identity of users within the ecosystem. Because digital certificates are used to identify the users to whom encrypted data is sent, or to verify the identity of the signer of information, protecting the authenticity and integrity of the certificate is imperative to maintain the trustworthiness of the system.

Certificate authorities (CAs) issue the digital credentials used to certify the identity of users. CAs underpin the security of a PKI and the services they support, and therefore can be the focus of sophisticated targeted attacks. In order to mitigate the risk of attacks against CAs, physical and logical controls as well as hardening mechanisms, such as hardware security modules (HSMs) have become necessary to ensure the integrity of a PKI.

PKI Deployment

PKIs provide a framework that enables cryptographic data security technologies such as digital certificates and signatures to be effectively deployed on a mass scale. PKIs support identity management services within and across networks and underpin online authentication inherent in secure socket layer (SSL) and transport layer security (TLS) for protecting internet traffic, as well as document and transaction signing, application code signing, and time-stamping. PKIs support solutions for desktop login, citizen identification, mass transit, mobile banking, and are critically important for device credentialing in the IoT. Device credentialing is becoming increasingly important to impart identities to growing numbers of cloud-based and internet-connected devices that run the gamut from smart phones to medical equipment.

Cryptographic Security

Using the principles of asymmetric and symmetric cryptography, PKIs facilitate the establishment of a secure exchange of data between users and devices – ensuring authenticity, confidentiality, and integrity of transactions. Users (also known as "Subscribers" in PKI parlance) can be individual end users, web servers, embedded systems, connected devices, or programs/applications that are executing business processes. Asymmetric cryptography provides the users, devices or services within an ecosystem with a key pair composed of a public and a private key component. A public key is available to anyone in the group for encryption or for verification of a digital signature. The private key on the other hand, must be kept secret and is only used by the entity to which it belongs, typically for tasks such as decryption or for the creation of digital signatures.

The Increasing Importance of PKIs

With evolving business models becoming more dependent on electronic transactions and digital documents, and with more Internet-aware devices connected to corporate networks, the role of a PKI is no longer limited to isolated systems such as secure email, smart cards for physical access or encrypted web traffic. PKIs today are expected to support larger numbers of applications, users and devices across complex ecosystems. And with stricter government and industry data security regulations, mainstream operating systems and business applications are becoming more reliant than ever on an organizational PKI to guarantee trust.

Encryption Algorithms and Key Management

Encryption is a process that uses algorithms to encode data as ciphertext. This ciphertext can only be made meaningful again, if the person or application accessing the data has the data encryption keys necessary to decode the ciphertext. So, if the data is stolen or accidentally shared, it is protected because it is indecipherable, thanks to data encryption.

Controlling and maintaining data encryption keys is an essential part of any data encryption strategy, because, with the encryption keys, a cybercriminal can return encrypted data to its original unencrypted state. An encryption key management system includes generation, exchange, storage, use, destruction and replacement of encryption keys.

The need for encryption key management

High-profile data losses and regulatory compliance requirements have caused a dramatic increase in the use of encryption to protect data in the enterprise. Encryption is the process of applying complex algorithms to data and then converting that data into streams of seemingly random alphanumeric characters. There are two basic types of cryptographic algorithms: symmetric, or private key, and asymmetric, or public key.

To protect their data and business-critical assets, enterprises might use many different and possibly incompatible encryption tools, resulting in the use of thousands of encryption keys. Each key must be securely generated and stored, because if an unauthorized or malicious user gains access to a key, they could be able to decrypt the encrypted data and then use that data for their own purposes.

In addition, the distribution of encryption keys must be controlled, and any losses or compromises must be addressed quickly and appropriately. It's also vital to ensure that each key is easily retrievable by authorized users.

To effectively manage all these aspects, encryption key management is vital. With an effective encryption key management system, organizations can efficiently generate, store, use, organize and manage their encryption keys. That's why encryption key management must be part of the enterprise data encryption and data protection strategy.

Best practices for encryption key management

Key management means protecting every encryption key from loss, corruption and unauthorized access throughout its lifecycle. Many processes can be used to control key management, including changing the keys regularly as well as managing how keys are assigned and who is authorized to get them. In addition, organizations must evaluate whether one key should be used for all data types or if each type should have its own key. They must also rotate keys to minimize the chances of keys being stolen or compromised because they've been used for a long time.

To generate secure encryption keys, it's important to use secure methods such as Advanced Encryption Standard (AES) encryption algorithms and random number generators. Also, the keys must not be hardcoded into any program code and must be securely distributed to authorized users only via secure connections.

Secure storage is vital so that the encryption keys can be reused for decryption more than once. A hardware security module (HSM) provides one of the most secure methods for encryption key storage. Keys can also be securely stored in the cloud using a cloud service provider's key management service. Ideally, deactivated keys should also be stored in a secure archive to enable the later decryption of encrypted data that uses those keys.

Having more than one person in charge of storing, backing up, referencing and rotating encryption keys is essential. The roles of key players should be defined, and the encryption key management policy should be accessible to everyone on an internal or intranet site. The policy should clearly state the methods and practices used in the organization to track key generation, access and use.

Encryption key management standards

The best-known encryption key management standard is the Key Management Interoperability Protocol (KMIP), developed by vendors and submitted to OASIS, the Organization for the Advancement of Structured Information Standards. The goal of KMIP is to allow users to attach any encryption device to a key management system.

KMIP enables and simplifies key lifecycle management. It can be used by both legacy and new cryptographic applications and works with many types of keys, including symmetric and asymmetric keys, authentication tokens, and digital certificates.

Distribution of Public Key

The public key can be distributed in four ways:

- ◉ Public announcement
- ◉ Publicly available directory
- ◉ Public-key authority
- ◉ Public-key certificates.

These are explained as following below:

Public Announcement

Here the public key is broadcasted to everyone. The major weakness of this method is a forgery. Anyone can create a key claiming to be someone else and broadcast it. Until forgery is discovered can masquerade as claimed user.

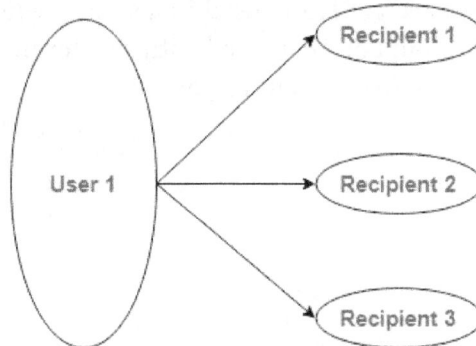

Public Announcement

Publicly Available Directory

In this type, the public key is stored in a public directory. Directories are trusted here, with properties like Participant Registration, access and allow to modify values at any time, contains entries like {name, public-key}. Directories can be accessed electronically still vulnerable to forgery or tampering.

Public Key Authority

It is similar to the directory but, improves security by tightening control over the distribution of keys from the directory. It requires users to know the public key for the directory. Whenever the keys are needed, real-time access to the directory is made by the user to obtain any desired public key securely.

Public Certification

This time authority provides a certificate (which binds an identity to the public key) to allow key exchange without real-time access to the public authority each time. The certificate is accompanied by some other info such as period of validity, rights of use, etc. All of this content is signed by the private key of the certificate authority and it can be verified by anyone possessing the authority's public key.

First sender and receiver both request CA for a certificate which contains a public key and other information and then they can exchange these certificates and can start communication.

Recent advancements in encryption key management

AWS Key Management Service enables users to create and manage cryptographic keys that protect data in the Amazon Web Services cloud. These keys can also be used in cryptographic operations, such as to sign and verify messages, generate hash-based message authentication codes, and generate random numbers for specific applications. Each key is protected and validated using HSMs. Organizations can track and audit their AWS keys for regulatory and compliance purposes via AWS CloudTrail.

AWS encryption keys are generally used in a single region. For example, data encrypted in one region would be encrypted with a different key than a replicated version of that data stored in a different region.

CHAPTER-6

SECURITY INFORMATION AND EVENT MANAGEMENT (SIEM)

The term SIEM was coined by Mark Nicolett and Amrit Williams, in Gartner's SIEM report, Improve IT Security with Vulnerability Management. They proposed a new security information system on the basis of two previous technologies: Security Information Management (SIM) and Security Event Management (SEM).

Several years later, Gartner introduced a vision of a next-gen SIEM that goes beyond rules and correlations. Next-gen SIEM incorporates two key technologies: user and entity behavior analytics (UEBA) and security orchestration and automation response (SOAR). These technologies enable complex threat identification, detection of lateral movement, and automated incident response as an integral part of a SIEM's functions.

The underlying principles of every SIEM system are to aggregate relevant data from multiple sources, identify deviations from the norm and take appropriate action. For example, when a potential issue is detected, a SIEM system might log additional information, generate an alert and instruct other security controls to stop an activity's progress.

Payment Card Industry Data Security Standard compliance originally drove SIEM adoption in large enterprises, but concerns over advanced persistent threats have led smaller organizations to look at the benefits SIEM tools can offer as well. Being able to look at all security-related data from a single point of view makes it easier for organizations of all sizes to spot unusual patterns.

At the most basic level, a SIEM system can be rules-based or employ a statistical correlation engine to make connections between event log entries. Advanced SIEM systems have evolved to include user and entity behavior analytics, as well as security orchestration, automation and response (SOAR).

SIEM systems work by deploying multiple collection agents in a hierarchical manner to gather security-related events from end-user devices, servers and network equipment, as well as specialized security equipment, such as firewalls, antivirus programs or intrusion prevention systems (IPSes). The collectors forward events to a centralized management console, where security analysts sift through the noise, connecting the dots and prioritizing security incidents.

In some systems, pre-processing can happen at edge collectors, with only certain events being passed through to a centralized management node. In this way, the volume of information being communicated and stored can be reduced. Although advancements in machine learning are helping systems flag anomalies more accurately, analysts must still provide feedback, continuously educating the system about the environment.

Working of SIEM

SIEM tools gather event and log data created by host systems throughout a company's infrastructure and bring that data together on a centralized platform. Host systems include applications, security devices, antivirus filters and firewalls. SIEM tools identify and sort the data into categories such as successful and failed logins, malware activity and other likely malicious activity.

The SIEM software generates security alerts when it identifies potential security issues. Using a set of predefined rules, organizations can set these alerts as a low or high priority.

For instance, a user account that generates 25 failed login attempts in 25 minutes could be flagged as suspicious but still be set at a lower priority because the login attempts were probably made by a user who had forgotten their login information.

However, a user account that generates 130 failed login attempts in five minutes would be flagged as a high-priority event because it's most likely a brute-force attack in progress.

Importance of SIEM

SIEM makes it easier for enterprises to manage security by filtering massive amounts of security data and prioritizing the security alerts the software generates.

SIEM software enables organizations to detect incidents that may otherwise go undetected. The software analyzes the log entries to identify signs of malicious activity. In addition, since the system gathers events from different sources across the network, it can re-create the timeline of an attack, enabling an organization to determine the nature of the attack and its effect on the business.

A SIEM system can also help an organization meet compliance requirements by automatically generating reports that include all the logged security events among these sources. Without SIEM software, the company would have to gather log data and compile the reports manually.

A SIEM system also enhances incident management by helping the company's security team to uncover the route an attack takes across the network, identify the sources that were compromised and provide the automated tools to prevent the attacks in progress.

Benefits of SIEM

Benefits of SIEM include the following:

- It shortens the time it takes to identify threats significantly, minimizing the damage from those threats.

- SIEM offers a holistic view of an organization's information security environment, making it easier to gather and analyze security information to keep systems safe. All an organization's data goes into a centralized repository where it's stored and easily accessible.

- Companies can use SIEM for a variety of use cases that revolve around data or logs, including security programs, audit and compliance reporting, help desk and network troubleshooting.

- SIEM supports large amounts of data so organizations can continue to scale out and add more data.

- SIEM provides threat detection and security alerts.

- It can perform detailed forensic analysis in the event of major security breaches.

Limitations of SIEM

Despite its benefits, SIEM also has the following limitations:

- It can take a long time to implement SIEM because it requires support to ensure successful integration with an organization's security controls and the many hosts in its infrastructure. It typically takes 90 days or more to install SIEM before it starts to work.

- It's expensive. The initial investment in SIEM can be in the hundreds of thousands of dollars. And the associated costs can add up, including the costs of personnel to manage and monitor a SIEM implementation, annual support and software or agents to collect data.

- Analyzing, configuring and integrating reports require the talent of experts. That's why some SIEM systems are managed directly within a security operations center, a centralized unit staffed by an information security team that deals with an organization's security issues.

- ⊙ SIEM tools usually depend on rules to analyze all the recorded data. The problem is that a company's network could generate thousands of alerts per day. It's difficult to identify potential attacks because of the number of irrelevant logs.

- ⊙ A misconfigured SIEM tool might miss important security events, making information risk management less effective.

Features and Capabilities of SIEM

Important features to consider when evaluating SIEM products include the following:

- ⊙ **Data aggregation.** Data is collected and monitored from applications, networks, servers and databases.

- ⊙ **Correlation.** Typically a part of SEM in a SIEM tool, correlation refers to the tool finding similar attributes between different events.

- ⊙ **Dashboards.** Data is collected and aggregated from applications, databases, networks and servers and is displayed in charts to help find patterns and to avoid missing critical events.

- ⊙ **Alerting.** If a security incident is detected, SIEM tools can notify users.

- ⊙ **Automation.** Some SIEM software might also include automated functions, such as automated security incident analysis and automated incident responses.

Users should also ask the following questions about SIEM product capabilities:

- ⊙ **Integration with other controls.** Can the system give commands to other enterprise security controls to prevent or stop attacks in progress?

- ⊙ **Artificial intelligence (AI).** Can the system improve its own accuracy through machine learning and deep learning?

- ⊙ **Threat intelligence feeds.** Can the system support threat intelligence feeds of the organization's choosing, or is it mandated to use a particular feed?

- ⊙ **Extensive compliance reporting.** Does the system include built-in reports for common compliance needs and provide the organization with the ability to customize or create new compliance reports?

- ⊙ **Forensic capabilities.** Can the system capture additional information about security events by recording the headers and contents of packets of interest?

SIEM tools and software

There are a wide variety of SIEM tools on market, but the following is just a sample:

- **Splunk**. Splunk is an on-premises SIEM system that supports security monitoring and offers continuous security monitoring, advanced threat detection, incident investigation and incident response.

- **IBM QRadar**. The IBM QRadar SIEM platform provides security monitoring for IT infrastructures. It features log data collection, threat detection and event correlation.

- **LogRhythm**. LogRhythm is a SIEM system for smaller organizations. It unifies Log Management, network monitoring and endpoint monitoring, as well as forensics and security analytics.

- **Exabeam**. Exabeam Inc.'s SIEM portfolio offers a data lake, advanced analytics and a threat hunter.

- **NetWitness**. The RSA NetWitness platform is a threat detection and response tool that includes data acquisition, forwarding, storage and analysis.

- **Datadog Cloud SIEM**. Datadog Cloud SIEM from Datadog Security is a cloud-native network and management system. The tool features both real-time security monitoring and log management.

- **Log360**. The Log360 SIEM tool offers threat intelligence, incident management and SOAR features. Log collection, analysis, correlation, alerting and archiving features are available in real time.

- **SolarWinds Security Event Manager**. The SolarWinds Security Event Manager SIEM tool automatically detects threats, monitors security policies and protects networks. The tool offers features such as integrity monitoring, compliance reporting and centralized log collection.

Best practices to implementing SIEM

Follow these best practices while implementing SIEM:

- Set understandable goals. The SIEM tool should be chosen and implemented based on security goals, compliance and the potential threat landscape of the organization.

- Apply data correlation rules. Data correlation rules should be implemented across all systems, networks and cloud deployments so data with errors in it can be more easily found.

- Identify compliance requirements. This helps ensure the chosen SIEM software is configured to audit and report on correct compliance standards.

⊙ List digital assets. Listing all digitally stored data across an IT infrastructure aids in managing log data and monitoring network activity.

⊙ Record incident response plans and workflows. This helps ensure teams can respond to security incidents rapidly.

⊙ Assign a SIEM administrator. A SIEM administrator ensures the proper maintenance of a SIEM implementation.

COLLECTING AND ANALYZING SECURITY DATA

Security is a challenging and strange property of software. Security is not about understanding how a customer might use the system; security is about ensuring that an attacker cannot abuse the system. Instead of defining what the system should do, security is about ensuring that system does not do something malicious. As a result, applying traditional software analytics to security leads to some unique challenges and caveats. In this chapter, we will discuss four "gotchas" of analyzing security data, along with vulnerabilities and severity scoring. We will describe a method commonly-used for collecting security data in open source projects. We will describe some of the state-of-the-art in analyzing security data today.

Security analytics is a cybersecurity approach that uses data collection, data aggregation and analysis tools for threat detection and security monitoring. An organization that deploys security analytics tools can analyze security events to detect potential threats before they can negatively affect the company's infrastructure and bottom line.

Security analytics combines big data capabilities with threat intelligence to help detect, analyze and mitigate insider threats, persistent cyber threats and targeted attacks from external bad actors.

Benefits of security analytics

Security analytics tools provide organizations with the following key benefits:

⊙ **Security incident and anomaly detection and response.** Security analytics tools analyze a wide range of data types, making connections between different events and alerts to detect security incidents or cyber threats in real time.

⊙ **Regulatory compliance.** Security analytics tools help enterprises comply with government and industry regulations, such as Health Insurance Portability and Accountability Act and Payment Card Industry Data Security Standard. Security analytics software can integrate a variety of data sources, giving organizations a single, unified view of data events across a variety of devices. This enables compliance managers to monitor regulated data and identify potential noncompliance.

- **Enhanced forensics capabilities.** Security analytics tools provide companies insights into where attacks originated from, how their systems were compromised, what assets were compromised and whether there was any data loss. These tools can also provide timelines for any incidents. The ability to reconstruct and analyze incidents can help organizations shore up their cybersecurity strategy to prevent similar incidents from happening again.

Security analytics tools

Security analytics tools detect behaviors that indicate malicious activity by collecting, normalizing and analyzing network traffic for threat behavior. Providers that specialize in security analytics offer machine learning tools for applying security models to traffic across a company's assets.

Security analytics tools include the following:

- WildFire from Palo Alto Networks detects and prevents zero-day malware using a combination of malware sandboxing, signature-based detection and malware blocking.

- Sumo Logic is a cloud-native, machine data analytics service that enables organizations to monitor, troubleshoot and resolve operational issues and security threats.

- Logz.io Security Analytics combines the ELK stack — a collection of three open source products: Elasticsearch, Logstash and Kibana — with advanced security analytics tools to help enterprises identify and remediate threats to their systems.

Security analytics use cases

Companies can deploy security analytics for a wide variety of reasons. Some common use cases are the following:

- Analyzing network traffic to detect patterns indicating potential attacks.
- Monitoring user behavior, including potentially suspicious activity.
- Detecting potential threats.
- Detecting Data exfiltration.
- Monitoring employees.
- Detecting insider threats.
- Identifying compromised accounts.
- Identifying improper user account usage, such as shared accounts.
- Investigating malicious activity.
- Demonstrating compliance during audits.
- Investigating cybersecurity incidents.

SIEM vs. security analytics

Security information and event management (SIEM) systems collect log data generated by monitored devices — e.g., network equipment, computers, storage, firewalls, etc. — to identify specific security-related events occurring on individual machines. They then aggregate this data to determine what's occurring across an entire system. This enables organizations to identify any variations in expected behavior so they can formulate and implement the necessary responses.

Legacy SIEM systems aren't built to handle modern continuous integration/continuous delivery (CI/CD) lifecycles based on frequent build and deployment cycles. As such, they can't handle the massive amounts of data these methods generate.

Unlike legacy SIEM systems, security analytics takes advantage of cloud-based infrastructure. And, since cloud storage providers can provide almost unlimited data storage that can scale according to an organization's needs, the company is not limited by the corporate data storage and retention policies. In addition, security analytics can collect and store data more efficiently. It's also better at handling modern DevOps practices and CI/CD systems.

Big data security analytics

IT security professionals must ensure that their companies' systems are secure, that cyber threat risks are kept to a minimum and that they are complying with data governance regulations. Consequently, one of their primary responsibilities is monitoring and analyzing huge amounts of log and event data from servers, network devices and applications.

Big data security analytics refers to the techniques and strategies used to analyze vast amounts of security data. Big data security analytics can be divided into two functional categories: performance and availability monitoring (PAM) and SIEM. PAM applications focus on managing operations data, while SIEM tools focus on log management, event management, behavioral analysis, database monitoring and application monitoring.

Big data security analytics tools can discover network devices and automatically collect each device's event and configuration data. Because big data analytics systems require a comprehensive view of the enterprise's security data, they have to integrate with other third-party security tools, as well as Active Directory or Lightweight Directory Access Protocol servers.

REAL-TIME MONITORING AND INCIDENT RESPONSE

Real-time monitoring employs applications and tools that track and record continuous snapshots of your network's overall performance. Organizations use real-time monitoring to track network activity, improve network security and identify potential problems as soon as they arise. Every business, regardless of size, can benefit from monitoring its network in real time.

Benefits of real-time monitoring?

Although it is a good business practice to monitor your network in real time, doing so also provides several advantages for small business owners.

Network security

Network security should be a top priority for any business. Monitoring your network in real time is a great way to support security compliance. Real-time monitoring can help you or your information technology (IT) department identify and resolve security problems as soon as they arise. These issues can include unusual or suspicious traffic, unauthorized requests or devices, cyberthreats or any other potentially harmful behavior on your network.

Network performance

Your network performance can be directly tied to the success of your business. For example, if you run an e-commerce business, you'll want to optimize your servers to avoid issues like downtime, bandwidth overload and long loading times. Monitoring your network in real time can reveal actionable insights about glitches and performance inefficiencies that need to be addressed.

Anthony Petecca, AVP of IT at StaffGlass, listed some of the most common network performance elements you can monitor and why they are important:

- **Bandwidth usage**: If you are sending or receiving more data than you planned, your network pipe could get overloaded, impacting overall performance.

- **Latency**: This is the time between a request and response of data. Latency is more important in some situations than others; for example, it's very relevant when you're playing a real-time game.

- **Network availability/uptime**: Knowing the actual uptime on your network allows you to confidently advertise your service-level agreement.

- **Speed**: The speed of your network will vary at any given point. Visibility into the speed you receive versus the expected speed is important to maintaining good network performance.

"Having real-time monitoring allows you to track performance over time to finely tune your network for ideal performance levels," Petecca told us. "With enough time passed, it also allows you to prepare for anticipated network spikes, such as Cyber Monday shopping."

Incident response time

"Not only do business leaders get to know the status of their network performance and security at all times, but when an incident happens, the real-time alerting allows for faster incident response," said Pieter VanIperen, founder and managing partner of PWV Consultants.

Businesses need to resolve incidents as soon as they arise, however big or small they appear to be. For example, it may seem obvious to resolve a data breach or a cyberattack immediately, but even something as seemingly inconsequential as a slow-loading website or an abundance of 404 web pages can severely impact your business. Monitoring your network in real time can help you catch these incidents as soon as they occur and respond immediately.

"Faster incident response means faster mitigation, which means less loss to the company," VanIperen added.

Employee productivity

Monitoring your network can increase employee productivity. For example, using real-time monitoring to optimize your network performance can enable your team to send company emails, work on projects and collaborate with colleagues more efficiently. You can also use real-time monitoring to track employee data transfer and protect any sensitive information they may be working with.

Cost savings

Up-to-date knowledge of your network's use can ultimately save you money. Instead of overspending on advanced software or unnecessary site speeds, you can gain a bird's-eye view of the exact technology and support you need. An optimized network can also help you make money, primarily if you work in e-commerce.

Use of real-time network monitoring

You can use real-time monitoring to increase your business's data security, network performance, employee productivity, customer satisfaction and reputation. There is a wide variety of monitoring applications, software and services available, so the specific tools you use (and the way you use them) will depend on your business needs.

"At the very minimum, I recommend that companies at least utilize real-time networking to monitor speeds and latency of the network," Petecca said. "Having the knowledge of a network slowdown before you see degradation within your company's performance can be the difference of tens, hundreds, thousands or even millions of dollars."

VanIperen said that real-time monitoring can help companies identify what is "normal" for their business and set alerts around those metrics.

"Ensuring that alerts are set around anything that is out of the business normal is key," he said. "When performance changes or there is a security alert, the system can notify you so that fixes can be implemented. This is why it is key to know what is normal for the business ¯ without knowing what is normal, business leaders have no idea how to set alerts."

Choose tools and resources for real-time monitoring

There are several monitoring applications on the market, which range in features, technical expertise and price. You should choose an affordable platform that is easy to use but advanced enough to support your infrastructure and monitoring needs.

VanIperen offered the following advice for businesses searching for the right monitoring tools:

- ⊙ Compare and vet all companies. Don't just look at cost; look at what you're getting for that cost. Ensure it's what your business needs and that your chosen company is reputable.

- ⊙ If possible, see if your cloud provider offers this service. All businesses should be using cloud services anyway, and your cloud provider may know what is normal for your business better than you do.

- ⊙ Like any technology, real-time monitoring is not foolproof or perfect. It is always best to use several tools to monitor your business and set multiple alert levels for different activities.

THREAT INTELLIGENCE INTEGRATION

Amidst an increasingly tumultuous cybersecurity landscape, threat intelligence vendors have become vital to protecting organizations and individuals. These vendors provide invaluable insights that empower organizations to safeguard their digital assets. However, it's essential to recognize that not all threat intelligence providers are created equal. This article will explore the crucial role of threat intelligence integration, discuss its challenges, and outline best practices for Security Operations Centers (SOCs) to maximize their security posture.

The Importance of Threat Intelligence Integration

Bolstering security operations relies on moving beyond mere data provision into threat intelligence integration. Organizations can proactively thwart a breach by integrating threat intelligence into security tools rather than reacting to it. Threat intelligence provides SOCs with the information to stay one step ahead of cybercriminals.

When threat intelligence is separate from security operations, organizations face many challenges. They must spend valuable time and resources correlating threat data, which can lead to missed signals and delayed responses. This fragmentation can leave security teams overwhelmed by an abundance of raw data, lacking the insights necessary for effective decision-making.

Real-time and accurate threat intelligence feeds are important, but they're not the lifeblood of effective cybersecurity. The faster organizations can receive, process, and act upon intelligence, the better they can protect their networks. Delayed or inaccurate information can prove detrimental in a landscape where every second counts.

Threat Intelligence Lifecycle

The intelligence lifecycle is a process to transform raw data into finished intelligence for decision making and action. You will see many slightly different versions of the intelligence cycle in your research, but the goal is the same, to guide a cybersecurity team through the development and execution of an effective threat intelligence program.

Threat intelligence is challenging because threats are constantly evolving – requiring businesses to quickly adapt and take decisive action. The intelligence cycle provides a framework to enable teams to optimize their resources and effectively respond to the modern threat landscape. This cycle consists of six steps resulting in a feedback loop to encourage continuous improvement:

Let's explore the 6 steps below:

Requirements

The requirements stage is crucial to the threat intelligence lifecycle because it sets the roadmap for a specific threat intelligence operation. During this planning stage, the team will agree on the goals and methodology of their intelligence program based on the needs of the stakeholders involved. The team may set out to discover:

- who the attackers are and their motivations
- what is the attack surface
- what specific actions should be taken to strengthen their defenses against a future attack

Collection

Once the requirements are defined, the team then sets out to collect the information required to satisfy those objectives. Depending on the goals, the team will usually seek out traffic logs, publicly available data sources, relevant forums, social media, and industry or subject matter experts.

Processing

After the raw data has been collected, it will have to be processed into a format suitable for analysis. Most of the time, this entails organizing data points into spreadsheets, decrypting files, translating information from foreign sources, and evaluating the data for relevance and reliability.

Analysis

Once the dataset has been processed, the team must then conduct a thorough analysis to find answers to the questions posed in the requirements phase. During the analysis phase, the team also works to decipher the dataset into action items and valuable recommendations for the stakeholders.

Dissemination

The dissemination phase requires the threat intelligence team to translate their analysis into a digestible format and present the results to the stakeholders. How the analysis is presented depends on the audience. In most cases the recommendations should be presented concisely, without confusing technical jargon, either in a one-page report or a short slide deck.

Feedback

The final stage of the threat intelligence lifecycle involves getting feedback on the provided report to determine whether adjustments need to be made for future threat intelligence operations. Stakeholders may have changes to their priorities, the cadence at which they wish to receive intelligence reports, or how data should be disseminated or presented.

Integration Best Practices for SOCs

Organizations looking to integrate threat intelligence into their SOC should follow these best practices:

Collection: Research Threat Intelligence Feeds

Timeliness and accuracy are non-negotiable in the world of threat intelligence. SOCs must prioritize feeds that deliver the most up-to-date and reliable information. Outdated or inaccurate data can lead to costly false alarms or missed genuine threats.

Selecting threat intelligence feeds with the highest fidelity is a strategic decision. SOCs should carefully evaluate vendors' sources, methodologies, and track records. High-fidelity feeds provide the most valuable insights and minimize the noise that can overwhelm security teams.

Prevention: Leveraging Knowledge from Other Organizations

The collective knowledge of the larger security community is a formidable asset. SOCs can benefit significantly from sharing and receiving threat intelligence with other organizations. Collaboration and information sharing enable more effective threat mitigation and a more robust defense posture.

SOCs can tap into the knowledge of the larger security community through various channels, including Information Sharing and Analysis Centers (ISACs), threat intelligence sharing platforms, and industry-specific forums. Building these connections can yield valuable insights and threat indicators.

Detection: Deploying Rules and Indicators of Compromise (IoCs)

Rules and Indicators of Compromise (IoCs) are critical tools for threat detection. SOCs should have a well-defined strategy for deploying these rules to identify suspicious activities and potential network threats. Effectively deploying rules based on threat intelligence requires a proactive approach. SOCs must continuously update and fine-tune their detection mechanisms to adapt to evolving threats. Automation and machine learning can enhance the efficiency of this process.

Response: Contextualizing and Analyzing Threat Data

Obtaining and analyzing threat data is the final piece of the puzzle. SOCs must detect threats and contextualize them to understand their potential impact. This step enables informed decision-making in responding to threats. Associating threat data with known threats and patterns helps SOCs assess the severity and urgency of incidents. This contextualization allows for more efficient response strategies, reducing the time it takes to neutralize threats.

Threat intelligence integration is paramount for effective security operations. It moves organizations beyond the realm of passive data collection into the realm of proactive threat mitigation. By following best practices such as selecting high-fidelity feeds, collaborating with the larger security community, deploying effective detection rules, and contextualizing threat data, SOCs can significantly enhance their security posture.

SOCs should seek to automatically collect, normalize, and prioritize threat intelligence integrated into a single security operations platform. This approach streamlines processes, reduces response times, and strengthens an organization's defense against cyber threats. In an era where cybersecurity is a top priority, integrating threat intelligence is not merely a choice but a necessity for safeguarding digital assets and maintaining business continuity.

Types of Threat Intelligence

The information can be straightforward, such as a malicious domain name, or complex, such as an in-depth profile of a known threat actor. Keep in mind that there is a maturity curve when it comes to intelligence represented by the three levels listed below. With each level, the context and analysis of CTI becomes deeper and more sophisticated, caters to different audiences, and can get more costly.

- Tactical intelligence
- Operational intelligence
- Strategic intelligence

Tactical Threat Intelligence

Challenge: Organizations often only focus on singular threats

Objective: Obtain a broader perspective of threats in order to combat the underlying problem

Tactical intelligence is focused on the immediate future, is technical in nature, and identifies simple indicators of compromise (IOCs). IOCs are things such as bad IP addresses, URLs, file hashes and known malicious domain names. It can be machine-readable, which means that security products can ingest it through feeds or API integration.

Tactical intelligence is the easiest type of intelligence to generate and is almost always automated. As a result, it can be found via open source and free data feeds, but it usually has a very short lifespan because IOCs such as malicious IPs or domain names can become obsolete in days or even hours.

It's important to note that simply subscribing to intel feeds can result in plenty of data, but offers little means to digest and strategically analyze the threats relevant to you. Also, false positives can occur when the source is not timely or of high fidelity.

Questions to ask yourself:

- Do you have an IOC feed?
- Are IOCs timely and relevant?
- Is malware analysis automated?

Operational Threat Intelligence

Challenge: Threat actors favor techniques that are effective, opportunistic, and low-risk

Objective: Engage in campaign tracking and actor profiling to gain a better understanding of the adversaries behind the attacks

In the same way that poker players study each other's quirks so they can predict their opponents' next move, cybersecurity professionals study their adversaries.

Behind every attack is a "who," "why," and "how." The "who" is called attribution. The "why" is called motivation or intent. The "how" is made up of the

TTPs the threat actor employs. Together, these factors provide context, and context provides insight into how adversaries plan, conduct, and sustain campaigns and major operations. This insight is operational intelligence.

Machines alone cannot create operational threat intelligence. Human analysis is needed to convert data into a format that is readily usable by customers. While operational intelligence requires more resources than tactical intelligence, it has a longer useful life because adversaries can't change their TTPs as easily as they can change their tools, such as a specific type of malware or infrastructure.

Operational intelligence is most useful for those cybersecurity professionals who work in a SOC (security operations center) and are responsible for performing day-to-day operations. Cybersecurity disciplines such as vulnerability management, incident response and threat monitoring are the biggest consumers of operational intelligence as it helps make them more proficient and more effective at their assigned functions.

Strategic Threat Intelligence

Challenge: Poor business and organizational decisions are made when the adversary is misunderstood

Objective: Threat intelligence should inform business decisions and the processes behind them

Adversaries don't operate in a vacuum — in fact, there are almost always higher level factors that surround the execution of cyber attacks. For example, nation-state attacks are typically linked to geopolitical conditions, and geopolitical conditions are linked to risk. Furthermore, with the adoption of financially motivated Big Game Hunting, cyber-crime groups are constantly evolving their techniques and should not be ignored.

Strategic intelligence shows how global events, foreign policies, and other long-term local and international movements can potentially impact the cyber security of an organization.

Strategic intelligence helps decision-makers understand the risks posed to their organizations by cyber threats. With this understanding, they can make cybersecurity investments that effectively protect their organizations and are aligned with its strategic priorities.

Strategic intelligence tends to be the hardest form to generate. Strategic intelligence requires human data collection and analysis that demands an intimate understanding of both cybersecurity and the nuances of the world's geopolitical situation. Strategic intelligence usually comes in the form of reports.

CHAPTER-7

WEB APPLICATION SECURITY

Web application security (also known as Web AppSec) is the idea of building websites to function as expected, even when they are under attack. The concept involves a collection of security controls engineered into a Web application to protect its assets from potentially malicious agents. Web applications, like all software, inevitably contain defects. Some of these defects constitute actual vulnerabilities that can be exploited, introducing risks to organizations. Web application security defends against such defects. It involves leveraging secure development practices and implementing security measures throughout the software development life cycle (SDLC), ensuring that design-level flaws and implementation-level bugs are addressed.

Web application security is the process of protecting websites and online services against different security threats that exploit vulnerabilities in an application's code. Common targets for web application attacks are content management systems (e.g., WordPress), database administration tools (e.g., phpMyAdmin) and SaaS applications.

Perpetrators consider web applications high-priority targets due to:

◉ The inherent complexity of their source code, which increases the likelihood of unattended vulnerabilities and malicious code manipulation.

◉ High value rewards, including sensitive private data collected from successful source code manipulation.

◉ Ease of execution, as most attacks can be easily automated and launched indiscriminately against thousands, or even tens or hundreds of thousands of targets at a time.

Organizations failing to secure their web applications run the risk of being attacked. Among other consequences, this can result in information theft, damaged client relationships, revoked licenses and legal proceedings.

COMMON WEB APPLICATION VULNERABILITIES

Web application vulnerabilities are typically the result of a lack of input/output sanitization, which are often exploited to either manipulate source code or gain unauthorized access.

Such vulnerabilities enable the use of different attack vectors, including:

Broken access control

Access controls define how users interact with data and resources including what they can read or edit. A broken access control vulnerability exists when a user has the ability to interact with data in a way that they don't need. For example, if a user should only be able to read payment details but can actually edit them, this is a broken access control. Malicious actors use this vulnerability to gain unauthorized access to systems, networks, and software. They can then escalate the privileges, give the user ID additional access within the ecosystem, to negatively impact data confidentiality, integrity, or availability.

Broken authentication

Broken authentication vulnerabilities also focus on user access. However, in this case, malicious actors compromise the information that confirms a user's identity, such as by stealing passwords, keys, or session tokens. The malicious actor gains unauthorized access to the systems, networks, and software because the company failed to adequately set appropriate identity and access management controls.

Carriage Return and Line Feed (CRLF) Injection

Carriage return is a command that indicates the start of a line of code, normally denoted as

- Line feed is a command that indicates the end of a line of code, normally denoted as

- Like many other software, each operating system uses a different combination of carriage return and line feed. When malicious actors engage in CRLF injections, the inserted code changes the way that the web application responds to commands. This can be used to either disclosure sensitive information or execute code.

Cipher transformation insecure

Cipher, a standard term for "encryption algorithm," is the math behind an encryption/decryption process. Transformation is the list of operations performed on an input to provide the expected output. So, a cipher transformation is the set of operations that turn unreadable encrypted data back to readable, decrypted data. A cipher transformation insecure vulnerability means that the encryption algorithm is easy to break, ultimately undermining the purpose of encryption in the first place.

Components with known vulnerabilities

Every web application relies on other components to work. For example, if you're running an application on an unpatched web/application server, the server is the component with known vulnerabilities. The Common Vulnerabilities and Exposures (CVE) list includes all known security vulnerabilities. Since malicious actors are aware of the list, they regularly look for components without the appropriate security patch updates. Once they can compromise one component of the web application, they can gain access to the application's data, too.

Cross-Origin Resource Sharing (CORS) Policy

Every web-based application uses a URL as a way to connect the user's browser to its server. One common protection is called a Same Origin Policy. According to this, the server will only respond to a URL that has the same protocol, top-level domain name, and path schema. This means that you can access http://company. com/page1 and http:/company.com/page2 because they both have the following in common:

- ◉ Protocol: HTTP

- ◉ Domain: Company.com

- ◉ Path schema: /page#

Although secure, the Same Origin Policy becomes restrictive when working with web-based applications that need access to resources that connect to subdomains or third-parties.

A CORS policy gives the browser permission to access these shared resources by creating a set of allowed HTTP headers considered "trusted." For example, an application may need to pull data from two databases on different web servers. Creating a specific "allowed" list becomes too much work as you add more servers. Since the application is "shared" by both servers, the organization creates a CORS policy that lets browsers connect to both. However, if a CORS policy is not well defined, then the policy might allow the servers to provide access when a malicious actor requests it.

Credentials management

User credentials consist of a user ID and password. To gain access to an application, the user must input both pieces of information into the login page. The application compares this data to that stored in its database. If both pieces match, then it grants the user access. However, databases often store this information in plaintext or use weak encryption. Poor credentials management makes it easy for attackers to steal credentials and use them to gain access to web applications.

Cross-site request forgery (CSRF)

A CSRF attack leverages social engineering methods to get a user to change information, like user name or password, in an application. Unlike malware or cross-site scripting (XXS) attacks, a CSRF requires a user to be logged into the application that uses only session cookies for tracking sessions or validating user requests. Once the user takes the intended action, the attacker leverages the browser to perform the rest of the attack, such as transferring funds, without the user realizing what happened. For example, as OWASP explained, the "buy now" feature on retail websites is easy to exploit through a CSRF attack because the attacker can use the cookies stored on the browser that saves the payment data to complete the attack.

Cross-site scripting (XSS)

Distinct from a CSRF which requires a user logged into an application to be tricked into doing something, an XSS attack requires the cybercriminal to insert code into a web page, usually in some element of the page like an image. When the user opens the web page on their browser, the malicious code downloads and executes in the browser. For example, the code may redirect users from a legitimate site to a malicious one.

Directory indexing

Web servers often list all the files stored on them in a single directory. If a user is trying to locate a specific file in a web application, they normally include the file name as part of the request. If that file is not available, the application will return a list of all indexed files, giving the user a way to choose something else.

However, web servers automatically index the files. If the application returns a list of all files stored, a malicious actor exploiting vulnerabilities in the directory index can gain access to information that can tell them more about the system. For example, it can tell them about naming conventions or personal user accounts. Both of these data points can be used to locate sensitive information or engage in credential theft attacks.

Directory traversal

Also called directory climbing, dot-dot-slash, and backtracking attack, the directory traversal method leverages the way in which an application gets data from the webserver. Generally, Access Control Lists (ACLs) limit user access to specific files within a root directory.

Consider a set of nested folders that follow this order:

- ⊙ **Root directory:** My Very Sensitive Data (MVSD)
- ⊙ **Inside MVSD folder:** Protecting from H@x0rs (PfH) folder
- ⊙ **Inside PfH folder:** My Password is Bad (MPiB) folder
- ⊙ **Inside MPiB folder:** H@x0rs Stole My Info file

Now, you might have an additional set of folders outside that root folder including Pictures, Videos, and Downloads. Unless you have access to each of these other root folders, you can't access the information they contain.

Web applications organize information the same way, even if you don't see it. In a directory traversal attack, malicious actors figure out the URL structure that the application uses to request files. Using the hypothetical above, that URL might be:

www.myinsecurewebapp.com/MyPas... ".asp?item=" indicates that this URL pulled the file "H@x0rsStoleMyInfo" from the "My Password is Bad" folder. Now, they know the structure of folders and how to start getting different files.

Using this structure, they add "../" at the end. The "../" indicates moving from one folder to one just above it in the hierarchy. The new request might look like this:

www.myinsecurewebapp.com/MyH@cking.asp?item=../

They keep adding the ../ until they gain access to another file. If they know the name of the file, such as an operating system file name, they might do this:

www.mywebsiteinfo.com/MyPasswordisBad.asp?item=../
genericoperatingsystemfile

At this point, they just keep adding more "../" after the equal sign until they get to the folder level and file they want.

Encapsulation

Unlike some of the other vulnerabilities that leverage web browser access to applications, encapsulation vulnerability exploits focus on weaknesses in the way a developer coded the application. The programming term encapsulation refers to bundling data and actions that can be taken on that data into a single unit. Encapsulation protects data by hiding details about how the code works which creates a better user interface. Users don't need to know how the application brings them data; they just need access to it.

For example, a developer can bundle access controls, like read/write permissions, into an application's ability to retrieve data. When the user requests information in the application, it returns only the data that they have permission to access.

However, if the developers fail to clearly define the boundaries between the data and the actions taken across different areas of the application, the application has an encapsulation vulnerability. Attackers exploit this by sending the application a request that they know will result in an error message. The error message gives them information about how the application works, enabling additional attack types such as a denial of service.

Error handling

Several different attack methods rely on how an application responds to abnormal inputs or conditions. One example of an error message is the "404 not found" message when you try to access a website. For most enterprise applications and systems, error messages provide valuable information about how to fix a problem. However, for web applications, too much information returned through an error message can give malicious actors that same information. Often, attackers send the web application a query that they know will return an error message. They usually do this during the reconnaissance phase, where they try to get as much information as possible so they can find exploitable vulnerabilities.

Failure to restrict URL access

As with many other web application vulnerabilities, this one also aligns with access control rights. Applications use URL restrictions to prevent non-privileged users from accessing privileged data and resources. Every clickable button in a web application directs to a URL. A failure to restrict access vulnerability means that while clicking the button in the application would prevent access, directly using the URL into the browser allows access. When an application fails to restrict URL access, malicious actors can use "forced browsing" for an attack.

For example, a web application might have a URL structure that looks like this:

⦿ www.insecurewebapp.com/failure... the attackers know that the last item in that URL is the data type, they can try to take guesses at the URL structure for a specific type of sensitive information.

⦿ www.insecurewebapp.com/failure... the application has a failure to restrict URL access vulnerability, plugging that URL directly into the browser gives the attacker access.

HTTP response splitting

HTTP response splitting is a type of CRLF injection attack. HTTP is the way that a browser sends queries and a server sends back responses. In an HTTP response splitting attack, the malicious actors use the CR and LF notations to manipulate how the browser and server "talk" to one another that sends a request but asks the server to "split" the response into different parts. Splitting the response into two parts gives the attacker control over what data the server sends in response to the second part of the request. When that requested data is sensitive or user ID data, the malicious attacker has completed the attack.

HTTP verb tampering

HTTP is the protocol that lets applications respond to requests and retrieve data. An HTTP verb is one of several actions that the application can use when querying the server. Common ones HTTP verbs include:

- **GET:** retrieves data from specified source
- **HEAD:** requests preview of specified resource
- **POST:** submits entity to specified resource, such as editing data
- **PUT:** transmits new data to the specified resource replacing the old information
- **DELETE:** deletes the specified resource entirely

Most web applications use HTTP verbs to authenticate users and manage access privileges. Malicious actors can bypass authentication and access controls intended to protect privileged information.

Improper certificate validation

SSL certificates bind a domain name, server name, or hostname to a company and location. For example, GoodSecureCo installs the SSL certificate data files on its US web servers. Every time a browser asks for data from the US web server, the SSL certificate checks to make sure that the user's browser connects with an approved owner. The two securely connect if the answer is yes.

When software refuses to validate or incorrectly validates the certificate, it has an improper certificate validation vulnerability. Most often, attackers create a false trusted entity that tricks the server or application into thinking the certificate is valid so it accepts the data transfer as legitimate. Often, malicious actors use improper certificate validation vulnerabilities as a way to install malware on endpoints.

Injection flaw

An injection flaw enables a variety of different attack methods. Any application that enables users to update a database, shell command, or operating system call can have an injection flaw. In computing, an interpreter is a program that takes a command, generates an instruction, and performs the action within the application.

Malicious actors use injection flaws to change the commands which leads to new and unintended actions within the application. Leveraging these flaws, attackers can create, read, update, or delete data.

Insecure cryptographic storage

Encrypting stored data is a common best practice for preventing unauthorized access to or use of sensitive information. Encryption takes information stored in a readable format, such as PlainText, then uses mathematical algorithms to scramble it, making it unreadable. Encryption typically requires an encryption key, which is the technology that applies the algorithm that scrambles the data and is also used to make the information readable again. However, if someone finds the encryption key, the protection no longer works.

The insecure cryptographic storage vulnerability means you have a problem with one or more of the following:

- Not encrypting all sensitive data
- Improper key storage and management
- Easy to crack encryption algorithms
- Internally-designed, untested algorithm

Insecure deserialization

Applications handle complex data structures. Serialization converts the structures into an object that can be stored and transmitted easily. For example, think about different actions that go into making a peanut butter and jelly sandwich:

- Get plate
- Get bread
- Open bread
- Take out bread 1
- Put bread 1 on plate
- Take out bread 2
- Put bread 2 on plate
- Get knife
- Get peanut butter
- Open peanut butter
- Get jelly
- Open jelly
- Get peanut butter on knife
- Put peanut butter on bread 1
- Get jelly on knife

⊙ Put jelly on bread 2

⊙ Smoosh bread 1 and bread 2 together with covered sides facing

You need all of these things to happen as part of making the sandwich, but they aren't necessarily step-by-step in this order. Having to send all 17 of these data points, like individual messages, every time someone asks for a peanut butter and jelly sandwich can be time-consuming to write down and send. Most likely, you'd group them in a document as "Peanut Butter and Jelly Sandwich" that you send when someone asks, similar to serialization. When the person opens the document, they can see each individual data point, similar to deserialization.

Deserialization is the process of reconstructing the original, expanded data structure. With a deserialization vulnerability, malicious actors can change the application logic or execute code remotely, one of the most serious attack types.

Insecure digest

Another cryptographic vulnerability, an insecure message-digest vulnerability reduces the effectiveness of encryption. A message-digest contains the cryptographic hash function, which is the algorithm that maps an arbitrary length of data to the fixed bit array, a way of compactly storing data. Unlike encryption that requires the sender and user to have keys, hash functions do not.

Malicious actors leverage insecure digest vulnerabilities to engage in a "hash collisions attack." The goal of the attack is to see if sending an input results in generating a duplicative hash. If the attackers brute force a shared hash, then they can offer a malicious file for download using this hash, which leaves the end-user assuming that the file is valid.

Insecure direct object references (IDOR)

Web application URLs can expose the format/pattern used for directing users to backend storage locations. For example, a URL might indicate the format/pattern for a record identifier in a storage system such as a database or file system.

Alone, the IDOR may be a low-risk issue. However, an IDOR in combination with a failed access control check gives attackers a way to successfully launch an enumeration attack.

Insufficient logging and monitoring

Insufficient logging and monitoring vulnerabilities occur when your data event logs fail to capture the necessary information that can prevent an attack. Every user, device, and resource generates an event log that tells your security team what is happening in your systems, networks, and applications.

Since successful attacks often use vulnerability probing during the reconnaissance stage, collecting the right event log data is a way to mitigate risk.

Common logging and monitoring weaknesses include:

- Failure to collect logs for auditable events like logins, failed logins, and high-value transactions
- Failure to generate an adequate and clear warning and error logs
- Failure to monitor application and API logs for abnormal activity
- Storing logs locally
- Failure to effectively set alerting thresholds and response escalation processes
- Lack of alert triggers during penetration tests and dynamic application security testing (DAST) scans
- Lack of real-time or near real-time application detection, escalation, and alerting functions

Insufficient session expiration

Session timeout is when an application automatically logs a user out after being idle for a specified amount of time. When an application is idle and open, attackers look to steal the credentials associated with the account.

Some examples of insufficient session expiration weaknesses include:

- Lack of session timeout
- Session timeouts that are longer than necessary
- Inability to trace session creation/destruction to analyze trends

Insufficient transport layer protection

Transport layer security (TLS) is the way that computer applications securely "talk" to one another on the internet. Some applications only use TLS during the authentication process, leaving data and ID session information exposed when someone uses the application.

Attackers can use this vulnerability to intercept data as it travels across the internet between the user's device and the application server.

Lightweight Directory Access Protocol (LDAP) injection

LDAP is a protocol that lets applications talk with directory services servers that store user IDs, passwords, and computer accounts. When applications accept user input and execute it, attackers can exploit the LDAP server by sending malicious requests.

Some examples of LDAP coding issues include:

- Excess access privileged assigned to LDAP accounts

- Lack of output regulation
- Inability to perform dynamic checks
- Lack of static source code analysis

Malicious code

Traditionally, code that intends to cause harm is considered malicious code. For example, people normally consider malicious code in terms of viruses, malware, and ransomware.

However, it also refers to code that can provide a backdoor into an application that lets people gain remote access to a computer. Lack of secure coding practices can lead to application backdoors. Although unintended, these programming errors make the web application vulnerable. Additionally, since modern applications often copy and paste code from one place to another, a mistake in one source can lead to the same malicious code being used in multiple applications.

Missing function level access control

Once users authenticate to an application, the function level access controls define the actions they can take within it. For example:

- www.insecurewebapp.com/genericusername/read
- www.insecurewebapp.com/SuperAd... on this example, Generic Username can read files in this application while Super Adminuser can edit within this application. Because the access rights are included in the URL, no one needs the authentication that protects these actions. Authenticated non-administrative users or unauthenticated users can type in a URL hoping to gain administrative access. For example, the malicious actors might try to type:
- www.insecurewebapp.com/SuperAd... missing function level access control means that the malicious actor doesn't need to authenticate to the system and can now delete data.

Missing PT_DENY_ATTACH

Although a bit more specific and technical than other web application vulnerabilities, this one is increasingly important as companies build out more mobile applications. A debugger is a program that helps application developers find errors in their coding. They often use debuggers to keep the application to prevent downtime from errors. However, malicious actors can leverage these same debuggers to learn how the application works and find ways to exploit them.

Process trace, more commonly called ptrace, is a system call that many debuggers and code analysis tools use. However, ptrace calls give tools a way to control their targets. The PT_DENY_ATTACH is a command for iOS mobile applications that prevents debuggers from attaching to applications. A missing PT_DENY_ATTACH command leaves an iOS mobile application at risk because malicious attackers can launch ptrace, connect to the application, and infiltrate it.

Operating System (OS) command injection

Some web applications make calls to operating systems so that they can communicate with the operating system or hardware. OS calls include functions like:

- Process control: monitoring what an application is doing and providing for termination
- File management: giving the application access to interact with files
- Device management: requesting or managing hardware like processing power
- Information maintenance: managing or maintaining information as part of keeping data updated
- Inter-process communication: coordinating processes for effective operation

Insecure OS command calls allow users to supply unvalidated inputs. In other words, the malicious actors can take the OS command call, add an additional query notation, and gain valuable information about how to exploit the application.

Race condition

Web application processes generally rely on a series of actions, run in order, to do a task. For example, consider the following process:

- Click Word icon
- Wait for Word to open
- Click "open file"
- Wait for list of file storage locations
- Look for file name you want
- Click file with the right name
- Wait for file to open in Word
- Edit document

You need to do these steps in that precise order so that you can write in a new Word document. Functionally, many applications rely on a similar approach, where each step relies on the completion of the previous one.

However, application tasks are often more complex and need to be faster. This means that they use multi-threaded and asynchronous order. For example, if you're collaborating in real-time with a co-worker on a document in a shared drive, you're both giving the application tasks. This is where the race condition vulnerability comes into play.

Incorrectly coded web applications might have logic adjusting for asynchronous actions but lack the appropriate controls. When this happens, malicious attackers can manipulate the timing of actions, which throws off the sequencing and leads to unexpected, often maliciously intended, application behaviors.

Remote code execution (RCE)

RCE vulnerabilities are coding mistakes in web applications that allow malicious actors to input code regardless of their geographic location. RCEs are a larger category of web application injection vulnerabilities where malicious actors insert their own code into an application that does not verify user inputs so that the server views it as legitimate application code. Generally, attackers will leverage unpatched commonly known vulnerabilities and input their code into the application.

Remote file inclusion (RFI)

Developers use "include" statements in their code to connect common directories to an application. For example, an application might want to pull information from a database. Instead of manually coding it to pull each file, the "include" statement can be used to connect to the entire source directory so that it can use everything stored there.

If a web application has an RFI vulnerability, malicious actors can direct the application to upload malware or other malicious code to the website, server, or database.

Security misconfiguration

One of the most prevalent web application vulnerabilities is the potential for a security misconfiguration. Generally, this vulnerability occurs when an organization fails to change default Security settings. For example, off-the-shelf software generally ships with a default administrative ID and password. Failure to change these is considered a security misconfiguration.

Typical security misconfigurations include:

- Use of default accounts/passwords
- Lack of secure password policy
- Unpatched software
- Lack of appropriate file and directory configurations

- ⊙ Leaving unused features, components, and other resources
- ⊙ Lack of encryption
- ⊙ Poor firewall policies

Sensitive data exposure

Unlike a data breach where a cybercriminal steals information, sensitive data exposure vulnerabilities leave information visible to the public.

Several sensitive exposure vulnerabilities exist, including:

- ⊙ Lack of Secure Sockets Layer (SSL) protocol that authenticates and encrypts data
- ⊙ Misconfigured cloud storage locations storing data in plaintext
- ⊙ Data transmitted in clear text
- ⊙ Outdated or weak encryption algorithms
- ⊙ Weak or default cryptography keys used

Session ID leakage

Session IDs are the unique identifiers that authenticate users and track their activities when they use a web application. Web application vulnerabilities that lead to session leakage include:

- ⊙ Storing the session ID in the query string. By storing the session ID in the part of the URL that asks the application to retrieve information from the database, sharing of that URL allows the recipient to inherit that session without new authentication.
- ⊙ Storing the session ID in HTTP cookies: By storing the session ID in the small data files that let a web server remember a web browser and using the unencrypted HTTP protocol, the application gives the attacker the ability to steal the session ID and impersonate the user.

SQL Injection

Structured Query Language (SQL) is a programming language for databases that enables data retrieval and manipulation for relational databases. A SQL injection vulnerability falls under the larger group of unvalidated user inputs. When cybercriminals send requests that they know are false, the web application returns an error message that gives them information about how the database is organized and protected.

Unrestricted File Upload

Web applications often incorporate file upload capabilities. For example, if you want to input data in bulk, you might upload a CSV file to a database. An unrestricted file upload vulnerability can be a lack of authentication/authorization when someone tries to upload a file. This means that the application fails to verify the user, giving malicious actors the ability to upload compromised files. Additionally, the application may fail to sanitize files prior to uploading, thus giving attackers a way to leave malicious content in the files, like macros that hide malware.

Additional file upload vulnerabilities include:

- Allows all file extensions
- Fails to authorize or authenticate users
- Fails to scan content to ensure the file type is expected
- Allows webserver to fetch files
- Stores files in a publicly accessible directory

Unvalidated automatic library activation

Developers use third-party libraries to save time when coding. Often, this allows them to use pre-tested code that speeds up the application development process. However, the use of publicly available, open-source code increases security risks, including:

- Abandoned projects that are no longer updated
- Lack of documented ownership increases the risk of malicious code added
- Monitoring for library updates to fix vulnerabilities

Since many applications involve third-party library dependencies, this vulnerability is becoming more common.

Unvalidated redirects and forwards

Web applications can use redirects or forwards after a user submits a form. For example, if your marketing website has a form so that visitors can download a whitepaper, the page redirects or forwards them to the "thank you" page when they submit the form. However, malicious actors can impersonate these redirected or forwarded page URLs to steal user information.

Examples of this vulnerability include web applications with:

- Large numbers of destination pages
- Fail to store full URLs
- Lack identifiers for these redirects/forwards
- Lack of identifiers used as request parameters
- Failure to filter out untrusted URL inputs

XML External Entities (XXE)

Extensible Markup Language (XML) describes data, like the contents of a webpage or database file. XML formatting allows applications to understand information and share data consistently. In order to read this data, you need to have an XML processor. Also referred to as an XML parser, these automated tools read files, transform the content, update databases, and deliver that content so the program can access it.

However, when web applications use XML format to transmit data between the browser and server, they often use APIs to process the data. Within the XML standard, storage units are called "entities." External entity refers to a storage unit that can access local or remote content.

An XXE vulnerability can arise from failure to:

- Know the source before accepting or uploading XML data
- Disable document type definitions (DTDs)
- Use less complex data formats like JSON
- Patch XML processors or underlying operating system
- Detect XXE in source code

WEB APPLICATION FIREWALLS (WAF)

Web application firewalls (WAFs) are hardware and software solutions used for protection from application security threats. These solutions are designed to examine incoming traffic to block attack attempts, thereby compensating for any code sanitization deficiencies.

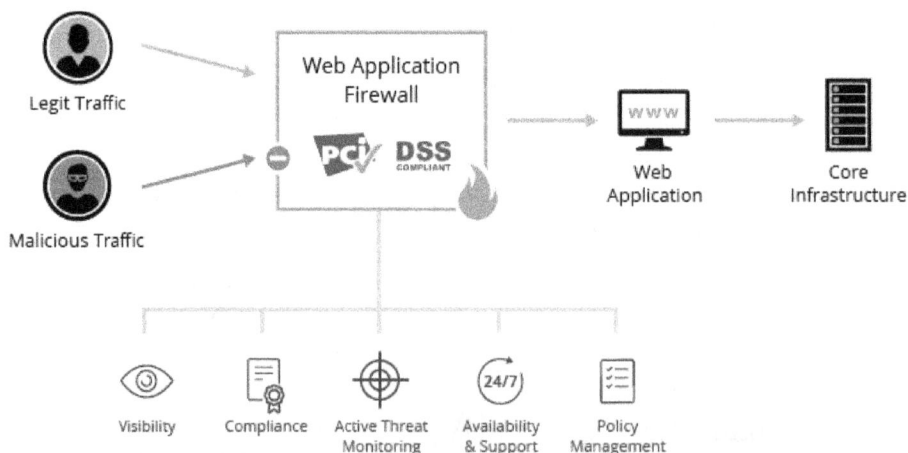

By securing data from theft and manipulation, WAF deployment meets a key criteria for PCI DSS certification. Requirement 6.6 states that all credit and debit cardholder data held in a database must be protected.

Generally, deploying a WAF doesn't require making any changes to an application, as it is placed ahead of its DMZ at the edge of a network. From there, it acts as a gateway for all incoming traffic, blocking malicious requests before they have a chance to interact with an application.

WAFs use several different heuristics to determine which traffic is given access to an application and which needs to be weeded out. A constantly-updated signature pool enables them to instantly identify bad actors and known attack vectors.

Almost all WAFs can be custom-configured for specific use cases and security policies, and to combat emerging (a.k.a., zero-day) threats. Finally, most modern solutions leverage reputational and behavior data to gain additional insights into incoming traffic.

WAFs are typically integrated with other security solutions to form a security perimeter. These may include distributed denial of service (DDoS) protection services that provide additional scalability required to block high-volume attacks.

Types of Web Application Firewalls

There are three primary ways to implement a WAF:

- ⊙ **Network-based WAF**—usually hardware-based, it is installed locally to minimize latency. However, this is the most expensive type of WAF and necessitates storing and maintaining physical equipment.

- ⊙ **Host-based WAF**—can be fully integrated into the software of an application. This option is cheaper than network-based WAFs and is more customizable, but it consumes extensive local server resources, is complex to implement, and can be expensive to maintain. The machine used to run a host-based WAF often needs to be hardened and customized, which can take time and be costly.

- ⊙ **Cloud-based WAF**—an affordable, easily implemented solution, which typically does not require an upfront investment, with users paying a monthly or annual security-as-a-service subscription. A cloud-based WAF can be regularly updated at no extra cost, and without any effort on the part of the user. However, since you rely on a third party to manage your WAF, it is important to ensure cloud-based WAFs have sufficient customization options to match your organization's business rules.

WAF Technology

A WAF can be built into server-side software plugins or hardware appliances, or they can be offered as a service to filter traffic. WAFs can protect web apps from malicious or compromised endpoints and function as reverse proxies (as opposed to a proxy server, which protects users from malicious websites).

WAFs ensure security by intercepting and examining every HTTP request. Illegitimate traffic can be tested using a variety of techniques, such as device fingerprinting, input device analysis, and CAPTCHA challenges, and if they appear not to be legitimate, they can be blocked.

WAFs are pre-loaded with security rules that can detect and block many known attack patterns – these typically include the top web app security vulnerabilities maintained by the Open Web Application Security Project (OWASP).

In addition, the organization can define custom rules and security policies to match their application business logic. It can require special expertise to configure and customize a WAF.

WAF Security Models

WAFs can use a positive or negative security model, or a combination of the two:

- ⦿ Positive security model—the positive WAF security model involves a whitelist that filters traffic according to a list of permitted elements and actions—anything not on the list is blocked. The advantage of this model is that it can block new or unknown attacks that the developer didn't anticipate.

- ⦿ Negative security model—the negative model involves a blacklist (or denylist) that only blocks specific items—anything not on the list is allowed. This model is easier to implement but it cannot guarantee that all threats are addressed. It also requires maintaining a potentially long list of malicious signatures. The level of security depends on the number of restrictions implemented.

Threat modelling

Threat modeling or threat assessment is the process of reviewing the threats to an enterprise or information system and then formally evaluating the degree and nature of the threats. Threat modeling is one of the first steps in application security and usually includes the following five steps:

- ⦿ rigorously defining enterprise assets;
- ⦿ identifying what each application does or will do with respect to these assets;
- ⦿ creating a security profile for each application;
- ⦿ identifying and prioritizing potential threats; and
- ⦿ documenting adverse events and the actions taken in each case.

In this context, a threat is any potential or actual adverse event that can compromise the assets of an enterprise. These include both malicious events, such as a denial-of-service attack, and unplanned events, such as the failure of a storage device.

Common application security weaknesses and threats

The most common application security weaknesses are well-known. Various organizations track them over time. The Open Web Application Security Project (OWASP) Top Ten list and the Common Weakness Enumeration (CWE) compiled by the information security community are two of the best-known lists of application weaknesses.

The OWASP list focuses on web application software. The CWE list focuses on specific issues that can occur in any software context. Its goal is to provide developers with usable guidance on how to secure their code.

SECURE CODING PRACTICES

Secure coding refers to the practice of writing software code in a manner that minimizes vulnerabilities and guards against potential cyber threats. It involves adhering to established coding standards, employing robust coding techniques, and leveraging security best practices throughout the software development lifecycle. Secure coding serves as a primary defense against malicious attacks and vulnerabilities that could otherwise compromise the confidentiality, integrity, and availability of software systems.

Insecure code, on the other hand, exposes web applications to a multitude of risks, ranging from injection attacks, cross-site scripting, and data breaches, to denial-of-service exploits and unauthorized access. Such vulnerabilities can lead to severe consequences, including the unauthorized disclosure of sensitive information, disruption of services, and damage to an organization's reputation. Therefore, embracing secure coding practices is not only a technical necessity but also a fundamental step towards building resilient and trustworthy web applications.

Firewall
Login page
Security Queation
Multi-Factor Authentication
Password Hasing
Access Authorization

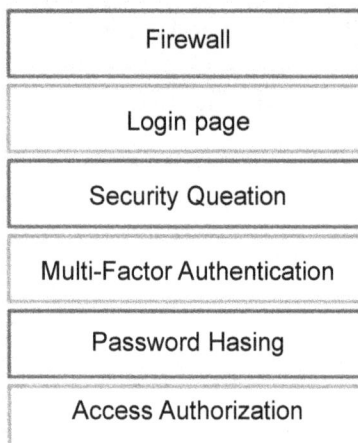

Example of multiple security layers used to protect applications

In this blog post we will explore five essential secure coding best practices:

- Input Validation and Sanitization
- Authentication and Authorization
- Secure Data Storage and Transmission
- The Principle of Least Privilege
- Regular Security Updates and Patching

Input Validation and Sanitization

Perhaps the most important practice is input validation which is the process of examining data that is entered into a software application to verify that it conforms to specified formats and criteria. For example, input validation would expect integers between 1 and 12 for the correct input for a month value. The goal of input validation is to prevent potentially malicious data from causing issues within the application. By validating inputs, developers can ensure that only data meeting predefined standards is accepted, reducing the risk of security vulnerabilities.

Input sanitization, on the other hand, involves cleaning or filtering input data to remove any characters, symbols, or elements that could potentially be exploited by attackers to inject malicious code or disrupt the applications behavior. An example of unusual characters includes quotation marks inside of a text field which may be indicative of an attack. Sanitization ensures that even if validation fails and potentially harmful data gets through, it is neutralized before being processed, displayed, or stored.

Both input validation and sanitization are vital for making web applications secure. Making sure that user inputs are trustworthy is crucial to stopping various online dangers. By carefully checking data against known standards and thoroughly cleaning it to remove any harmful parts, developers can stop vulnerabilities like SQL injection and cross-site scripting attacks. This method acts as a strong shield, making web applications strong against unauthorized access and keeping user information safe.

Authentication and Authorization

Authentication is the process of verifying the identity of a user, system, or entity attempting to access a particular resource or system. It ensures that the individual or entity is who they claim to be. In the context of web applications, authentication involves validating user credentials, such as usernames and passwords, and sometimes additional factors like security tokens or biometric data. Authentication prevents unauthorized individuals from gaining access to sensitive information or functionalities.

In contrast, authorization determines what actions an authenticated user is allowed to perform within the system. It specifies the permissions and privileges associated with a user's identity. Authorization ensures that authenticated users only have access to the resources, features, and data that they are entitled to use. This prevents users from overstepping their boundaries and helps protect sensitive information from being accessed or manipulated by unauthorized parties.

In essence, authentication confirms who you are, while authorization defines what you are allowed to do once your identity is confirmed. Both authentication and authorization are crucial components of web application security, working together to ensure that only legitimate users can access appropriate resources and perform authorized actions.

Secure Data Storage and Transmission

Secure data storage refers to the practice of safeguarding sensitive information, such as user credentials, personal data, and confidential documents, in a way that prevents unauthorized access, tampering or theft. This involves using encryption, access controls, and other techniques to ensure that data is stored in a protected manner.

Secure data transmission involves ensuring that data transferred between users and the web application or between different components of the application is encrypted and cannot be intercepted or manipulated by malicious actors during transit. This is typically achieved using protocols like HTTPS, which encrypts data exchanged between a user's browser and web server.

Secure data storage and transmission are integral to the over security posture of web applications. Implementing robust encryption, access controls, and following best practices for data handling contribute significance to a web application's ability to protect user data and maintain its integrity.

The Principle of Least Privilege

The Principle of Least Privilege is a fundamental security concept that mandates that any user, process, or entity should be granted the minimum necessary access rights, permissions, and privileges required to perform their tasks and nothing more. Applying this principle aims to reduce the potential impact of security breaches. By limiting the scope of access, the attack surface available to potential threats is minimized, making it more difficult for attackers to exploit vulnerabilities or gain unauthorized access to critical systems, data, or resources.

In the context of web applications, following the Principle of Least Privilege involves designing and implementing role-based access controls, employing proper authentication and authorization mechanisms, and continuously reviewing and adjusting permissions as needed. While it may require additional effort to carefully define and manage access levels, the benefits far outweigh the potential risks associated with granting excessive privileges.

Regular Security Updates and Patching

Regular security updates and patching involves consistently updating software components, libraries, frameworks, and the underlying infrastructure to address known vulnerabilities and security weaknesses. This practice is crucial for maintaining the security and integrity of web applications over time.

Incorporating regular security updates and patching into the development process is a proactive approach that demonstrates a commitment to security and helps protect web applications from evolving cyber threats.

Embracing Secure Coding

In today's digital landscape, secure coding in web applications is not just a choice but a necessity. The principles discussed above form a robust framework for building and maintaining secure web applications. Implementing input validations, authentication and authorization, secure data handling, the principle of least privilege, and regular updates enhances application security. These practices collectively counter cyber threats, safeguard data, and build user trust. By combining thoughtful practices and ongoing improvement, web applications can confidently navigate the digital realm, upholding privacy and reliability.

CHAPTER-8

CLOUD SECURITY TECHNOLOGIES

The main purpose of cloud security is to secure cloud computing systems. It requires establishing measures that keep data private and secure across cloud infrastructure, platforms, and applications. Cloud security may encompass one or more of the following responsibilities:

⦿ Data security

⦿ Governance (policies on threat prevention, detection, and mitigation)

⦿ Access management

⦿ Compliance

⦿ Disaster recovery (DR) and business continuity (BC) planning

Cloud security is usually a collaborative effort between cloud providers and customers. A cloud customer may be an individual, a small-to-medium business (SMB), or an enterprise.

Cloud providers or vendors are trusted to secure the underlying computing infrastructure—including servers and connections. Vendors are also expected to provide customers with the capabilities needed to secure their workloads and data.

The most common and widely adopted cloud computing services are:

⦿ **IaaS (Infrastructure-as-a-Service):** Offers a hybrid approach, which allows organizations to manage some of their data and applications on-premises. At the same time, it relies on cloud providers to manage servers, hardware, networking, virtualization and storage needs.

⦿ **PaaS (Platform-as-a-Service):** Gives organizations the ability to streamline their application development and delivery. It does so by providing a custom application framework that automatically manages operating systems, software updates, storage and supporting infrastructure in the cloud.

◉ **SaaS (Software-as-a-Service):** Provides cloud-based software hosted online and typically available on a subscription basis. Third-party providers manage all potential technical issues, such as data, middleware, servers and storage. This setup helps minimize IT resource expenditures and streamline maintenance and support functions.

Cloud security tools

Many of the same tools used in on-premises environments should be used in the cloud, although cloud-specific versions of them may exist. These tools and mechanisms include encryption, IAM and single sign-on (SSO), data loss prevention (DLP), intrusion prevention and detection systems (IPSes/IDSes) and public key infrastructure (PKI).

Some cloud-specific tools include the following:

◉ **Cloud workload protections platforms (CWPPs).** A CWPP is a security mechanism designed to protect workloads — for example, VMs, applications or data — in a consistent manner.

◉ **Cloud access security brokers (CASBs).** A CASB is a tool or service that sits between cloud customers and cloud services to enforce security policies and, as a gatekeeper, add a layer of security.

◉ **Cloud security posture management (CSPM).** CSPM is a group of security products and services that monitor cloud security and compliance issues and aim to combat cloud misconfigurations, among other features.

Secure Access Service Edge (SASE) and zero-trust network access (ZTNA) are also emerging as two popular cloud security models/frameworks.

Security as a Service, often shortened to SaaS or SECaaS, is a subset of software as a service. The Cloud Security Alliance (CSA) defined 10 SECaaS categories:

◉ IAM

- DLP
- web security
- email security
- security assessments
- intrusion management
- security information and event management (SIEM)
- encryption
- BC/disaster recovery (BCDR)
- network security

These include services such as firewall as a service, cloud-based virtual private networks (VPNs) and key management as a service (KMaaS).

How to secure data in the cloud

The steps required to secure data in the cloud vary. Factors, including the type and sensitivity of the data to be protected, cloud architecture, accessibility of built-in and third-party tools, and number and types of users authorized to access the data must be considered.

Some general best practices to secure business data in the cloud include the following:

- Encrypt data at rest, in use and in motion.
- Use two-factor authentication (2FA) or multifactor authentication (MFA) to verify user identity before granting access.
- Adopt cloud edge security protections, including firewalls, IPSes and antimalware.
- Isolate cloud data backups to prevent ransomware threats.
- Ensure data location visibility and control to identify where data resides and to implement restrictions on whether data can be copied to other locations inside or outside the cloud.
- Log and monitor all aspects of data access, additions and changes.

Emerging cybersecurity tools should also be considered to help secure data in clouds. These include network detection and response (NDR) and artificial intelligence (AI) for IT operations (AIOps). Both tools collect cloud infrastructure health and cybersecurity information. AI then analyzes data and alerts administrators of abnormal behavior that could indicate a threat.

Top cloud security challenges

Many of the traditional cybersecurity challenges also exist in the cloud. These can include the following:

- ◉ insider threats
- ◉ data loss
- ◉ data breaches
- ◉ IAM
- ◉ key management
- ◉ access control
- ◉ phishing
- ◉ malware
- ◉ shadow IT
- ◉ distributed denial-of-service (DDoS) attacks
- ◉ insecure application programming interfaces (APIs)

As for cloud security challenges specifically, administrators have to deal with issues that include the following:

- ◉ cloud account hijacking;
- ◉ lack of cloud visibility and control;
- ◉ working with cloud security tools that in-house administrators may be unfamiliar with;
- ◉ tracking and monitoring where data is located both in transit and at rest;
- ◉ misconfigurations;
- ◉ weak cloud control plane;
- ◉ challenges understanding the shared responsibility model;
- ◉ nefarious use of cloud services;
- ◉ multi-tenancy concerns;
- ◉ incompatibilities with on-premises environments;
- ◉ cloud compliance; and
- ◉ cloud governance.

Security administrators must have plans and processes in place to identify and curb emerging cloud security threats. These threats typically revolve around newly discovered exploits found in applications, OSes, VM environments and other network infrastructure components. To handle these security challenges and eliminate emerging threats, organizations must quickly and properly update and patch software that they control.

It's also important to establish communications channels between in-house IT and CSP staff. In-house staff should subscribe to, monitor and digest the CSP's security bulletin stream. If coordination between the customer and CSP is required to handle a security incident, well-documented communications channels must be established and continuously updated so time isn't wasted when working through a security breach.

SECURING CLOUD INFRASTRUCTURE

Cloud infrastructure security is the practice of securing resources deployed in a cloud environment and supporting systems.

Public cloud infrastructure is, in many ways, more vulnerable than on-premises infrastructure because it can easily be exposed to public networks, and is not located behind a secure network perimeter. However, in a private or hybrid cloud, security is still a challenge, as there are multiple security concerns due to the highly automated nature of the environment, and numerous integration points with public cloud systems.

Cloud infrastructure is made up of at least 7 basic components, including user accounts, servers, storage systems, and networks. Cloud environments are dynamic, with short-lived resources created and terminated many times per day. This means each of these building blocks must be secured in an automated and systematic manner. Read on to learn best practices that can help you secure each of these components.

Public Cloud Security

In a public cloud, the cloud provider takes responsibility for securing the infrastructure, and provides tools that allow the organization to secure its workloads. Your organization is responsible for:

- Securing workloads and data, fully complying with relevant compliance standards, and ensuring all activity is logged to enable auditing.

- Ensuring cloud configurations remain secure, and any new resources on the cloud are similarly secured, using automated tools such as a Cloud Security Posture Management (CSPM) platform.

- Understanding which service level agreements (SLA), supplied by your cloud provider, deliver relevant services and monitoring.

- If you use services, machine images, container images, or other software from third-party providers, performing due diligence on their security measures and replacing providers if they are insufficient.

Private Cloud Security

The private cloud model gives you control over all layers of the stack. These resources are commonly not exposed to the public Internet. This means that you can achieve a certain level of security using traditional mechanisms that protect the corporate network perimeter. However, there are additional measures you should take to secure your private cloud:

⊙ Use cloud native monitoring tools to gain visibility over any anomalous behavior in your running workloads.

⊙ Monitor privileged accounts and resources for suspicious activity to detect insider threats. Malicious users or compromised accounts can have severe consequences in a private cloud, because of the ease at which resources can be automated.

⊙ Ensure complete isolation between virtual machines, containers, and host operating systems, to ensure that compromise of a VM or container does not allow compromise of the entire host.

⊙ Virtual machines should have dedicated NICs or VLANs, and hosts should communicate over the network using a separate network interface.

⊙ Plan ahead and prepare for hybrid cloud by putting security measures in place to ensure that you can securely integrate with public cloud services

Hybrid Cloud Security

Hybrid clouds are a combination of on-premise data center, public cloud, and private cloud. The following security considerations are important in a hybrid cloud environment:

⊙ Ensure public cloud systems are secured using all the best practices.

⊙ Private cloud systems should follow private cloud security best practices, as well as traditional network security measures for the local data center.

⊙ Avoid separate security strategies and tools in each environment—adopt a single security framework that can provide controls across the hybrid environment.

⊙ Identify all integration points between environments, treat them as high-risk components and ensure they are secured.

IDENTITY AND ACCESS MANAGEMENT (IAM)

There is a saying in the cybersecurity world that goes like this "No matter how good your chain is it's only as strong as your weakest link." and exactly hackers use the weakest links in the organization to infiltrate. They usually use phishing attacks to infiltrate an organization and if they get at least one person to fall for it, it's a serious turn of events from thereon. They use the stolen credentials to plant back doors, install malware or exfiltrate confidential data, all of which will cause serious losses for an organization.

How Identity and Access Management Works?

AWS(Amazon Web Services) will allows you to maintain the fine-grained permissions to the AWS account and the services provided Amazon cloud. You can manage the permissions to the individual users or you can manage the permissions to certain users as group and roles will helps you to manage the permissions to the resources.

Users

- ⊙ Roles
- ⊙ Groups
- ⊙ Policies

With these new applications being created over the cloud, mobile and on-premise can hold sensitive and regulated information. It's no longer acceptable and feasible to just create an Identity server and provide access based on the requests. In current times an organization should be able to track the flow of information and provide least privileged access as and when required, obviously with a large workforce and new applications being added every day it becomes quite difficult to do the same. So organizations specifically concentrate on managing identity and its access with the help of a few IAM tools. It's quite obvious that it is very difficult for a single tool to manage everything but there are multiple IAM tools in the market that help the organizations with any of the few services given below.

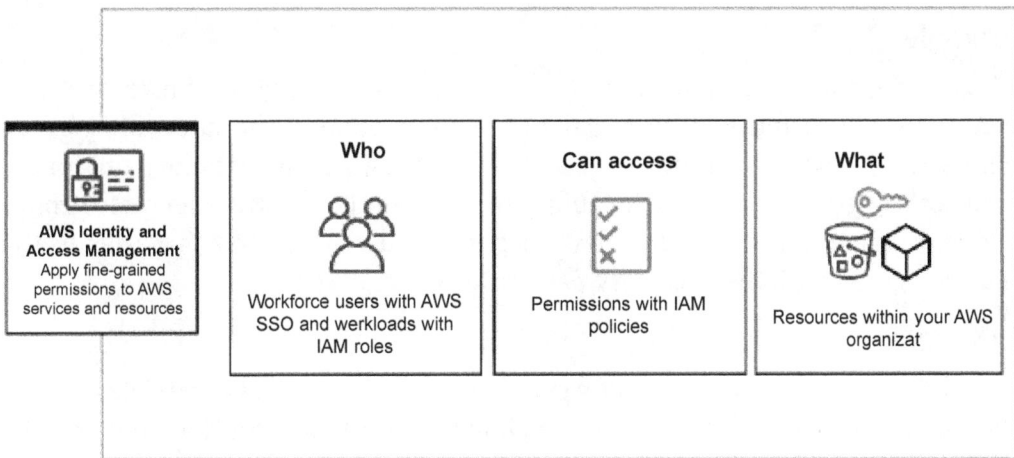

| AWS Identity and Access Management
Apply fine-grained permissions to AWS services and resources | **Who**
Workforce users with AWS SSO and werkloads with IAM roles | **Can access**
Permissions with IAM policies | **What**
Resources within your AWS organizat |

Components of Identity and Access Management (IAM)

IAM Identities Classified as

⊙ IAM Users

⊙ IAM Groups

⊙ IAM Roles

Root user

The root user will automatically be created and granted unrestricted rights. We can create an admin user with fewer powers to control the entire Amazon account.

IAM Users

We can utilize IAM users to access the AWS Console and their administrative permissions differ from those of the Root user and if we can keep track of their login information.

Example

With the aid of IAM users, we can accomplish our goal of giving a specific person access to every service available in the Amazon dashboard with only a limited set of permissions, such as read-only access. Let's say user-1 is a user that I want to have read-only access to the EC2 instance and no additional permissions, such as create, delete, or update. By creating an IAM user and attaching user-1 to that IAM user, we may allow the user access to the EC2 instance with the required permissions.

IAM Groups

A group is a collection of users, and a single person can be a member of several groups. With the aid of groups, we can manage permissions for many users quickly and efficiently.

Example

Consider two users named user-1 and user-2. If we want to grant user-1 specific permissions, such as the ability to delete, create, and update the auto-calling group only, and if we want to grant user-2 all the necessary permissions to maintain the auto-scaling group as well as the ability to maintain EC2,S3 we can create groups and add this user to them. If a new user is added, we can add that user to the required group with the necessary permissions.

IAM Roles

While policies cannot be directly given to any of the services accessible through the Amazon dashboard, IAM roles are similar to IAM users in that they may be assumed by anybody who requires them. By using roles, we can provide AWS Services access rights to other AWS Services.

Example

Consider Amazon EKS. In order to maintain an autoscaling group, AWS eks needs access to EC2 instances. Since we can't attach policies directly to the eks in this situation, we must build a role and then attach the necessary policies to that specific role and attach that particular role to EKS.

IAM Policies

IAM Policies can manage access for AWS by attaching them to the IAM Identities or resources IAM policies defines permissions of AWS identities and AWS resources when a user or any resource makes a request to AWS will validate these policies and confirms whether the request to be allowed or to be denied. AWS policies are stored in the form of Jason format the number of policies to be attached to particular IAM identities depends upon no.of permissions required for one IAM identity. IAM identity can have multiple policies attached to them.

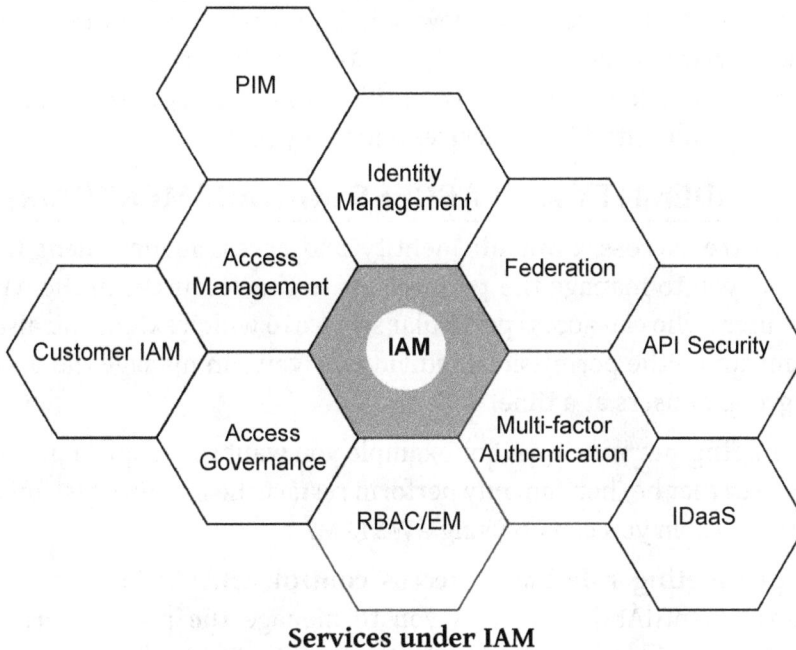

Services under IAM

Access management for AWS resourcesIdentity management

- ⦿ Access management
- ⦿ Federation
- ⦿ RBAC/EM
- ⦿ Multi-Factor authentication
- ⦿ Access governance
- ⦿ Customer IAM
- ⦿ API Security

- ⊙ IDaaS – Identity as a service
- ⊙ Granular permissions
- ⊙ Privileged Identity management – PIM (PAM or PIM is the same)

More About the Services: Looking into the services on brief, Identity management is purely responsible for managing the identity lifecycle. Access management is responsible for the access to the resources, access governance is responsible for access request grant and audits. PIM or PAM is responsible for managing all the privileged access to the resources. The remaining services either help these services or help in increasing the productivity of these services.

Market for IAM: Current situation of the market, there are three market leaders (Okta, SailPoint and Cyberark) who master one of the three domains (Identity Management, Identity Governance and Privilege access management), according to Gartner and Forrester reports. These companies have developed solutions and are still developing new solutions that allow an organization to manage identity and its access securely without any hindrances in the workflow. There are other IAM tools, Beyond Trust, Ping, One login, Centrify, Azure Active Directory, Oracle Identity Cloud Services and many more.

USE CASES IDENTITY AND ACCESS MANAGEMENT(IAM)

- ⊙ **Resource Access Control:** Identity and access management (IAM) will allows you to manage the permissions to the resources in the AWS cloud like users who can access particular serivce to which extent and also instead of mantaing the permissions individually you can manage the permissions to group of users at a time.

- ⊙ **Managing permissions:** For example you want to assign an permission to the user that he/her can only perform restart the instance task on AWS EC2 instance then you can do using AWS IAM.

- ⊙ **Implemneting role-based access control(RBAC):** Identity and Access Management(IAM) will helps you to manage the permissions based on roles Roles will helps to assign the the permissions to the resourcesw in the AWS like which resources can access the another resource according to the requirement.

- ⊙ **Enabling single sign-on (SSO):** Identity and Access Management will helps you to maintain the same password and user name which will reduce the effort of remembering the different password.

CLOUD SECURITY BEST PRACTICES

As businesses become more dependent on cloud technologies and computing environments grow more complex, the need to secure cloud infrastructure is becoming increasingly important. The following cloud infrastructure best practices can help organizations adopt a robust security posture that protects critical IT assets, sensitive data, and intellectual property.

Use strong authentication methods

Passwords alone do not provide enough security. Users typically choose short passwords that are easy to remember, often using the same password to access multiple websites or applications. Weak passwords are easy for hackers to guess and contribute to 81% of all data breaches. Stolen and reused login credentials also pose a significant security threat, comprising 80% of all hacking incidents.

To secure cloud infrastructure, companies should use strong authentication methods, such as multi-factor authentication (MFA) or biometrics. Requiring users to provide additional evidence to verify their identity significantly reduces the risk of cyberattacks. Bad actors can rarely meet the second authentication requirement, which prevents them from gaining access to user accounts that have permission to access sensitive data and use critical enterprise applications and services.

Limit users' access to resources

A strong security posture not only keeps unauthorized users out; it also limits the resources authorized users can access. Organizations that give users more access than they need risk unintentional data loss caused by users' careless actions. Even greater damage can result if bad actors gain access to zombie accounts or malicious insiders compromise data or steal the company's intellectual property.

Use the following infrastructure security best practices to protect sensitive data and resources from unauthorized access:

- Deploy an identity access management solution that simplifies credential management and centralizes authentication.

- When provisioning new users, grant granular permissions individually based on each user's role and business needs.

- Leverage the principle of least privilege to ensure each user has access only to the resources their job requires.

- To reduce the risk of cyberattacks that exploit zombie accounts, use a modern tool that deprovisions users automatically when they leave the organization.

- Perform routine security audits. Verify and update individual, group, and role-based permissions. Make sure no users have accumulated more permissions than they need.

Enable real-time monitoring and logging

While segmentation capabilities give cloud computing a significant security advantage, the accelerated adoption of cloud technologies has created an ever-expanding attack surface. In the first half of 2022, the incidence of cyberattacks rose by 42%. As threats become increasingly sophisticated and breaches become increasingly expensive, it is more important than ever for companies to employ real-time monitoring and comprehensive logging capabilities.

To detect irregular usage patterns and potential threats, use modern tools that provide visibility across all platforms and devices, including cloud infrastructure. Continuously monitor system activity and user behavior in real-time, and respond to alerts promptly. Be sure to enable logging for all critical IT assets. That way, IT teams will have all the information they need to identify potential threats and can respond quickly to any security incidents that may occur.

Provide cybersecurity training to employees

While monitoring user activity helps identify irregular usage and potentially malicious behavior, ongoing employee training plays a key role in every company's security strategy. All users should have at least a basic understanding of security protocols. Train users in security best practices so they will know how to protect their login credentials from theft or misuse and how to practice good password hygiene.

Leverage advanced training sessions to raise awareness of common cybersecurity risks, such as phishing attacks, online fraud, spoof domains that replicate popular trusted websites, and social engineering scams that trick users into disclosing sensitive information. With 75% of phishing attacks originating from cloud-based email servers and a record-breaking 1,097,811 phishing attacks in the second quarter of 2022, phishing should be top of mind for everyone.

Accounts

Service accounts in the cloud are typically privileged accounts, which may have access to critical infrastructure. Once compromised, attackers have access to cloud networks and can access sensitive resources and data.

Service accounts may be created automatically when you create new cloud resources, scale cloud resources, or stand up environments using infrastructure as code (IaC). The new accounts may have default settings, which in some cases means weak or no authentication.

Use identity and access management (IAM) to set policies controlling access and authentication to service accounts. Use a cloud configuration monitoring tool to automatically detect and remediate non-secured accounts. Finally, monitor usage of sensitive accounts to detect suspicious activity and respond.

Servers

While a cloud environment is virtualized, behind the scenes it is made up of physical hardware deployed at multiple geographical locations. This includes physical servers, storage devices, load balancers, and network equipment like switches and routers.

Here are a few ways to secure a cloud server, typically deployed using a compute service like Amazon EC2:

- **Control inbound and outbound communication**—your server should only be allowed to connect to networks, and specific IP ranges needed for its operations. For example, a database server should not have access to the public internet, or any other IP, except those of the application instances it serves.

- **Encrypt communications**—whether communications go over public networks or within a secure private network, they should be encrypted to avoid man in the middle (MiTM) attacks. Never use unsecured protocols like Telnet or FTP. Transmit all data over HTTPS, or other secure protocols like SCP (Secure Copy) or SFTP (Secure FTP).

  - **Use SSH keys**—avoid accessing cloud servers using passwords, because they are vulnerable to brute force attacks and can easily be compromised. Use SSH keys, which leverage public/private key cryptography for more secure access.

  - **Minimize privileges**—only users or service roles that absolutely need access to a server should be granted access. Carefully control the access level of each account to ensure it can only access the specific files and folders, and perform specific operations, needed for their role. Avoid using the root user—any operation should be performed using identified user accounts.

Hypervisors

A hypervisor runs on physical hardware, and makes it possible to run several virtual machines (VMs), each with a separate operating system.

All cloud systems are based on hypervisors. Therefore, hypervisors are a key security concern, because compromise of the hypervisor (an attack known as hyperjacking) gives the attacker access to all hosts and virtual machines running on it.

In public cloud systems, hypervisor security is the responsibility of the cloud provider, so you don't need to concern yourself with it. There is one exception—when running virtualized workloads on a public cloud, using systems like VMware Cloud, you are responsible for securing the hypervisor.

In private cloud systems, the hypervisor is always under your responsibility. Here are a few ways to ensure your hypervisor is secure:

- Ensure machines running hypervisors are hardened, patched, isolated from public networks, and physically secured in your data center

- Assign least privileges to local user accounts, carefully controlling access to the hypervisor

- Harden, secure, and closely monitor machines running the virtual machine monitor (VMM) and virtualization management software, such as VMware vSphere

- Secure and monitor shared hardware caches and networks used by the hypervisor

- Pay special attention to hypervisors in development and testing environments—ensure appropriate security measures are applied when a new hypervisor is deployed to production

Storage

In cloud systems, virtualization is used to abstract storage from hardware systems. Storage systems become elastic pools of storage, or virtualized resources that can be provisioned and scaled automatically.

Here are a few ways to secure your cloud storage services:

- Identify which devices or applications connect to cloud storage, which cloud storage services are used throughout the organization, and map data flows.

- Block access to cloud storage for internal users who don't need it, and eliminate shadow usage of cloud services by end users.

- Classify data into sensitivity levels—a variety of automated tools are available. This can help you focus on data stored in cloud storage that has security or compliance implications.

- Remove unused data—cloud storage can easily scale and it is common to retain unnecessary data, or entire data volumes or snapshots that are no longer used. Identify this unused data and eliminate it to reduce the attack surface and your compliance obligations.

- Carefully control access to data using identity and access management (IAM) systems, and applying consistent security policies for cloud and on-premises systems.

- Use cloud data loss prevention (DLP) tools to detect and block suspicious data transfers, data modification or deletion, or data access, whether malicious or accidental.

Databases

Databases in the cloud can easily be exposed to public networks, and almost always contain sensitive data, making them an imminent security risk. Because databases are closely integrated with the applications they serve and other cloud systems, those adjacent systems must also be secured to prevent compromise of the database.

Here are a few ways to improve security of databases in the cloud:

- **Hardening configuration and instances**—if you deploy a database yourself in a compute instance, it is your responsibility to harden the instance and securely configure the database. If you use a managed database service, these concerns are typically handled by the cloud provider.

- **Database security policies**—ensure database settings are in line with your organization's security and compliance policies. Map your security requirements and compliance obligations to specific settings on cloud database systems. Use automated tools like CSPM to ensure secure settings are applied to all database instances.

- **Network access**—as a general rule, databases should never be exposed to public networks and should be isolated from unrelated infrastructure. If possible, a database should only accept connections from the specific application instances it is intended to serve.

- **Permissions**—grant only the minimal level of permissions to users, applications and service roles. Avoid "super users" and administrative users with blanket permissions. Each administrator should have access to the specific databases they work on.

- **End user device security**—security is not confined to the cloud environment. You should be aware what endpoint devices administrators are using to connect to your database. Those devices should be secured, and you should disallow connections from unknown or untrusted devices, and monitor sessions to detect suspicious activity.

Network

Here are a few ways you can secure cloud networks:

Cloud systems often connect to public networks, but also use virtual networks to enable communication between components inside a cloud. All public cloud providers let you set up a secure, virtual private network for your cloud resources (called a VPC in Amazon and a VNet in Azure).

- Use security groups to define rules that define what traffic can flow between cloud resources. Keep in mind that security groups are tightly connected to compute instances, and compromise of an instance grants access to the security group configuration, so additional security layers are needed.

- ⊙ Use Network Access Control Lists (ACL) to control access to virtual private networks. ACLs provide both allow and deny rules, and provide stronger security controls than security groups.

- ⊙ Use additional security solutions such as firewalls as a service (FWaaS) and web application firewalls (WAF) to actively detect and block malicious traffic.

- ⊙ Deploy Cloud Security Posture Management (CSPM) tools to automatically review cloud networks, detect non-secure or vulnerable configurations and remediate them.

Kubernetes

When running Kubernetes on the cloud, it is almost impossible to separate the Kubernetes cluster from other cloud computing layers. These include the application or code itself, container images, compute instances, and network layers. Each layer is built on top of the previous layer, and all layers must be protected for defense in depth.

The Kubernetes project recommends approaching security from four angles, known as the "4 Cs":

- ⊙ **Code**—ensuring code in containers is not malicious and uses secure coding practices

- ⊙ **Containers**—scanning container images for vulnerabilities, and protecting containers at runtime to ensure they are configured securely according to best practices

- ⊙ **Clusters**—protecting Kubernetes master nodes and ensuring cluster configuration is in line with security best practices

- ⊙ **Cloud**—using cloud provider tools to secure the underlying infrastructure, including compute instances and virtual private clouds (VPC)

Compliance with security best practices, industry standards and benchmarks, and internal organizational strategies in a cloud-native environment also face challenges.

In addition to maintaining compliance, organizations must also provide evidence of compliance. You need to adjust your strategy so that your Kubernetes environment fits the controls originally created for your existing application architecture.

CHAPTER-9

IDENTITY AND ACCESS MANAGEMENT (IAM)

Identity and access management provides control over user validation and resource access. Commonly known as IAM, this technology ensures that the right people access the right digital resources at the right time and for the right reasons.

IAM basic concepts

To understand IAM, you must be familiar with some fundamental concepts:

◉ A **digital resource** is any combination of applications and data in a computer system. Examples of digital resources include web applications, APIs, platforms, devices, or databases.

◉ he core of IAM is **identity**. Someone wants access to your resource. It could be a customer, employee, member, participant, and so on. In IAM, a **user** account is a digital identity. User accounts can also represent non-humans, such as software, Internet of Things devices, or robotics.

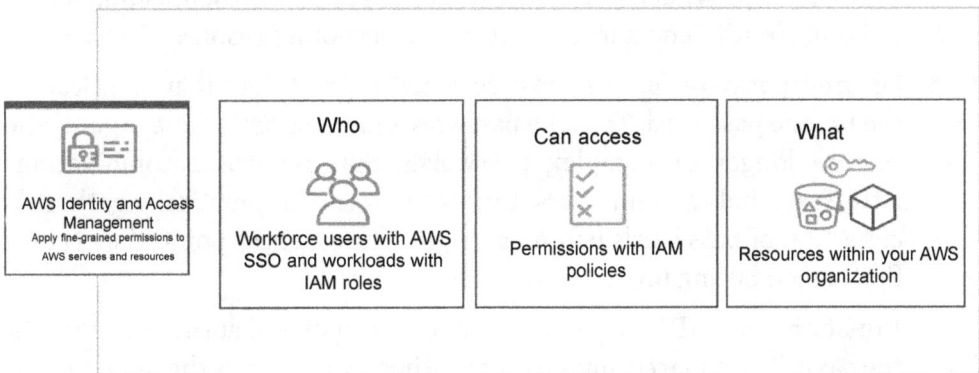

	Who	Can access	What
AWS Identity and Access Management Apply fine-grained permissions to AWS services and resources	Workforce users with AWS SSO and workloads with IAM roles	Permissions with IAM policies	Resources within your AWS organization

Identity and Access Management

- **Authentication** is the verification of a digital identity. Someone (or something) authenticates to prove that they're the user they claim to be.

- **Authorization** is the process of determining what resources a user can access.

IAM technologies and tools

IAM technologies are designed to simplify the user provisioning and account setup process. These systems should reduce the time it takes to complete these processes with a controlled workflow that decreases errors and the potential for abuse while allowing automated account fulfillment. An IAM system should also allow administrators to instantly view and change evolving access roles and rights.

These systems should balance the speed and automation of their processes with the control that administrators need to monitor and modify access rights. Consequently, to manage access requests, the central directory needs an access rights system that automatically matches employee job titles, business unit identifiers and locations to their relevant privilege levels.

Multiple review levels can be included as workflows to enable the proper checking of individual requests. This simplifies setting up appropriate review processes for higher-level access as well as easing reviews of existing rights to prevent privilege creep, which is the gradual accumulation of access rights beyond what users need to do their jobs.

IAM systems should be used to provide flexibility to establish groups with specific privileges for specific roles so that access rights based on employee job functions can be uniformly assigned. The system should also provide request and approval processes for modifying privileges because employees with the same title and job location may need customized, or slightly different, access.

Types of digital authentication

With IAM, enterprises can implement a range of digital authentication methods to prove digital identity and authorize access to corporate resources.

- **Unique passwords.** The most common type of digital authentication is the unique password. To make passwords more secure, some organizations require longer or complex passwords that require a combination of letters, symbols and numbers. Unless users can automatically gather their collection of passwords behind a single sign-on entry point, they typically find remembering unique passwords onerous.

- **Pre-shared key (PSK).** PSK is another type of digital authentication where the password is shared among users authorized to access the same resources — think of a branch office Wi-Fi password. This type of authentication is less secure than individual passwords. A concern with shared passwords like PSK is that frequently changing them can be cumbersome.

- **Behavioral authentication.** When dealing with highly sensitive information and systems, organizations can use behavioral authentication to get far more granular and analyze keystroke dynamics or mouse-use characteristics. By applying artificial intelligence, a trend in IAM systems, organizations can quickly recognize if user or machine behavior falls outside of the norm and can automatically lock down systems.

- **Biometrics.** Modern IAM systems use biometrics for more precise authentication. For instance, they collect a range of biometric characteristics, including fingerprints, irises, faces, palms, gaits, voices and, in some cases, DNA. Biometrics and behavior-based analytics have been found to be more effective than passwords.

When collecting and using biometric characteristics, companies must consider the ethics in the following areas:

- data security (accessing, using and storing biometric data);

- transparency (implementing easy-to-understand disclosures);

- optionality (providing customers a choice to opt in or out); and

- biometric data privacy (understanding what constitutes private data and having rules around sharing with partners.

One danger in relying heavily on biometrics is if a company's biometric data is hacked, then recovery is difficult, as users can't swap out facial recognition or fingerprints like they can passwords or other non-biometric information.

Another critical technical challenge of biometrics is that it can be expensive to implement at scale, with software, hardware and training costs to consider.

Before getting attached to passwordless IAM, make sure you understand the pros and cons of biometric authentication.

Implementing IAM in the enterprise

Before any IAM system is rolled out into the enterprise, businesses need to identify who within the organization will play a lead role in developing, enacting and enforcing identity and access policies. IAM impacts every department and every type of user (employee, contractor, partner, supplier, customer, etc.), so it's essential the IAM team comprises a mix of corporate functions.

IT professionals implementing an IAM system largely on-premises and largely for employees should become familiar with the OSA IAM design pattern for identity management, SP-010. The pattern lays out the architecture of how various roles interact with IAM components as well as the systems that rely on IAM. Policy enforcement and policy decisions are separated from one another, as they are dealt with by different elements within the IAM framework.

Organizations that want to integrate non-employee users and make use of IAM in the cloud in their architecture should follow these steps for building an effective IAM architecture, as explained by expert Ed Moyle:

- Make a list of usage, including applications, services, components and other elements users will interact with. This list will help validate that usage assumptions are correct and will be instrumental in selecting the features needed from an IAM product or service.

- Understand how the organization's environments, such as cloud-based applications and on-premises applications, link together. These systems might need a specific type of federation (Security Assertion Markup Language OpenID Connect, for instance).

- Know the specific areas of IAM most important to the business. Answering the following questions will help:
  - Is multifactor authentication needed?
  - Do customers and employees need to be supported in the same system?
  - Are automated provisioning and deprovisioning required?
  - What standards need to be supported?

Implementations should be carried out with IAM best practices in mind, including documenting expectations and responsibilities for IAM success. Businesses also should make sure to centralize security and critical systems around identity. Perhaps most important, organizations should create a process they can use to evaluate the efficacy of current IAM controls.

Trying to staff your enterprise security team with IAM experts? Use these 17 job interview questions — and answers — to find the best hires.

IAM risks

IAM is not without risks, which can include IAM configuration oversights. Expert Stephen Bigelow outlined five oversights that should be avoided, including incomplete provisioning, poor process automation and insufficient reviews. He also explained that paying attention to the principle of least privilege is essential to ensuring proper security.

Biometrics, as mentioned above, also poses security challenges, including data theft. Collecting and keeping only data that is necessary lessens that risk. Organizations should know what biometric data they have, what they need, how to get rid of what they don't require, and how and where data is stored.

Cloud-based IAM can be of concern when the provisioning and deprovisioning of user accounts aren't handled correctly, if there are too many vulnerable inactive assigned user accounts, and if there is a sprawl in admin accounts. Organizations need to ensure lifecycle control over all aspects of cloud-based IAM to prevent malicious actors from gaining access to user identities and passwords.

At the same time, features like multifactor authentication might be more easily deployed in a cloud-based service like IDaaS than they would be on premises because of their complexity.

Audit capabilities act as a check to ensure that when users switch roles or leave the organization, their access changes accordingly.

IT professionals can pursue IAM-specific and broader security certifications to be able to assess their organization's security posture and ward off threats. Read this comparison of the top IAM certifications.

Authentication and authorization

It's common to confuse authentication and authorization because they seem like a single experience to users. They are two separate processes: authentication proves a user's identity, while authorization grants or denies the user's access to certain resources.

You can think of authentication and authorization as the security system for an office building. Users are the people who want to enter the building. Resources that people want to access are areas in the building: floors, rooms, and so on.

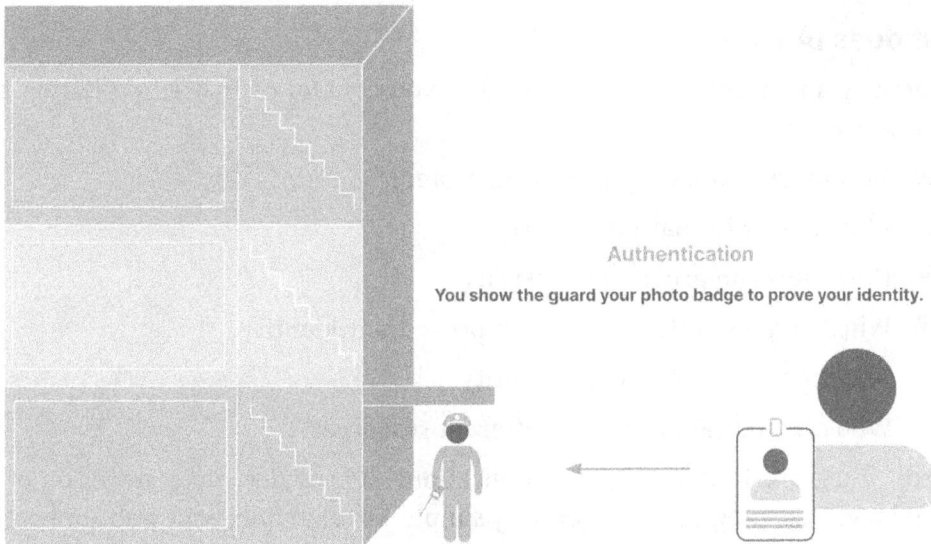

Authentication

You show the guard your photo badge to prove your identity.

Authentication: When you enter the building, you must show your photo ID badge to the security guard. The guard compares the photo on the badge to your face. If they match, the guard lets you through the door to try to access different areas of the building. The guard doesn't tell you what rooms you can access; they only get proof that you are who you claim to be. This is authentication: confirming user identity.

Authorization: In this scenario, imagine the elevators and doorways in the building have key sensors for access. The chip in your badge gives you access only to the first floor, which your company occupies. If you swipe your badge to enter any other floor, your access is denied. You can access your private office but not those belonging to your colleagues. You can enter the supply room but not the server room. This is authorization: granting and denying access to different resources based on identity.

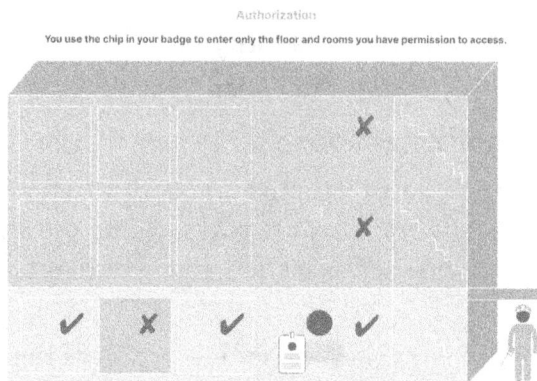

Authorization
You use the chip in your badge to enter only the floor and rooms you have permission to access.

To learn more about authentication and authorization, read Authentication vs. Authorization.

What does IAM do?

Identity and access management gives you control over user validation and resource access:

- How users become a part of your system
- What user information to store
- How users can prove their identity
- When and how often users must prove their identity
- The experience of proving identity
- Who can and cannot access different resources

You integrate IAM with your application, API, device, data store, or other technology. This integration can be very simple. For example, your web application might rely entirely on Facebook for authentication, and have an all-or-nothing authorization policy. Your app performs a simple check: if a user isn't currently logged in to Facebook in the current browser, you direct them to do so. Once authenticated, all users can access everything in your app.

It's unlikely that such a simple IAM solution would meet the needs of your users, organization, industry, or compliance standards. In real life, IAM is complex. Most systems require some combination of these capabilities:

- ◉ **Seamless signup and login experiences**—Smooth and professional login and signup experiences occur within your app, with your brand's look and language.

- ◉ **Multiple sources of user identities**—Users expect to be able to log in using a variety of social (such as Google or Linkedin), enterprise (such as Microsoft Active Directory), and other identity providers.

- ◉ **Multi-factor authentication (MFA)**—In an age when passwords are often stolen, requiring additional proof of identity is the new standard. Fingerprint authentication and one-time passwords are examples of common authentication methods. To learn more, read Multi-Factor Authentication (MFA).

- ◉ **Step-up authentication**—Access to advanced capabilities and sensitive information require stronger proof of identity than everyday tasks and data. Step-up authentication requires additional identity verification for selected areas and features. To learn more, read Add Step-up Authentication.

- ◉ **Attack protection**—Preventing bots and bad actors from breaking into your system is fundamental to cybersecurity. To learn more, read Attack Protection.

- ◉ **Role-based access control (RBAC)**—As the number of users grows, managing the access of each individual quickly becomes impractical. With RBAC, people who have the same role have the same access to resources. To learn more, read Role-Based Access Control.

Facing this level of complexity, many developers rely on an IAM platform like Auth0 instead of building their own solutions.

How does IAM work?

"Identity and access management" is not one clearly defined system. IAM is a discipline and a type of framework for solving the challenge of secure access to digital resources. There's no limit to the different approaches for implementing an IAM system. This section explores elements and practices in common implementations.

Identity providers

In the past, the standard for identity and access management was for a system to create and manage its own identity information for its users. Each time a user wanted to use a new web application, they filled in a form to create an account. The application stored all of their information, including login credentials, and performed its own authentication whenever a user signed in.

As the internet grew and more and more applications became available, most people amassed countless user accounts, each with its own account name and password to remember. There are many applications that continue to work this way. But many others now rely on identity providers to reduce their development and maintenance burden and their users' effort.

An identity provider creates, maintains, and manages identity information, and can provide authentication services to other applications. For example, Google Accounts is an identity provider. They store account information such as your user name, full name, job title, and email address. Slate online magazine lets you log in with Google (or another identity provider) rather than go through the steps of entering and storing your information anew.

identity and access management importance

IAM initiatives can help fulfill several use cases spanning cybersecurity, business operations and more.

Digital transformation

With the rise of multi-cloud environments, AI and automation and remote work, digital transformation means that companies need to facilitate secure access for more types of users to more types of resources in more locations.

IAM systems can centralize access management for all these users and resources, including nonemployee and nonhuman users. A growing number of IAM platforms now incorporate or integrate with CIAM tools, enabling organizations to manage access for internal and external users from the same system.

Workplace identity and access management

Businesses today maintain remote and hybrid workforces, and the average corporate network features a mix of legacy on-prem systems and newer cloud-based apps and services. IAM solutions can streamline access control in these complex environments.

Features like SSO and adaptive access allow users to authenticate with minimal friction while protecting vital assets. Organizations can manage digital identities and access control policies for all systems from a single, central IAM solution. Rather than deploying different identity tools for different assets, comprehensive IAM systems create a single source of truth, management and enforcement for the entire IT environment.

IT management and network administration

IAM systems, particularly those that support SSO, allow users to access multiple services with a single identity instead of creating different accounts for each service. This significantly reduces the number of user accounts that IT teams must manage. The growth of bring your own identity (BYOI) solutions, which allow users to manage their own identities and port them between systems, may also help simplify IT management.

IAM systems can streamline the process of assigning user permissions by using RBAC methods that automatically set user privileges based on role and responsibilities. IAM tools can give IT and security teams a single platform for defining and enforcing access policies for all users.

Regulatory compliance

Standards like GDPR, PCI-DSS and SOX require strict policies around who can access data and for what purposes. IAM systems allow companies to set and enforce formal access control policies that meet those standards. Companies can also track user activity to prove compliance during an audit.

Network and data security

According to IBM's *Cost of a Data Breach* report, credential theft is a leading cause of data breaches. Hackers often target overprovisioned accounts with higher permissions than they need. These accounts are usually less protected than admin accounts, but they allow hackers to access vast swaths of the system.

IAM can help thwart credential-based attacks by adding extra authentication layers so that hackers need more than just a password to reach sensitive data. Even if a hacker gets in, IAM systems help prevent lateral movement. Users only have the permissions that they need and no more. Legitimate users can access all the resources that they need on demand while malicious actors and insider threats are limited in what they can do.

Authentication and authorization standards

Authentication and authorization standards are open specifications and protocols that provide guidance on how to:

- Design IAM systems to manage identity
- Move personal data securely
- Decide who can access resources

These IAM industry standards are considered the most secure, reliable, and practical to implement:

OAuth 2.0

OAuth 2.0 is a delegation protocol for accessing APIs and is the industry-standard protocol for IAM. An open authorization protocol, OAuth 2.0 lets an app access resources hosted by other web apps on behalf of a user without ever sharing the user's credentials. It's the standard that allows third-party developers to rely on large social platforms like Facebook, Google, and Twitter for login. To learn more, read OAuth 2.0 Authorization Framework.

Open ID Connect

A simple identity layer that sits on top of OAuth 2.0, OpenID Connect (OIDC) makes it easy to verify a user's identity and obtain basic profile information from the identity provider. OIDC is another open standard protocol. To learn more, read OpenID Connect Protocol.

JSON web tokens

JSON web tokens (JWTs) are an open standard that defines a compact and self-contained way for securely transmitting information between parties as a JSON object. JWTs can be verified and trusted because they're digitally signed. They can be used to pass the identity of authenticated users between the identity provider and the service requesting the authentication. They also can be authenticated and encrypted. To learn more, read JSON Web Tokens.

Security Assertion Markup Language (SAML)

Security Assertion Markup Language (SAML) is an open-standard, XML-based data format that lets businesses communicate user authentication and authorization information to partner companies and enterprise applications that their employees use. To learn more, read SAML.

Web Services Federation (WS-Fed)

Developed by Microsoft and used extensively in their applications, this standard defines the way security tokens can be transported between different entities to exchange identity and authorization information. To learn more, read Web Services Federation Protocol.

Why use an IAM platform?

Why do so many developers choose to build on an identity and access management platform instead of building their own solution from the ground up?

User expectations, customer requirements, and compliance standards introduce significant technical challenges. With multiple user sources, authentication factors, and open industry standards, the amount of knowledge and work required to build a typical IAM system can be enormous. A strong IAM platform has built-in support for all identity providers and authentication factors, offers APIs for easy integration with your software, and relies on the most secure industry standards for authentication and authorization.

Authentication is the process of determining that a user, human or nonhuman, is who they claim to be. When a user logs in to a system or requests access to a resource, they submit credentials to vouch for their identity. For example, a human user might enter a password, while a nonhuman user might share a digital certificate. The IAM system checks these credentials against the central database. If they match, access is granted.

While a username and password combination is the most basic form of authentication, it's also one of the weakest. For that reason, most IAM implementations today use more advanced authentication methods.

Multi-factor authentication (MFA) requires users to provide two or more authentication factors to prove their identities. Common factors include a security code that is sent to the user's phone, a physical security key or biometrics like fingerprint scans.

SINGLE SIGN-ON (SSO)

Single sign-on (SSO) allows users to access multiple apps and services with one set of login credentials. The SSO portal authenticates the user and generates a certificate or token that acts as a security key for other resources. SSO systems use open protocols like Security Assertion Markup Language (SAML) to share keys freely between different service providers.

Adaptive authentication

Adaptive authentication, also called risk-based authentication, uses AI and machine learning to analyze user behavior and change authentication requirements in real time as risk level changes. By requiring stricter authentication for riskier activity, risk-based authentication schemes make it harder for hackers or insider threats to reach critical assets.

A user logging in from their usual device and location may only need to enter their password, as this routine situation poses little risk. That same user logging in from an untrusted device or trying to view especially sensitive information may need to supply more factors, as the user is now engaging in riskier behavior.

Once a user is authenticated, the IAM system checks the privileges that are connected to their digital identity in the database. The IAM system **authorizes** the user to only access the resources and perform the tasks that their permissions allow.

Identity governance

Identity governance is the process of tracking what users do with access rights. IAM systems monitor users to ensure that they don't abuse their privileges and to catch hackers who may have snuck into the network.

Identity governance is important for regulatory compliance. Companies typically craft their access policies to align with security mandates like the General

Data Protection Regulation (GDPR) or the Payment Card Industry Data Security Standard (PCI-DSS). By tracking user activity, IAM systems help companies ensure that their policies work as intended. IAM systems can also produce audit trails to help companies prove compliance or pinpoint violations as needed.

Cloud identity and access management

Increasingly, identity and access management solutions have been moving off-premises and adopting a software-as-a-service (SaaS) model. Called "identity-as-a-service" (IDaaS) or "authentication-as-a-service" (AaaS), these cloud-based IAM solutions offer a few capabilities that on-premises tools may lack.

IDaaS tools can be useful in complex corporate networks where distributed users log in from various devices (Windows, Mac, Linux and mobile) to access resources located on site and in private and public clouds. While on-premises IAM tools may not readily accommodate so many different users and resources across locations, IDaaS often can.

IDaaS can also help organizations extend IAM services to contractors, customers and other nonemployee roles. This can help simplify IAM implementations, as the company doesn't need to use different systems for different users.

IDaaS tools also allow companies to outsource some of the more time- and resource-intensive aspects of IAM like creating new user accounts and authenticating access requests and identity governance.

Single Sign-On (SSO)

Single sign-on (SSO) is an authentication method that enables users to securely authenticate with multiple applications and websites by using just one set of credentials.

How Does SSO Work?

SSO works based upon a trust relationship set up between an application, known as the service provider, and an identity provider, like OneLogin. This trust relationship is often based upon a certificate that is exchanged between the identity provider and the service provider. This certificate can be used to sign identity information that is being sent from the identity provider to the service provider so that the service provider knows it is coming from a trusted source. In SSO, this identity data takes the form of tokens which contain identifying bits of information about the user like a user's email address or a username.

The login flow usually looks like this:

- ◉ A user browses to the application or website they want access to, aka, the Service Provider.

- The Service Provider sends a token that contains some information about the user, like their email address, to the SSO system, aka, the Identity Provider, as part of a request to authenticate the user.

- The Identity Provider first checks to see whether the user has already been authenticated, in which case it will grant the user access to the Service Provider application and skip to step 5.

- If the user hasn't logged in, they will be prompted to do so by providing the credentials required by the Identity Provider. This could simply be a username and password or it might include some other form of authentication like a One-Time Password (OTP).

- Once the Identity Provider validates the credentials provided, it will send a token back to the Service Provider confirming a successful authentication.

- This token is passed through the user's browser to the Service Provider.

- The token that is received by the Service Provider is validated according to the trust relationship that was set up between the Service Provider and the Identity Provider during the initial configuration.

- The user is granted access to the Service Provider.

When the user tries to access a different website, the new website would have to have a similar trust relationship configured with the SSO solution and the authentication flow would follow the same steps.

Types of SSO configurations

Some SSO services use protocols, such as Kerberos or Security Assertion Markup Language (SAML):

- In a Kerberos-based setup, once user credentials are provided, a ticket-granting ticket (TGT) is issued. The TGT fetches service tickets for other applications the user wants to access, without asking the user to reenter credentials.

- SAML is an Extensible Markup Language standard that facilitates the exchange of user authentication and Authorizationdata across secure domains. SAML-based SSO services involve communications among the user, an identity provider that maintains a user directory and a service provider.

- Smart card-based SSO asks an end user to use a card holding the sign-in credentials for the first login. Once the card is used, the user does not have to reenter usernames or passwords. SSO smart cards store either certificates or passwords.

SSO security risks

Although single sign-on is a convenience to users, it presents risks to enterprise security. An attacker who gains control over a user's SSO credentials is granted access to every application the user has rights to, increasing the amount of potential damage.

In order to avoid malicious access, SSO should be coupled with Identity governance. Organizations can also use two-factor authentication (2FA) or multifactor authentication with SSO to improve security.

Social SSO

Google, LinkedIn, Apple, Twitter and Facebook offer popular SSO services that enable end users to log in to third-party applications with their social media authentication credentials. Although social single sign-on is a convenience to users, it can present security risks because it creates a single point of failure that can be exploited by attackers.

Many security professionals recommend end users refrain from using social SSO services because, once attackers gain control of a user's SSO credentials, they can access all other applications that use the same credentials.

Enterprise SSO

Enterprise single sign-on (eSSO) software and services are password managers with client and server components that log a user on to target applications by replaying user credentials. These credentials are almost always a username and password. Target applications do not need to be modified to work with the eSSO system.

Advantages and disadvantages of SSO

Advantages of SSO include the following:

- ◉ Users need to remember and manage fewer passwords and usernames for each application.

- ◉ The process of signing on and using applications is streamlined — no need to reenter passwords.

- ◉ The chances of phishing are lessened.

- ◉ IT help desks are likely to see fewer complaints or trouble about passwords.

Disadvantages of SSO include the following:

- ◉ It does not address certain levels of security each application sign-on may need.

- ◉ If availability is lost, users are locked out of all systems connected to SSO.

⊙ If unauthorized users gain access, they could access more than one application.

MULTI-FACTOR AUTHENTICATION (MFA)

Multi-factor Authentication (MFA) is an authentication method that requires the user to provide two or more verification factors to gain access to a resource such as an application, online account, or a VPN. MFA is a core component of a strong identity and access management (IAM) policy. Rather than just asking for a username and password, MFA requires one or more additional verification factors, which decreases the likelihood of a successful cyber attack.

Why is multifactor authentication important?

One of the biggest shortcomings of traditional user ID and password logins is that passwords can be easily compromised, potentially costing organizations millions of dollars. Brute-force attacks are also a real threat, as bad actors can use automated tools to guess various combinations of usernames and passwords until they find the right sequence.

Step 1: User name and password entered   **Step 2:** Pin from phone app entered   **Step 3:** Fingerprint verified

Multi-Factor Authentication (MFA)

Although locking an account after a certain number of incorrect login attempts can help protect an organization, hackers have numerous other methods for system access and carrying out cyber attacks. This is why a multifactor authentication process is so important, as it can help reduce security risks.

MFA authentication methods

An authentication factor is a category of credential used for identity verification. For MFA, each additional factor is intended to increase the assurance that an entity involved in some kind of communication or requesting access to a system is who — or what — it says it is. The use of multiple forms of authentication can help make a hacker's job more difficult.

The three most common categories, or authentication factors, are often described as something you know, or the knowledge factor; something you have, or the possession factor; and something you are, or the inherence factor. MFA works by combining two or more factors from these categories.

Knowledge factor

Knowledge-based authentication typically requires the user to answer a personal security question. Knowledge factor technologies generally include passwords, four-digit personal identification numbers (PINs) and one-time passwords (OTPs). Typical user scenarios include the following:

- Swiping a debit card and entering a PIN at the grocery checkout.
- Downloading a virtual private network client with a valid digital certificate and logging into the VPN before gaining access to a network.
- Providing answers to personal security questions — such as mother's maiden name or previous address — to gain system access.

Possession factor

Users must have something specific in their possession to log in, such as a badge, token, key fob or a mobile phone subscriber identity module (SIM) card. For mobile authentication, a smartphone often provides the possession factor in conjunction with an OTP app.

Possession factor technologies include the following:

- Security tokens, which are small hardware devices that store a user's personal information and are used to authenticate that person's identity electronically. The device may be a smart card or an embedded chip in an object such as a Universal Serial Bus (USB) drive or wireless tag.
- Software tokens, which are software-based security applications that generate a single-use login PIN. Software tokens are often used for mobile multifactor authentication, in which the device itself — such as a smartphone — provides the possession factor authentication.

Typical possession factor user scenarios include the following:

- Mobile authentication, where end users receive a code on their smartphone to gain or grant access — variations include text messages and phone calls sent to a user as an out-of-band method, smartphone OTP apps, SIM cards and smart cards with stored authentication data.
- Attaching a USB hardware token to a desktop that generates an OTP and using it to log in to a VPN client.

Inherence factor

Any biological traits the user has that are confirmed for login. Inherence factor technologies include the following biometric verification methods:

- Retina or iris scan.
- Fingerprint scan.

- Voice authentication.
- Hand geometry.
- Digital signature scanners.
- Facial recognition.
- Earlobe geometry.

Biometric device components include a reader, a database and software to convert the scanned biometric data into a standardized digital format and to compare match points of the observed data with stored data.

Typical inherence factor scenarios include the following:

- Using a fingerprint or facial recognition to access a smartphone.
- Providing a digital signature at a retail checkout.
- Identifying a criminal using earlobe geometry.

User location is often suggested as a fourth factor for authentication. Again, the ubiquity of smartphones can help ease the authentication burden: Users typically carry their phones, and all basic smartphones have Global Positioning System tracking, providing credible confirmation of the login location.

Time-based authentication is also used to prove a person's identity by detecting presence at a specific time of day and granting access to a certain system or location. For example, bank customers cannot physically use their ATM card in the U.S. and then in Russia 15 minutes later. These types of logical locks can be used to help prevent many cases of online bank fraud.

Pros and cons of MF

Multifactor authentication was introduced to harden security access to systems and applications through hardware and software. The goal was to authenticate the identity of users and to assure the integrity of their digital transactions. The downside to MFA is that users often forget the answers to the personal questions that verify their identity, and some users share personal ID tokens and passwords. MFA has other benefits and disadvantages.

Pros

- Adds layers of security at the hardware, software and personal ID levels.
- Can use OTPs sent to phones that are randomly generated in real time and are difficult for hackers to break.
- Can reduce security breaches by up to 99.9% over passwords alone.
- Can be easily set up by users.
- Enables businesses to opt to restrict access for time of day or location.
- Has a scalable cost, as there are expensive and highly sophisticated MFA tools but also more affordable ones for small businesses.

- Improves security measures and response for companies, as they can set up a multifactor authentication system to actively generate an alert whenever questionable login attempts are detected.

- Provides adaptive authentication, which helps with changing workplaces as more and more employees work remotely.

- Helps with meeting Health Insurance Portability and Accountability Act and compliance requirements, which require only authorized and restricted access to sensitive information, such as personal medical records.

Cons

- Requires a phone to get a text message code.

- Hardware tokens can get lost or stolen.

- Phones can get lost or stolen.

- The biometric data calculated by MFA algorithms for personal IDs, such as thumbprints, aren't always accurate and can create false positives or negatives.

- MFA verification can fail if there's a network or internet outage.

- MFA techniques must constantly be upgraded to protect against cybercriminals who work incessantly to break them.

Multifactor authentication vs. two-factor authentication

When authentication strategies were first introduced, the intent was to enforce security but to also keep it as simple as possible. Users were asked to supply only two forms of security keys that would inform a system that they were authentic and authorized users. Common forms of 2FA were user ID and password or automated teller machine (ATM) bank card and PIN.

Unfortunately, hackers quickly discovered ways to buy or break passwords or skim debit cards at ATMs. This prompted companies and cybersecurity vendors to look for more hardened forms of user authentication that used additional security factors for verification.

While MFA requires at least two authentication factors, if not more, 2FA only requires two. Therefore, all 2FA is MFA, but not the other way around.

Adaptive multifactor authentication

Adaptive multifactor authentication is a security approach that chooses which authentication factors to apply to a user's login attempt based on business rules and contextual information. It's also referred to as adaptive MFA or risk-based authentication.

Traditional MFA uses set credentials and a second factor, but adaptive MFA is a bit more advanced, as it automatically adapts authentication by considering several variables such as user location, device being used, number of failed login attempts, user behavior and environment. This strategy makes it harder for hackers to gain unauthorized access, since authentication is coordinated with the degree of risk.

Addressing the challenges of multifactor authentication

Users might be reluctant to adopt MFA, since it presents certain usability challenges such as remembering several passwords to log in. Along with user resistance, there could be other obstacles with MFA, including integration problems. Consequently, the goal of MFA is to simplify authentication for users.

The following four approaches are being used to simplify MFA:

- ◉ **Adaptive MFA.** As described above, this approach applies knowledge, business rules or policies to user-based factors, such as device or location. For example, a corporate VPN knows that it's OK for a user to sign on from home because it sees the user's location and can determine the risk of misuse or compromise. But an employee who accesses the VPN from a coffee shop will trigger the system and be required to enter MFA credentials.

- ◉ **Single sign-on (SSO).** This one-stop authentication method enables users to maintain one account that automatically logs them into multiple applications or websites with a single ID and password. SSO works by establishing the user's identity and then sharing this information with each application or system that requires it.

- ◉ **Push authentication.** This is an automated mobile device authentication technique where the security system automatically issues a third, single-use identification passcode or push notification to the user's mobile device. For example, users who want to access a secured system enter their user ID and password and a security system automatically issues a third, single-use identification code to their mobile device. Users enter that code into the system to gain access. Push authentication simplifies MFA by providing users with a third code, eliminating the need to remember it.

- ◉ **Passwordless authentication.** Passwordless authentication forgoes the use of conventional passwords in favor of additional authentication factors such as hardware tokens or biometrics, including fingerprints and face recognition. Remembering passwords is hard, so this makes it easier for users to authenticate as well as improves the security posture of an organization, as most phishing attacks target password vulnerabilities for unauthorized access.

CHAPTER-10

MOBILE SECURITY

Mobile device management (MDM) is a type of security software that enables organizations to secure, monitor, manage, and enforce policies on employees' mobile devices. MDM is important because it helps protect the corporate network and data from cyberattacks and breaches that may occur due to the use of personal or unsecured devices in the workplace. MDM also allows employees to work more efficiently and productively by providing them with access to business applications and tools on their own devices. MDM works by using a server management console and an agent on each device to communicate and apply policies.

Designed to manage and secure mobile devices, such as smartphones, tablets, and laptops, that are used within an organization. MDM solutions allow businesses to control and monitor mobile devices remotely, ensuring data security, enforcing corporate policies and streamlining device management processes.

Tabnova mobile device management (MDM) is a type of software that helps organizations manage and secure their mobile devices, such as tablets, smartphones, and laptops. Tabnova MDM works by using a server management console and an agent on each device to communicate and apply policies. Tabnova MDM also provides solutions for different verticals, such as education, healthcare, retail, hospitality, and transportation. Tabnova MDM offers features such as kiosk mode, location tracking, remote wipe, and app management.

MOBILE DEVICE MANAGEMENT (MDM)

Mobile application management

Device management doesn't end with configuring policies, retrieving asset information, and securing your devices. Application management is just as important as setting up employees' mobile devices.

With RMM Central, you can:

⊙ Create your own enterprise app catalog.

⊙ Manage and distribute both in-house and third-party applications.

⊙ Integrate with the Apple Volume Purchase Program (VPP) and Google's Play for Work, allowing simple distribution of commercial apps.

⊙ Blacklist and whitelist mobile applications.

⊙ Audit your app inventory.

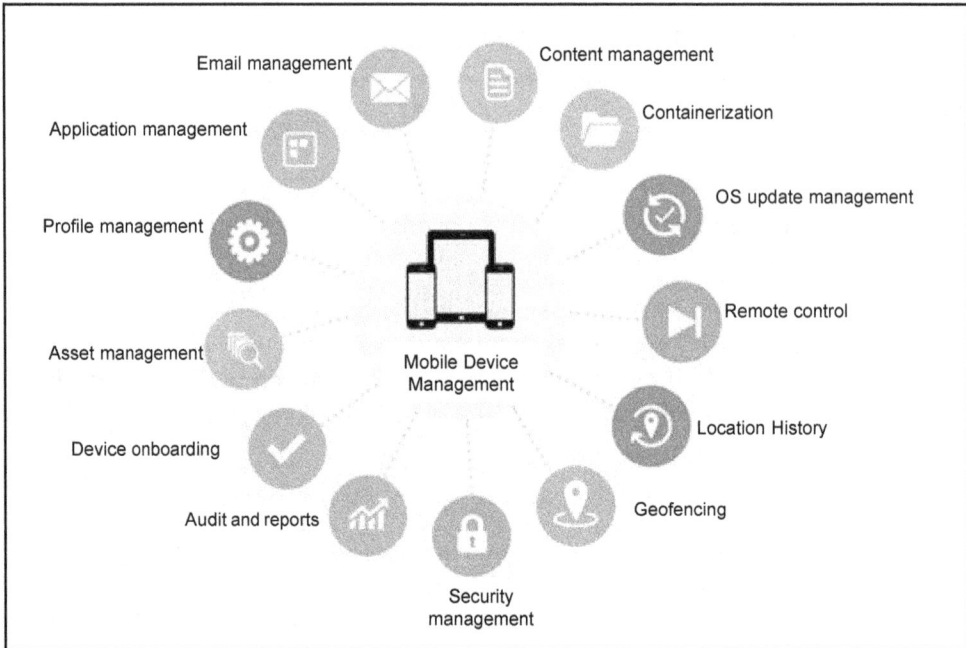

Mobile Device Management

Mobile security management

No two enterprises are the same—enforce stringent policies at various levels to suit your specific security needs.

With RMM Central's mobile security management feature, you can:

⊙ Enforce device passcodes to prevent unauthorized access.

⊙ Remotely lock devices to prevent the misuse of lost or stolen devices.

⊙ Track devices in real time with geo-location tracking.

⊙ Wipe a device's data completely to make it as good as new.

⊙ Perform a corporate wipe to remove corporate data only, leaving personal data intact. This feature is most useful in bring your own device (BYOD) environments, where employees access corporate data on their personal devices.

Profile management

Protect corporate resources by configuring and enforcing policies on mobile devices.

With RMM Central, you can create and configure policies and profiles for different departments or roles.

With RMM Central's profile and policy management feature, you can:

- Configure policy and profile settings for accessing enterprise resources.
- Restrict the use of applications such as the camera, YouTube, browsers, and more.
- Regulate access to corporate accounts including email, Wi-Fi, and VPN accounts.
- Create a logical group of devices based on department or location. You can also create groups to distinguish corporate devices from employees' personal devices. Apply policies or restrictions and distribute apps to all devices in a group.

Mobile content management

When employees use mobile devices for work, they need access to corporate resources on their devices.

RMM Central allows admins to remotely share documents to employees' devices, all without compromising security.

With RMM Central, you can:

- Create a content repository to store documents.
- Distribute documents in various formats, including DOC, PDF, PPTX, and more.
- Restrict document sharing between unmanaged devices.

Email management

RMM Central lets you securely manage corporate emails through platform containerization and Exchange ActiveSync. With mobile email management, you can configure, secure, and manage corporate email accounts for both enterprise-owned and personal devices.

With RMM Central, you can:

- Set up email security policies over the air.
- Containerize data to prevent unauthorized apps from accessing email data.
- Restrict users from modifying or removing their corporate email account.

- Selectively wipe corporate email accounts.

Containerization

In a BYOD environment, employees can perform work-related tasks with their personal mobile devices. However, BYOD management only works if you can effectively manage these devices and protect your data from being compromised.

RMM Central gives you the ability to set policies and restrictions to keep enterprise data safe. RMM Central allows you to containerize in the following ways:

- Enroll devices based on ownership.
- Create separate groups and define policies for BYOD and corporate devices.
- Wipe corporate data while leaving user data untouched, and secure corporate data when employees leave your organization.

Kiosk mode

Lock down mobile devices to run a single app or a select set of apps. RMM Central supports lockdown functions for both iOS and Android devices.

With RMM Central, you can:

- Permit access to only a limited selection of apps.
- Create a customized homepage with only the permitted apps.
- Restrict access to the task manager and status bar.

Audits and reports

Tracking and analyzing asset information helps you protect sensitive corporate data. RMM Central provides out-of-the-box reports that allow you to audit devices.

With RMM Central's reporting capabilities, you can:

- Scan devices to ensure they are compliant with company policy.
- Obtain granular details about the apps running on managed devices.
- Generate predefined or customized reports immediately or at a scheduled time.

Asset management

Unlike traditional workstations that reside within the physical workspace of an enterprise, mobile devices are used from multiple locations, complicating the process of managing and controlling them.

With RMM Central, you can:

- Track and analyze asset information to protect sensitive corporate data.
- Retrieve complete information about devices, including device details, certificates, installed apps, and more.

- Gain complete visibility on devices with out-of-the-box reports.
- Remotely troubleshoot mobile devices in real time.

Device enrollment

RMM Central serves as an endpoint management solution that works across many device environments, providing necessary security protocols so that unauthorized users can't gain access to your corporate network.

You can enroll devices manually or automatically, enroll devices in bulk, or have users self-enroll their mobile devices.

RMM Central offers:

- Automatic, manual, or over-the-air (OTA) device enrollment.
- Bulk enrollment of mobile devices using a CSV file.
- Authentication of enrollment with a one-time passcode or users' Active Directory credentials.

APP SECURITY AND CONTAINERIZATION

Application security is a set of measures designed to prevent data or code at the application level from being stolen or manipulated. It involves security during application development and design phases as well as systems and approaches that protect applications after deployment. A good application security strategy ensures protection across all kinds of applications used by any stakeholder, internal or external, such as employees, vendors, and customers.

Importance of Application Security

Today's applications are not only connected across multiple networks, but are also often connected to the cloud, which leaves them open to all cloud threats and vulnerabilities. Today, organizations are embracing additional security at the application level rather than only at the network level because application security gives them visibility into vulnerabilities that may help in preventing cyberattacks.

Security controls are a great baseline for any business' application security strategy. These controls can keep disruptions to internal processes at a minimum, respond quickly in case of a breach and improve application software security for businesses. They can also be tailored to each application, so a business can implement standards for each as needed. Reducing security risks is the biggest benefit of application security controls.

Application Security Controls

Application security controls are techniques that improve the security of applications at the code level, reducing vulnerability. These controls are designed to respond to unexpected inputs, such as those made by outside threats. With application security controls, the programmers have more agency over responses to unexpected inputs. Application security helps businesses stave off threats with tools and techniques designed to reduce vulnerability.

Application security controls are steps assigned to developers to implement security standards, which are rules for applying security policy boundaries to application code. One major compliance businesses must follow is the National Institute of Standards and Technology Special Publication (NIST SP), which provides guidelines for selecting security controls.

There are different **types of application security controls** designed for different security approaches that include:

- **Authentication**: Confirming if a user's identity is valid; necessary to enforce identity-based access.

- **Encryption**: Converting information or data into code to prevent unauthorized access; can involve individual files or an entire project.

- **Logging**: Examining user activity to audit incidents of suspicious activity or breach.

- **Validity Checks**: Making sure data entered and processed meets specific criteria.

- **Access Controls**: Limiting access to applications based on IP addresses or otherwise authorized users.

Challenges of Modern Application Security

Some of the challenges presented by modern application security are common, such as inherited vulnerabilities and the need to find qualified experts for a security team. Other challenges involve looking at security as a software issue and ensuring security through the application security life cycle. It is important to be aware of these challenges before beginning application security processes.

Common challenges for modern application security are bound to occur for any business interested in secure applications, and include the following:

- **Inherited vulnerabilities**: Companies often rely on software and code from outside sources, and these are likely to contain vulnerabilities.

- **Third-party and open-source vulnerabilities**: Open-source software might contain components of code that pose security risks and have IP risks from restrictive licenses.

- **dopting a DevSecOps approach**: A DevSecOps approach is the process of incorporating security measures through every phase of the IT process, also known as shift-left.

- **Finding qualified experts**: Security teams play a vital role in application security and finding experts or training security teams already in place is necessary.

- **Lack of a centralized management tool**: Without a centralized tool to support development teams, a business will either have extra overhead dealing with each siloed application team, or a lack of insight into reporting for applications.

Application Security Tools

Application security tools involve various types of security testing for different kinds of applications. Security testing has evolved since its inception and there is a right time to use each security tool. A modern business needs to secure applications to keep its data safe.

There are a variety of application security tools available:

- **Runtime Application Self-Protection**: RASP provides personalized application protections based on insight into internal data.

- **Software Composition Analysis**: SCA is a process that automatically detects open-source software in code to evaluate security, compliance and quality.

- **Static Application Security Testing**: SAST is a security testing method to analyze source code for vulnerability.

- **Dynamic Application Security Testing**: DAST provides insight into how applications behave during production.

- **Interactive Application Security Testing**: IAST is used to analyze code during testing run by automation and human testers.

- **Mobile Application Security Testing**: MAST products are designed to identify vulnerability in applications on mobile platforms.

- **Cloud-Native Application Protection Platform**: CNAPP is the practice of cloud-native applications and infrastructure.

Application Security Best Practices

The security best practices for web applications involve using security teams, tools and application security controls in tandem. Whether a business needs cloud security, web application security or API security, the security best practices provide a helpful guideline.

Perform a Threat Assessment of your code and applications.

Have an inventory of all your assets and highlight the most sensitive ones. Additionally, stay on top of the most common threats and vulnerabilities that can target these assets so you can appropriately plan.

Adopt a Shift-Left Approach

Adopting a shift-left approach is essential to including security throughout the application development process (DevSecOps).

Prioritize Remedial Operations

Prioritize remedial operations to resolve threats after identifying them. Using CVSS ratings among other criteria while performing a threat assessment will help you prioritize operations more effectively.

Measure Application Security Results with Frequent Testing

Test frequently and identify which are the most important metrics for your organization. Ensure that metrics are reasonable and easy to understand so that they can be used to determine if the application security program is compliant and if it will reduce risk.

Manage Privileges

Manage and limit privileges by adopting the Principle of Least Privilege (POLP) so those who have access to code and applications are the right teams.

Containerization

Imagine a situation where every application you wish to run comes with its own environment – carrying not just the core software but also its dependencies, configurations, and libraries. This encapsulated package is what we call a 'container'. Containerization, therefore, is the method of packaging, distributing, and managing applications and their environments as a singular unit.

Containerization: Cultivating a Secure Application Deployment Ecosystem

Containerization is more than just a mechanism for packaging applications—it's a comprehensive system that fosters a controlled, monitored, and secure environment for deploying applications. Here's a closer look at how this comes to fruition:

- ⊙ **Immutable Infrastructure:** Containers are typically designed to be immutable, meaning once they're built, they don't change. Instead of patching or updating a container, a new version is built and the old one is replaced. This approach:

- Reduces inconsistencies: Every deployment is consistent since it starts with a fresh container.

- Minimizes vulnerabilities: By regularly replacing containers with updated versions, potential security vulnerabilities can be addressed at the source.

◉ **Microservices Architecture Compatibility:** Containerization naturally complements the microservices architecture, where an application is broken down into smaller, independent services. This alignment brings:

- Enhanced security granularity: Each microservice, being in its container, can have security policies tailored to its specific function.

- Reduced attack surface: Even if a malicious actor compromises one microservice, the damage is contained, preventing system-wide breaches.

◉ **Centralized Management with Orchestration Tools:** Tools like Kubernetes provide centralized orchestration for containerized applications, ensuring:

- Automated security updates: With centralized management, security patches can be rolled out seamlessly across multiple containers.

- Efficient monitoring: Unusual behaviors or vulnerabilities can be detected swiftly, triggering automated responses to neutralize threats.

◉ **Least Privilege Principle:** Containers can be configured to operate on the 'least privilege' principle, where they only have the minimum permissions necessary to function. This minimizes potential damage if a container is compromised.

◉ **Network Segmentation:** With container orchestration platforms, it's possible to define intricate networking rules. This allows for:

- Isolated communication: Containers can be set up so that they only communicate with specific containers, reducing potential pathways for malicious activities.

- Enhanced data protection: Sensitive data can be isolated in containers with particularly stringent communication rules, ensuring it's shielded from potential breaches.

◉ **Continuous Integration and Continuous Deployment (CI/CD) Alignment:** The agility of containerization dovetails neatly with CI/CD pipelines. This synchronicity means:

- Swift vulnerability rectification: If a security flaw is detected, it can be fixed in the development phase, and a new container can be deployed rapidly, minimizing exposure.

- Regular security scanning: Containers can be scanned for vulnerabilities at every stage of the CI/CD pipeline, ensuring only secure containers reach the deployment phase.

- In the intricate dance of modern software deployment, containerization stands out, not just as a method of packaging but as a comprehensive philosophy that prioritizes security at every step. Its principles, when applied judiciously, can significantly elevate the security posture of any organization.

Best Practices for Securing Containers

Containers, while inherently secure in their design, can be further fortified by following a set of best practices. Here are some foundational steps to ensure the utmost security of containerized applications:

- **Regularly Update Container Images:** Maintain a regular update schedule for your container images. This ensures that you benefit from the latest security patches and avoid potential vulnerabilities. Remember, an outdated container image can be a security risk.

- **Implement Image Scanning:** Adopt automated tools that scan container images for vulnerabilities. Such scans should be an integral part of your CI/CD pipeline, ensuring that no vulnerable images make it to production.

- **Use Minimal Base Images:** Instead of using bloated, generic images, opt for minimal base images that only contain the essential components your application needs. This reduces the potential attack surface.

- **Control Container Capabilities:** By default, containers might have more privileges than they require. Limit these by defining and assigning only the necessary capabilities, ensuring the principle of least privilege is upheld.

- **Network Segmentation:** Set up network policies that define which containers can communicate with others. This not only enhances performance but also limits potential vectors for malicious activities.

- **Limit Resource Usage:** Use control groups (cgroups) to set resource limits on containers, preventing any single container from monopolizing system resources or initiating Denial-of-Service (DoS) attacks from within.

- **Use Read-Only Filesystems:** Where feasible, deploy containers with read-only filesystems. This ensures that the container's file system cannot be tampered with or written to during runtime.

- **Monitor Runtime Behavior:** Implement monitoring solutions that keep an eye on container behavior during runtime. Any deviation from expected behavior can be an indication of a compromise and should trigger alerts.

- **Secure Container Orchestration:** If you're using orchestration tools like Kubernetes, ensure that their configurations are hardened. This includes securing API endpoints, using role-based access control (RBAC), and encrypting sensitive data.

- **Regularly Audit and Review:** Periodically review and audit container configurations, deployment protocols, and security policies. The landscape of security is ever-evolving, and continuous assessment ensures that you remain a step ahead of potential threats.

By proactively embracing these practices, organizations can further enhance the inherent security advantages of containerization, ensuring that their applications remain robust, resilient, and shielded from a myriad of threats.

Challenges and Limitations of Containerization

While containerization boasts an impressive array of security and operational benefits, it's not without its challenges and limitations. Understanding these is crucial for organizations aiming to deploy containers effectively:

- **Complexity in Management:** The initial shift to containerization can seem daunting, especially for larger applications. Orchestrating numerous containers, each with its configurations, inter-dependencies, and communication requirements, demands a higher level of management skill and oversight.

- **Persistent Data Storage:** Containers are ephemeral by nature, which can pose challenges for applications requiring persistent data storage. Integrating and managing storage solutions in such transient environments necessitates strategic planning.

- **Security Misconceptions:** There's a common misconception that containers are completely secure by default. While they do offer inherent security advantages, they're not invulnerable. Relying solely on their native security without additional measures can lead to vulnerabilities.

- **Overhead and Performance:** While containers are lightweight compared to traditional virtual machines, running many of them simultaneously can introduce overhead. Performance optimization becomes crucial, especially when managing resources for a multitude of containers.

- **Inter-container Dependencies:** As applications grow and evolve, so do their inter-container dependencies. Managing these intricacies, ensuring smooth communication and operation, can become a substantial challenge.

- **Vendor Lock-in Concerns:** With various container tools and platforms available, there's a risk of becoming too reliant on a specific vendor's ecosystem. This can limit flexibility and complicate migrations in the future.

- **Networking Challenges:** Creating secure and efficient networking configurations for containers, especially in multi-container setups, can be intricate. It requires careful planning to ensure both security and performance.

- **Evolving Ecosystem:** The container ecosystem, though robust, is still evolving. This means that standards, best practices, and tooling are continually changing, which can pose adaptation challenges for organizations.

- **Skill Gap:** As with any emerging technology, there exists a skill gap in the market. Organizations may find it challenging to source or train professionals proficient in container management and security.

Recognizing these challenges and limitations is the first step in effectively navigating the container landscape. With informed strategies and a comprehensive understanding of both the pros and cons, organizations can harness the full potential of containerization while mitigating its associated risks.

Harnessing the Power of Containers

In the dynamic world of software deployment and development, the potential of containerization cannot be understated. As we've traversed its multifaceted realm, from understanding its core principles to evaluating its real-world impact, a consistent theme emerges: containerization offers a promising avenue for enhancing application security. Its holistic approach to software deployment — encapsulating applications in isolated, efficient, and easily managed units — is a formidable response to the challenges of the digital age. By integrating containers into their infrastructure, organizations can fortify their defenses against breaches, ensure more consistent application performance, and pivot rapidly in the face of emerging vulnerabilities. But as with all technological advancements, the true power of containerization lies in informed and strategic implementation. It's a tool, and like any tool, its effectiveness is determined by the hands that wield it. As we look forward to a digital future rife with both opportunities and challenges, containerization stands as a beacon, guiding us toward more secure, scalable, and resilient application landscapes.

SECURING BRING YOUR OWN DEVICE (BYOD) ENVIRONMENTS

BYOD (bring your own device) is a policy that enables employees in an organization to use their personally owned devices for work-related activities. Those activities include tasks such as accessing emails, connecting to the corporate network and accessing corporate apps and data. Smartphones are the most common mobile device an employee might take to work, but they also take their own tablets, laptops and USB drives into the workplace.

With more and more people working remotely and using personal devices, it's imperative for companies to execute and enforce BYOD policies. BYOD is not simply to eliminate the need for employees to carry two phones; a BYOD policy is designed to ensure that the employees use strong security practices when connecting to the company network.

While some organizations might endorse BYOD, others might see it as a facet of shadow IT, which indicates a hardware or software component that's not supported by the IT department.

Define a BYOD policy

Defining a BYOD (Bring Your Own Device) policy is a crucial step in managing the security and efficiency of IT services within an organisation. This policy sets the framework for how personal devices can be used in a corporate setting, outlining the responsibilities of both the employer and the employees, while ensuring compliance with legal and security standards.

A real-world example of this can be seen in the approach taken by IBM. As a global leader in technology, IBM implemented a BYOD policy that balances security with flexibility. Their policy outlines specific requirements for devices being used for work purposes, including mandatory use of encryption and regular security updates. Additionally, IBM's policy provides guidelines on which types of corporate data can be accessed and stored on personal devices, and it mandates the use of secure connections when accessing company networks.

IBM's policy also includes a clear outline of the support provided by the company for personal devices used for work purposes. This includes assistance with setting up access to corporate networks and resources, as well as guidance on adhering to security protocols. However, it also makes it clear that the primary responsibility for the maintenance and security of the device remains with the employee.

By establishing such a comprehensive BYOD policy, IBM has been able to leverage the advantages of a flexible work environment while maintaining a strong security posture. Their approach serves as a valuable model for other organisations looking to navigate the complexities of a BYOD environment.

When crafting a BYOD (Bring Your Own Device) policy, several critical elements must be considered to ensure it is effective, secure, and user-friendly. These elements include:

- **Security Requirements**: The policy should specify the minimum-security standards for devices that access the organisation's network. This often includes requirements for passwords, encryption, and antivirus software. Additionally, the policy should address how to handle lost or stolen devices and the protocol for remote wiping of data in such cases.

- **Acceptable Use**: Clearly outline what constitutes acceptable and unacceptable use of personal devices for work purposes. This includes guidelines on the types of applications that can be installed, the handling of company data, and restrictions on using the device during work hours for personal activities.

- **Privacy Considerations**: It's important to strike a balance between monitoring for security purposes and respecting employee privacy. The policy should clarify what data the company can access and monitor on personal devices and under what circumstances.

- **Support and Maintenance**: Define the scope of technical support that the company will provide for personal devices. This includes assistance with setup, access to corporate resources, and troubleshooting. The policy should also clarify the employee's responsibility for maintaining and updating their device.

- **Compliance and Legal Issues**: Address compliance with relevant laws and regulations, especially those related to data protection and privacy. The policy should also cover the legal implications of using a personal device for work purposes.

- **Reimbursement and Costs**: Outline any reimbursement policies for costs incurred by employees, such as data plans or software purchases necessary for work.

- **Device and Software Standards**: Specify any requirements or restrictions on the types of devices and software versions that are permitted to connect to the corporate network.

- **Training and Awareness**: Include provisions for training employees on the BYOD policy, emphasising the importance of security practices and the proper use of personal devices in the workplace.

- **Exit Strategy**: Define procedures for when an employee leaves the company or changes their device, including the removal of company data and access rights from the personal device.

⊙ **Regular Reviews and Updates**: Ensure the policy remains relevant and effective by scheduling regular reviews and updates to address new technologies, security threats, and changes in the regulatory environment.

By incorporating these elements, a BYOD policy can provide a robust framework for managing the use of personal devices in a corporate setting, safeguarding company data while accommodating the flexibility that BYOD offers.

BYOD Security Risks

Following are three of the most severe risks affecting BYOD devices.

Data Leakage and Loss

When employees use personal devices at work, any access to the corporate network can pose a risk—whether the employee is performing routine activities like logging into a work email account, or more sensitive activities such as viewing financial or HR records.

Attackers can gain access to a lost or stolen device, or compromise a device via phishing or malware while it is still owned by the employee. At that point, attackers have three main options to do damage:

⊙ Steal data stored locally on the device

⊙ Use credentials stored on the device to access the corporate network

⊙ Destroy data on the device

The second option is especially dangerous, because a compromised account can initially appear to be a legitimate user accessing corporate systems.

The third option can be mitigated by cloud backup systems, but these must be setup carefully or they can also become an attack vector.

Device Infection

Smartphones are commonly infected by malware, and in most cases, smartphone users are not aware their phone is infected. What's even more worrying is that, because mobile users install a large number of applications and may use them only occasionally, they may be careless about terms of service or permissions they grant to new applications.

On desktop or laptop computers, operating system vulnerabilities pose the biggest risk. Most users are not diligent about updating their operating system with the latest security patches. A first priority in any BYOD program is to identify the current OS running on employee devices, and ensuring they apply the latest updates.

Lastly, antivirus software is used unevenly by users on their personal devices. Some devices may not be protected at all, and others may be protected by free or unknown antivirus programs of questionable effectiveness

Mixing Personal and Business Use

With BYOD, it is inevitable that employees will perform both work and personal tasks on the same device. Your organization won't have control over websites visited by employees, some of which may be malicious or compromised, or install questionable applications. Devices may be used by the employee's children or other members of their household, and may be used to connect to unsecured wireless networks—the list of potential threats is endless.

Security Measures for BYOD Security

Given the major risks posed by BYOD devices, here are a few basic measures organizations can take to improve security on these devices.

Application Control

Some devices and operating systems provide control over the applications installed on a device. For example:

- iOS devices can block access to the Apple App Store
- Android Enterprise makes it possible to customize Google Play to show only approved applications

However, applying such restrictions on applications on a user's personal device is not practical. Employees are likely to resist these types of measures, and expect that they should be able to freely use their personal device when off work.

Containerization

Containerization is a way to divide each part of a device into its own protected environment, each with a different password, security policies, applications and data. This can allow employees to use the device without restrictions, while preventing security risks to the corporate network.

When a user logs in to a containerized work environment, they cannot access their personal applications and other features that the container does not manage. Containerization is a powerful solution that, on the one hand, prevents employees from using unapproved applications while connected to corporate systems, and on the other hand, does not restrict employees from free use of their personal device.

Android Enterprise makes it possible to set up separate, containerized environments for work and personal applications. This gives organizations full control over the work environment, without encroaching on the employee's free use of their personal applications.

Perception Point's Advanced Browser Security is a solution that provides all the security benefits of having separate physical devices for privileged and non-privileged work, without the inherent hassles and costs when users juggle between multiple devices. Cyber criminals that breach the general workspace are completely contained within it and cannot laterally move to the other protected environment. They cannot reach the host or privileged OS, and they can't even see that it exists.

Encrypting Data at Rest and in Transit

BYOD causes sensitive data to be retrieved and viewed on systems outside an organization's control. Therefore, it is crucial to encrypt data at rest and in transit. Encryption allows you to protect the content of sensitive files even in the worst case of device theft or compromise.

In practice, encrypting all data transmitted to employee devices can be challenging. Security and operations teams must take into account all scenarios in which a user downloads or saves a file on the local computer, such as downloading email attachments or retrieving files from corporate cloud storage. In all these cases, software on the BYOD device must ensure the data is encrypted.

Another concern is that encryption can slow down day-to-day operations, hurt productivity and frustrate users. In addition, any malfunction in the encryption process can block users out of critical files they need to do their jobs.

BYOD Security Best Practices
Educate Employees

Define a BYOD security policy, and even more importantly, take the time to educate users about it. Users should clearly understand what they can and cannot do on their personal devices, why the security measures are important, and what are the consequences of violating the policy.

Employees should undergo mandatory security training. A primary goal of employee education is to explain that security threats are a danger to the organization and to the employees themselves, and that by following the policy, they are improving safety for themselves, their colleagues, and helping to prevent catastrophic data breaches that can threaten the organization.

Separate Personal and Business Data

When employees use a device for business activities, a primary concern is privacy. A device can contain sensitive personal files or information, which the employee does not want to share with their workplace. At the same time, sensitive business data stored on the device must be protected and accessible only to the employee. Whether containerization solutions are used or not, the BYOD policy should clearly state how to separate personal and business information and prevent unwanted exposure.

Have a Solution in Place for Lost Devices

If a device is lost or stolen, employees must immediately report it to their manager or IT department. IT needs to be prepared for the necessary actions such as remote device lock, data wipe, password reset, and auto-wipe for critical applications. The protocol for device loss or theft should be clearly defined in the BYOD policy and employees should be fully aware of it.

Ensure Secure Network Connectivity

If an employee is connected to the Internet or public Wi-Fi, attackers can eavesdrop on business activities. Encourage employees to connect their equipment to a secure network, not just in the office, but also on the go. In any event, they should only connect to the corporate network via a secured, encrypted virtual private network (VPN).

BYOD Security with Perception Point's Advanced Browser Security

Perception Point Advanced Browser Security adds enterprise-grade security to standard browsers like Chrome, Edge, and Safari. The solution fuses advanced threat detection with browser-level governance and DLP controls providing organizations of all sizes with unprecedented ability to detect, prevent and remediate web threats including sophisticated phishing attacks, ransomware, exploits, Zero-Days, and more.

By transforming the organizational browser into a protected work environment, the access to sensitive corporate infrastructure and SaaS applications is secure from data loss and insider threats. The solution is seamlessly deployed on the endpoints via a browser extension and is managed centrally from a cloud-based console. There is no need to tunnel/proxy traffic through Perception Point.

Enhanced browser-level DLP capabilities deter malicious insiders, partners and contractors and include:

- Clipboard controls (preventing copy and paste);
- Printing controls;
- Configurable download/upload restrictions;
- Watermarking;
- Smart blur of sensitive web apps/data to prevent accidental external screen capture and shoulder surfing;
- User activity monitoring and visibility into all installed browser extensions across the organization;
- SaaS app login visibility, enabling the organization's admins and security teams to view the usage of unsanctioned web apps

The all-included managed Incident Response service is available for all customers 24/7. Perception Point's team of cybersecurity experts will manage incidents, provide analysis and reporting, and optimize detection on-the-fly. The service drastically minimizes the need for internal IT or SOC team resources, reducing the time required to react and mitigate web-borne attacks by up to 75%.

Customers deploying the solution will experience fewer breaches, while providing their users with a better experience as they have the freedom to browse the web, use SaaS applications that they require, and access privileged corporate data, confidently, securely, and without added latency.

Zero Trust Architecture (ZTA) and Attribute-Based Access Control (ABAC) Impacts

Zero Trust Architecture (ZTA) and Attribute-Based Access Control (ABAC) indeed introduce significant changes to device management, particularly in a BYOD environment. These frameworks shift the focus from traditional perimeter-based security models to more dynamic, context-aware approaches. Let's explore how they influence device management:

Zero Trust Architecture:

- **Continuous Verification**: ZTA operates on the principle of "never trust, always verify." This means every request for access to resources is authenticated, authorised, and encrypted, regardless of where the request originates or what device is used. This continuous verification impacts device management by requiring robust identity and access management (IAM) solutions.

- **Micro-Segmentation**: ZTA often involves micro-segmentation of networks, where access to resources is limited to what is necessary for a specific job role or task. This limits the potential damage that can be caused if a device is compromised.

- **Device Compliance and Health Checks**: Devices in a Zero Trust environment may undergo regular compliance and security posture checks. This ensures that only devices meeting specific security criteria can access network resources.

Attribute-Based Access Control:

- **Dynamic Access Decisions**: ABAC uses policies that evaluate attributes (user, device, and environmental factors) to make access decisions. This means that device management must account for various attributes of the devices, such as the device type, location, security status, and more.

- ⊙ **Contextual and Fine-Grained Control**: Access decisions in ABAC are more granular and context-dependent. This requires device management strategies to be more adaptive and responsive to changes in device attributes.

- ⊙ **Enhanced Data Security**: With ABAC, the access to sensitive data can be more precisely controlled based on device attributes, user roles, and other contextual information, leading to enhanced data security.

A real-world example of how Zero Trust and ABAC change device management can be seen in Google's BeyondCorp initiative. Google implemented a Zero Trust security model that allows employees to work more securely from virtually any location without the need for a traditional VPN. This model relies heavily on verifying the trustworthiness of the devices used to access its internal systems. Google's approach involves continuous evaluation of device attributes and user credentials to make real-time access decisions, significantly altering the traditional landscape of device management and network access.

In summary, the adoption of Zero Trust Architecture and Attribute-Based Access Control profoundly impacts device management by introducing more dynamic, context-aware, and granular control mechanisms. These changes necessitate a more sophisticated approach to managing and securing devices in a BYOD environment, focusing on continuous assessment and real-time decision-making based on a wide array of attributes and factors.

Segregate your network

Segregating your network is a vital security measure in managing IT infrastructure, especially in environments that support Bring Your Own Device (BYOD) policies. Network segregation involves dividing a network into smaller, distinct segments or subnetworks. This approach limits the access of devices to only the necessary areas of the network, thereby reducing the potential impact of security breaches and improving overall network performance and management.

Key aspects of network segregation include:

- ⊙ **Creating Subnetworks**: Dividing the network into smaller subnets can help isolate different types of traffic and user groups. For example, a separate network segment can be created for BYOD devices, keeping them distinct from the core corporate network.

- ⊙ **Implementing VLANs**: Virtual Local Area Networks (VLANs) are often used to segregate networks at the data link layer. VLANs can separate traffic based on factors like device type, user role, or application type.

- ⊙ **Access Control Lists (ACLs):** ACLs are used to control which devices can communicate with each other within the network. This helps in limiting the access of BYOD devices to only those resources they are authorised to use.

- ⊙ **Firewall and Intrusion Prevention Systems (IPS):** Firewalls and IPS can be configured to enforce network segregation policies, monitoring and controlling the traffic between different network segments.

- ⊙ **Physical Separation for Sensitive Data:** In some cases, particularly for highly sensitive data, physical network separation might be used, where completely separate network infrastructures are created.

A real-world example of network segregation is the approach taken by a large healthcare provider in the United States. To protect sensitive patient data and ensure compliance with regulations like HIPAA, the healthcare provider implemented a network segregation strategy. They created separate VLANs for different departments and user groups, including a dedicated VLAN for BYOD devices used by staff and visiting practitioners. This segregation ensured that BYOD devices had no direct access to sensitive patient data systems.

Moreover, they used ACLs to fine-tune the access permissions, ensuring that devices on the BYOD network could only access necessary applications and services, like email and certain internal web resources. They also deployed firewalls and IPS at strategic points between network segments to monitor and control traffic, preventing any unauthorised access to restricted areas of the network.

By implementing these segregation measures, the healthcare provider was able to enhance the security of their network, mitigate the risks associated with BYOD devices, and ensure a high level of compliance with industry regulations. Network segregation, therefore, plays a crucial role in enhancing the overall security posture of an organisation, particularly in environments where personal devices are used for accessing corporate resources.

Educate your employees

Educating employees is a fundamental aspect of ensuring the security and efficiency of IT systems, particularly in environments that embrace Bring Your Own Device (BYOD) policies. Proper education and training help employees understand the risks associated with using personal devices for work and the best practices to mitigate these risks. This education is not just about disseminating information; it's about fostering a culture of security awareness and responsibility among all staff members.

Key components of employee education in BYOD environments include:

- **Understanding BYOD Policies**: Employees should be thoroughly educated about the organisation's BYOD policy. This includes understanding the rules, the rationale behind them, and the consequences of non-compliance.

- **Security Best Practices**: Training sessions should cover essential security practices, such as using strong passwords, recognising phishing attempts, and securing devices with up-to-date antivirus software.

- **Data Management**: Employees must understand how to handle corporate data on their devices, including what can be downloaded, how to store it securely, and how to share it safely.

- **Device Maintenance**: Regular updates and maintenance of personal devices should be emphasised as part of the training, highlighting the importance of installing security patches and updates.

Real-world examples of effective employee education in BYOD environments

- **IBM**: IBM has a comprehensive BYOD program that includes extensive training and resources for employees. They provide online courses, regular updates, and resources that cover security best practices, data management, and compliance. IBM's emphasis on continuous education helps maintain a high level of security awareness among its workforce.

- **Intel Corporation** : Intel offers its employees training modules that cover various aspects of BYOD security. Their program includes scenario-based learning, where employees are presented with different situations involving BYOD and guided on how to respond appropriately. This practical approach helps employees understand the real-world implications of their actions.

- **Salesforce** : Salesforce takes a proactive approach by integrating security education into their corporate culture. They use engaging and interactive methods, such as gamification and rewards, to encourage employees to participate in security training programs. This approach not only educates employees but also makes learning about security an engaging and ongoing process.

These examples demonstrate that effective employee education on BYOD is not just about providing information; it's about engaging employees in a way that makes them active participants in the company's security culture. Regular training, interactive learning experiences, and continuous updates are key to ensuring that employees are well-informed and motivated to adhere to best practices in BYOD security.

Monitor and audit your IT services

Monitoring and auditing IT services are crucial components of a robust IT security strategy, especially in environments with Bring Your Own Device (BYOD) policies. Effective monitoring and auditing help in identifying potential security threats, ensuring compliance with policies, and assessing the overall performance and health of IT systems. These practices involve regularly reviewing system logs, user activities, network traffic, and compliance with established IT policies.

Key aspects of monitoring and auditing IT services include:

- ⊙ **Regular System Audits:** Conducting routine audits of IT systems to ensure they are secure and comply with industry standards and regulations.

- ⊙ **Network Traffic Analysis:** Monitoring network traffic to detect unusual patterns or activities that could indicate a security breach or misuse of resources.

- ⊙ **Access and Authentication Logs:** Reviewing logs to track who is accessing what resources, when, and from where, which is particularly important in BYOD environments.

- ⊙ **Compliance Monitoring:** Ensuring that both company-owned and personal devices comply with the organisation's IT policies and security standards.

- ⊙ **Incident Response and Reporting:** Having mechanisms in place to respond to security incidents and regularly reporting on audit findings to relevant stakeholders.

Real-world examples of effective monitoring and auditing of IT services include:

- ⊙ **Cisco Systems:** Cisco employs a comprehensive monitoring system that includes real-time analysis of network traffic and user behaviour. Their system is designed to quickly detect and respond to anomalies and potential security threats. Cisco also uses advanced data analytics to understand usage patterns and optimise network performance.

- ⊙ **Microsoft :** Microsoft's approach to monitoring IT services includes the use of their own cloud-based tools, like Azure Monitor and Azure Security Center. These tools provide continuous monitoring and advanced threat detection capabilities. Microsoft's monitoring strategy is designed to be proactive, using machine learning and AI to predict and prevent security incidents before they occur.

- ⊙ **Amazon Web Services (AWS) :** AWS provides its customers with extensive monitoring and auditing tools such as AWS CloudTrail and Amazon

CloudWatch. These services enable AWS users to track user activity and API usage, monitor their AWS environments, and receive alarms to detect unusual activity. AWS's approach emphasises the importance of visibility and control in cloud-based IT environments.

These examples showcase the importance of continuous monitoring and regular audits in maintaining the security and efficiency of IT services. For companies with BYOD policies, these practices are even more crucial as they help manage the additional complexities and security challenges brought about by personal devices accessing corporate resources. Monitoring and auditing provide insights into the operational health of IT services, help in detecting and responding to threats promptly, and ensure adherence to internal policies and external regulations.

Review and update your IT services

Reviewing and updating IT services is an essential ongoing process for any organisation, particularly in the dynamic landscape of technology and cybersecurity. This process involves regularly assessing the effectiveness, security, and efficiency of IT services and systems, and making necessary updates to ensure they meet the evolving needs of the business and its security requirements. This practice is especially critical in environments with Bring Your Own Device (BYOD) policies, where the variety of devices and the rapid pace of technological change can quickly render existing protocols obsolete.

Key aspects of reviewing and updating IT services include:

- ◉ **Technology Assessments**: Evaluating current technologies against emerging trends and industry standards to identify areas for improvement or upgrade.

- ◉ **Security Updates**: Regularly updating security measures to protect against new threats and vulnerabilities.

- ◉ **Policy Revisions**: Continuously revising IT and BYOD policies to reflect changes in technology, business operations, and regulatory requirements.

- ◉ **Performance Analysis**: Assessing the performance of IT services to identify inefficiencies or bottlenecks and implementing enhancements.

- ◉ **Stakeholder Feedback**: Gathering feedback from users and stakeholders to understand the effectiveness of IT services and areas that require attention.

Real-world examples of organisations that effectively review and update their IT services include:

- ◉ **Google** : Google is known for its continuous innovation in IT services. They regularly review and update their services, incorporating the latest technologies and security measures. For example, Google constantly updates its G Suite services with new features and security enhancements, ensuring that they remain effective for businesses of all sizes.

- ⊙ **IBM:** IBM has a long-standing practice of regularly reviewing and updating its IT services. This includes not only their hardware and software offerings but also their internal IT policies and infrastructure. IBM regularly assesses its cybersecurity measures and updates them to address new threats, a practice that is crucial given the vast amount of sensitive data they handle.

- ⊙ **Salesforce:** Salesforce regularly updates its CRM platform with new features and security enhancements. They conduct periodic reviews to ensure their services remain at the cutting edge, particularly in terms of data security and regulatory compliance. This is crucial for maintaining the trust of their large customer base, which includes businesses handling sensitive customer data.

These examples illustrate the importance of a proactive approach to managing IT services. By continuously reviewing and updating their IT infrastructure, policies, and services, organisations can ensure that they are not only meeting current needs but are also prepared for future challenges and opportunities. This is especially important in the context of BYOD environments, where the diversity of devices and the pace of change require a dynamic and responsive IT management strategy.

Emerging future trends in BYOD technology and architecture

The landscape of Bring Your Own Device (BYOD) technology and architecture is continuously evolving, influenced by emerging technologies and changing work patterns. Several key trends are shaping the future of BYOD:

- ⊙ **Increased Use of Artificial Intelligence and Machine Learning:** AI and machine learning are being integrated into BYOD management solutions for predictive analytics, improved security, and personalised user experiences. These technologies can help in detecting and responding to security threats in real-time, as well as in managing device performance and user behaviour patterns.

- ⊙ **5G and Enhanced Connectivity:** The rollout of 5G networks is expected to significantly impact BYOD, offering higher speeds and more reliable connectivity. This will enhance the capabilities of mobile devices used for work, facilitating smoother video conferencing, faster data transfer, and more efficient remote work.

- ⊙ **Expansion of Edge Computing:** With edge computing, data processing is performed closer to where it is needed, reducing latency and improving response times. In a BYOD context, this means quicker access to corporate resources and applications, enhancing productivity for remote and mobile workers.

◉ **Advanced Cybersecurity Measures**: As the BYOD landscape expands, so does the complexity of cybersecurity. Future trends include more sophisticated encryption techniques, biometric security features, and the use of blockchain for secure, decentralised management of devices and data.

◉ **Increased Emphasis on Employee Privacy**: With growing concerns around data privacy, future BYOD architectures will likely place a greater emphasis on protecting employee privacy. This could include more robust data segregation techniques, ensuring that personal data on employee-owned devices is not accessed or monitored by employers.

◉ **Cloud-Native Applications and Infrastructure**: The shift towards cloud-native applications and infrastructure is facilitating more efficient BYOD management. Cloud-native technologies offer scalability, flexibility, and seamless integration across different devices and platforms.

◉ **Zero Trust Security Models**: The adoption of Zero Trust architectures in BYOD environments is becoming more prevalent. In this model, trust is never assumed, regardless of whether a device is internal or external to the organisation. Access to resources is granted based on strict identity verification and context.

◉ **Virtual and Augmented Reality for Workflows**: As VR and AR technologies mature, they are expected to become more integrated into BYOD environments for specific industries, offering immersive and interactive ways for employees to engage with work-related tasks.

◉ **Sustainability in Device Management**: There's a growing trend towards sustainable IT practices, which includes considering the environmental impact of BYOD. This might involve promoting the use of energy-efficient devices or implementing policies to encourage sustainable practices among employees.

◉ **Integration with IoT Devices**: As the Internet of Things (IoT) continues to grow, there will likely be an increased integration of IoT devices within BYOD policies, expanding the scope of devices that need to be managed and secured.

These trends indicate a future where BYOD is more integrated, secure, and efficient, powered by advanced technologies that enhance both the user experience and the organisation's ability to manage diverse and complex device environments.

6G and beyond, technology trends at the cutting edge of BYOD

The development and eventual deployment of 6G technology, expected around 2030, is poised to bring transformative changes across various sectors. While still in the early stages of research and conceptualisation, 6G is predicted to have several significant impacts:

- ⊙ **Unprecedented Speeds:** 6G networks are expected to offer significantly higher data speeds than 5G, potentially reaching terabits per second. This would enable extremely fast data transfers and new levels of connectivity.

- ⊙ **Enhanced Mobile Broadband:** With its higher capacity and speed, 6G will further enhance mobile broadband experiences, enabling more immersive augmented reality (AR) and virtual reality (VR) applications, ultra-high-definition video, and more sophisticated mobile gaming.

- ⊙ **Internet of Everything (IoE):** 6G could facilitate the IoE, where virtually every device, vehicle, and building is connected and communicating with each other, leading to smarter cities, automated transportation, and highly efficient energy management systems.

- ⊙ **Ultra-Reliable Low Latency Communications (URLLC):** 6G will likely provide even lower latency than 5G, crucial for applications requiring real-time feedback, such as remote surgery, autonomous vehicles, and advanced industrial automation.

- ⊙ **Advanced AI Integration:** The combination of 6G's high speeds and low latency could enable more powerful and seamless integration of AI technologies, allowing for more sophisticated machine learning applications and real-time data analytics.

- ⊙ **Enhanced Remote Sensing Capabilities:** 6G may offer improved remote sensing capabilities for environmental monitoring, agriculture, and disaster response, using advanced satellite communication and wireless sensing technologies.

- ⊙ **Quantum Communication and Computing:** 6G could leverage developments in quantum communications and computing, potentially offering unparalleled levels of data security and computational power.

- ⊙ **Impact on Global Connectivity:** 6G could bring high-speed, reliable internet to remote and rural areas, potentially reducing the digital divide and promoting global connectivity.

- ⊙ **Challenges in Health and Environment:** As with any new technology, 6G will bring challenges in terms of health and environmental impacts, which will need to be carefully studied and managed.

- ⊙ **Regulatory and Ethical Considerations:** The expansive capabilities of 6G will likely raise complex regulatory, privacy, and ethical issues, necessitating new policies and frameworks.

- ⊙ **Economic and Societal Impacts:** 6G has the potential to drive significant economic growth, create new industries and job opportunities, and impact various aspects of society, from education to healthcare.

While the exact capabilities and impacts of 6G are still speculative, it's clear that this technology could drive significant advancements and pose new challenges, requiring careful consideration and planning by governments, industries, and societies worldwide.

CHAPTER-11

INTERNET OF THINGS (IOT) SECURITY

Internet of Things (IoT) security is based on a cybersecurity strategy to protect IoT devices and the vulnerable networks they connect to from cyber attacks. IoT devices have no built-in security. IoT security is needed to help prevent data breaches because IoT devices transfer data over the internet unencrypted and operate undetected by standard cybersecurity systems.

Along with the meaning of IoT Security, it is important to understand the many challenges facing enterprises when dealing with IoT security issues. IoT devices were not built with security in mind. The ongoing proliferation and diversity of IoT devices and communications channels increases the potential for your organization to be exposed to cyber threats.

Unfortunately, there is no way to install security software on most IoT devices. IoT devices may even ship with malware on them that infects the network when they connect. This is why network security is a priority for IoT security.

Many network security solutions do not have the ability to detect connected IoT devices or show which devices are communicating on the network. The following sections explore these and other big IoT security challenges including:

- Weak authentication and authorization
- Lack of encryption
- Vulnerabilities in firmware and software
- Insecure communications
- Difficulty in patching and updating devices

IoT devices are used in multiple sectors and industries, including:

⊙ **Consumer applications** – IoT consumer products include smartphones, smart watches and smart homes, which control everything from air conditioning to door locks, all from a single device.

⊙ **Business applications** – Businesses use a wide range of IoT devices, including smart security cameras, trackers for vehicles, ships and goods, as well as sensors that capture data about industrial machinery.

⊙ **Governmental applications** – Governmental IoT applications include devices used to track wildlife, monitor traffic congestion and issue natural disaster alerts.

The number of IoT devices worldwide now numbers in the billions. Their increased presence in our daily lives has led to increased scrutiny of their inherent security issues, which we will be exploring here.

Management of Internet of Things devices

To function as intended, IoT devices need to be managed both internally, (e.g., software maintenance) and externally (i.e., their communication with other devices).

This is accomplished by connecting every IoT device to a management unit, known as a command and control (C&C) center. Centers are responsible for software maintenance, configurations, firmware updates to patch bugs and vulnerabilities, as well as the provisioning and authentication of tasks, such as device enrollment.

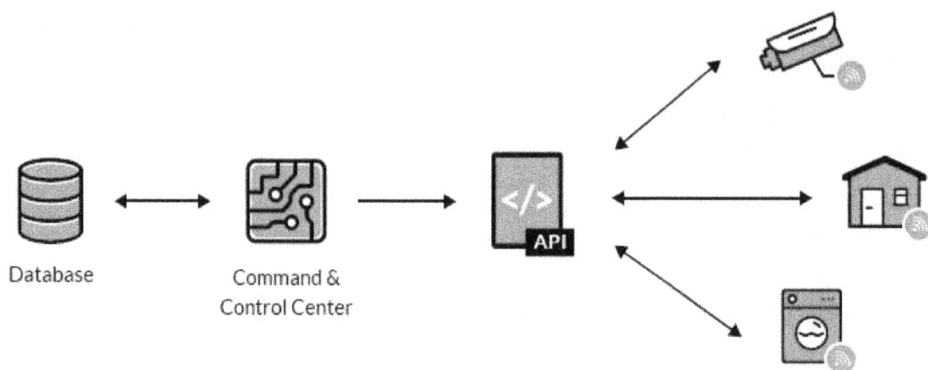

Database   Command &
                  Control Center

Communication between devices is enabled via application program interface (API). Once a device's manufacturer exposes its API, other devices or applications can use it to gather data and communicate. Some APIs even allow control over devices. For example, a building manager can use an API to remotely lock doors inside a specific office.

The IoT/ICS Device

IoT and ICS devices are considered end points. In other words, they are devices at the end of a communications chain that starts with a person or robotics device, and ends in cloud platforms and data centers. IoT and ICS devices don't just appear out of thin air. They are designed, developed and managed, just like any other computer. Figure 1 provides an overview of the elements inside of a typical IoT device.

- **Firmware:** Read-only memory embedded in the device that provides low-level control of the hardware. It can be updated, but usually not programmed. Communicates between each of the elements in the device as well as other networked devices.

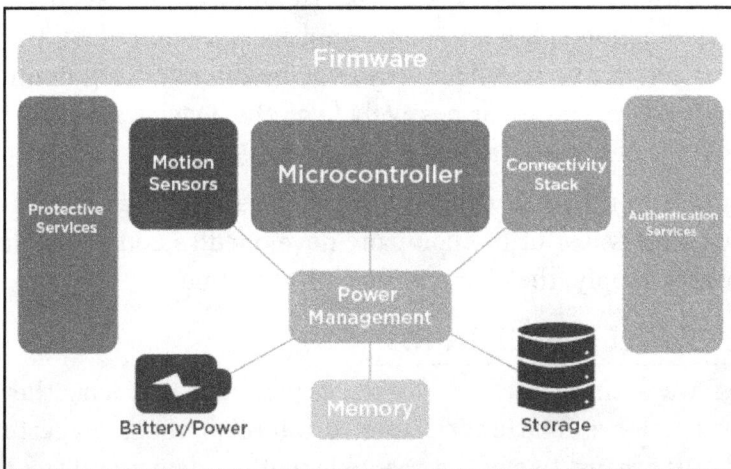

- **Protective services:** A portion of the device's firmware or operating system that provides security functionality, including the ability to isolate processes so that they can't be used to defeat security, and encryption.

- **Motion sensors:** The combined hardware and software used to track how the device is moved. Can include detection of simple movement (e.g., moving the device back and forth, or up and down), or satellite connectivity (e.g., Global Positioning System or GLONASS).

- **Microcontroller:** The processor used to run the software and provide the "brains" of the unit.

- **Connectivity stack:** Responsible for providing network connectivity. Networking capabilities can include Bluetooth, mobile (e.g., 3G, 4G, 5G), Zigbee, LoRA, SigFox or WiFi.

- **Authentication services:** When included, provides the ability for the IoT device to verify and validate users, network traffic or processes.

- ⊙ **Power management:** If the device requires significant use of power, functionality that manages power usage, as well as the charging of the device.

- ⊙ **Battery/power:** The physical capability to store power, as well as receive power from a remote source.

- ⊙ **Memory:** The working "muscle" of the IoT device, in that it provides the ability to store working data, machine code and information that is then addressed by the processor.

- ⊙ **Storage:** Provides the ability to capture and keep data for relatively long periods of time. Such information can include storing the location(s) the IoT device wearer/operator took the device, information about other devices that have connected with it and information entered by the user. Such information can be added actively (e.g., by the user programming the IoT/ OT device on purpose), or passively (e.g., the device capturing the motions and actions of the wearer/user).

It doesn't matter if that device is a webcam, the smartwatch or the Raspberry pi device your local water utility company developed to control devices for your community water supply, the elements remain the same.

SECURITY CHALLENGES IN IOT

The more ways there are for devices to connect to each other, the more opportunities there are for threat actors to intercept them. Hypertext Transfer Protocol and APIs are just two of the channels that IoT devices rely on that hackers can intercept.

The IoT umbrella doesn't strictly include internet-based devices either. Appliances that use Bluetooth technology also count as IoT devices and, therefore, require IoT security.

The following IoT security challenges continue to threaten the financial safety of both individuals and organizations:

- ⊙ **Remote exposure.** Unlike other technologies, IoT devices have a particularly large attack surface due to their internet-supported connectivity. While this accessibility is extremely valuable, it also gives hackers the opportunity to interact with devices remotely. This is why hacking campaigns, such as phishing, are particularly effective. IoT security, including cloud security, has to account for a large number of entry points to protect assets.

- ⊙ **Lack of industry foresight.** As organizations continue with digital transformations, so too have certain industries and their products. The automotive and healthcare industries have expanded their selection of IoT devices to become more productive and cost-efficient. This digital revolution, however, has also resulted in a greater technological dependence than ever before. While normally not an issue, a reliance on technology can amplify the consequences of a successful data breach. What makes this concerning is that these industries are now relying on pieces of technology that are inherently more vulnerable: IoT devices. Not only that, but many healthcare and automotive companies weren't prepared to invest the amount of money and resources required to secure these devices. This lack of industry foresight has unnecessarily exposed many organizations and manufacturers to increased cybersecurity threats.

- **Resource constraints.** Not all IoT devices have the computing power to integrate sophisticated firewalls or antivirus software. In fact, some devices can barely connect to other devices. IoT devices that have adopted Bluetooth technology, for example, have suffered from a recent wave of data breaches. The automotive industry, once again, has been one of the markets hit the hardest.

- **Weak default passwords.** IoT devices often come with weak passwords, and most consumers might not be aware that they need to be replaced with more secure ones. If default passwords aren't changed on IoT devices, it can leave them vulnerable to brute-force and other hacking attacks.

- **Multiple connected devices.** Most households today have multiple interconnected devices. The drawback of this convenience is that, if one device fails due to a security misconfiguration, the rest of the connected devices in the same household go down as well.

- **Lack of encryption.** Most network traffic originating from IoT devices is unencrypted, which increases the possibility of security threats and data breaches. These threats can be avoided by ensuring all the devices are secured and encrypted.

A cybersecurity expert hacked a Tesla Model X in less than 90 seconds by taking advantage of a massive Bluetooth vulnerability. Other cars that rely on wireless key fobs to open and start have experienced similar attacks. Threat actors have found a way to scan and replicate the interface of these fobs to steal vehicles without so much as triggering an alarm. If technologically advanced machinery, such as a Tesla vehicle, is vulnerable to an IoT data breach, then so is any other smart device.

SECURING IOT DEVICES AND NETWORKS

Enterprises can use the following tools and technologies to improve their data protection protocols and security posture:

- **Introduce IoT security during the design phase.** Of the IoT security risks and issues discussed, most can be overcome with better preparation, particularly during the research and development process at the start of any consumer-, enterprise- or industrial-based IoT (IIoT) device development. Enabling security by default is critical, along with providing the most recent operating systems and using secure hardware.

⊙ IoT developers should be mindful of cybersecurity vulnerabilities throughout each stage of development — not just the design phase. The car key hack, for instance, can be mitigated by the driver placing their fob in a metal box or away from the windows and hallways in their home.

⊙ **PKI and digital certificates.** PKI can secure client-server connections between multiple networked devices. Using a two-key asymmetric cryptosystem, PKI can facilitate the encryption and decryption of private messages and interactions using digital certificates. These systems help to protect the clear text information input by users into websites to complete private transactions. E-commerce wouldn't be able to operate without the security of PKI.

⊙ **Network security.** Networks provide a huge opportunity for threat actors to remotely control IoT devices. Because networks involve both digital and physical components, on-premises IoT security should address both types of access points. Protecting an IoT network includes ensuring port security, disabling port forwarding and never opening ports when not needed; using antimalware, firewalls, intrusion detection systems and intrusion prevention systems; blocking unauthorized IP addresses; and ensuring systems are patched and up to date.

⊙ **API security.** APIs are the backbone of most sophisticated websites. They enable travel agencies, for example, to aggregate flight information from multiple airlines into one location. Unfortunately, hackers can compromise these channels of communication, making API security necessary for protecting the integrity of data being sent from IoT devices to back-end systems and ensuring only authorized devices, developers and apps communicate with APIs. T-Mobile's 2018 data breach exposed the consequences of poor API security. Due to a leaky API, the mobile giant exposed the personal data of more than 2 million customers, including billing ZIP codes, phone numbers and account numbers.

Additional IoT security methods

Other ways to introduce IoT security include the following:

⊙ **Network access control (NAC).** NAC can help identify and inventory IoT devices connecting to a network. This provides a baseline for tracking and monitoring devices.

- **Segmentation.** IoT devices that need to connect directly to the internet should be segmented into their own networks and have restricted access to the enterprise network. Network segments should monitor for anomalous activity, taking action if an issue is detected.

- **Security gateways.** Acting as an intermediary between IoT devices and the network, security gateways have more processing power, memory and capabilities than the IoT devices themselves, which lets them add features such as firewalls to ensure hackers can't gain access to the IoT devices they connect.

- **Patch management and continuous software updates.** It's critical to provide a way to update devices and software either over network connections or through automation. Having a coordinated disclosure of vulnerabilities is also important for updating devices as soon as possible. Consider end-of-life strategies as well.

- **Training.** IoT and operational system security are new to many existing security teams. Security staff must keep up to date with new or unknown systems, learn new architectures and programming languages, and be ready for new security challenges. C-level and cybersecurity teams should receive regular cybersecurity training to keep up with modern threats and security measures.

- **Team integration.** Along with training, integrating disparate and regularly siloed teams can be useful. For example, having programming developers work with security specialists can help ensure the proper controls are added to devices during the development phase.

- **Consumer education.** Consumers must be made aware of the dangers of IoT systems and provided steps to stay secure, such as updating default credentials and applying software updates. Consumers can also play a role in requiring device manufacturers to create secure devices and refusing to use those that don't meet high-security standards.

- **Enforcement and automation of zero-trust policies.** The zero-trust model dictates that all users — whether inside or outside the organization's network — must be verified, authorized and continually evaluated for security configuration and posture before being given access to applications and data. Automating zero-trust policies and enforcing them across the board can help mitigate security threats against IoT devices.

- **Multifactor authentication (MFA).** MFA adds an extra layer of security by requiring more than one form of identification when requesting access to a device or network. By enforcing MFA policies, both enterprises and home users can improve the security of IoT devices.

⦿ **Machine learning (ML).** ML technology can be used to secure IoT devices by automating the management and scanning of devices throughout the entire network. Since every device connected to the network is scanned, it stops assaults automatically before IT teams are alerted. That's what happened in 2018 when Microsoft Windows Defender software stopped a Trojan malware attack in 30 minutes.

LOT SECURITY BEST PRACTICES

Securing IoT applications is not a one-time event. It requires careful planning, taking proactive actions, and regular monitoring.

Learn the Most Likely Threats

Threat modeling involves identifying, evaluating, and prioritizing potential vulnerabilities in IoT applications. This makes it possible to recommend security activities, allowing IT managers to integrate IoT applications into their overall security strategy. The security model must evolve to accurately reflect the IoT application's state.

Understand and Prioritize the Risks

Classify and prioritize IoT risks according to their level of concern and implement the relevant acts. Many technology teams neglect this aspect of aligning risk with real business scenarios and potential outcomes. A failure or breach of a single IoT application may seem insignificant to an IT department, but it can have a significant financial impact on a company.

Update IoT Apps Regularly

Administrators need to deploy updates to IoT applications as quickly as is feasible to ensure overall network security. Only use approved and verified updates, and when updating apps remotely, use a secure networking approach like a VPN to encrypt all the update streams. A secure public key infrastructure (PKI) enables authentication of devices and systems.

Use a Service Mesh

A service mesh is a dedicated infrastructure layer that controls communication between services in a network. A service mesh controls the distribution of service requests within an application. Common functions provided by a service mesh include service discovery, load balancing, encryption, and disaster recovery. A service mesh can make communication between services fast, reliable, and secure.

Ensure Network Security

Secure communication protocols, firewalls, and encryption contribute to protecting IoT applications from malicious access. It is important to check devices, standards, and communication protocols used across the network to guarantee security and add IoT applications to regular application security testing processes.

Enable Strong Authentication

A robust password protection strategy is critical for IoT applications, and this includes developing secure password generation and update processes. It is critical to change the default passwords of IoT devices and applications. Where possible, multiple authentication factors should be used in addition to passwords. Using the encrypted TLS communication protocol reduces the chance of authentication data being compromised at any point.

Encrypt Data in Transit

Protect data from attackers by encrypting data between IoT devices, applications, and backend systems. This includes encrypting data both in transit and at rest and using the PKI security model to ensure that both sender and receiver are authenticated by the system prior to transmission.

Secure Control Apps

Systems and applications that can access IoT applications must also be properly secured. This prevents the client (an IoT device or system) from being compromised by an external attack and prevents the attack from propagating downstream.

Ensure API Integrations Are Secure

APIs are a popular means of pushing and pulling data between systems and applications. This is another way attackers can connect to IoT applications. When only authorized devices and applications can communicate with an API, threats are easier to detect. IT admins should also use API versioning to identify outdated or duplicate versions of an API and eliminate them.

Monitor All IoT Apps

Monitoring your IoT application is the final step in securing it. Monitoring IoT applications allows organizations to detect and respond to potential security issues in a timely manner, improving incident response and minimizing the impact of an attack or breach. It also helps organizations meet compliance requirements and build customer trust by demonstrating a commitment to security.

CHAPTER-12

INCIDENT RESPONSE AND CYBERSECURITY FORENSICS

Digital forensics and incident response are branches of cybersecurity that involve identifying, investigating, containing, remediating and potentially testifying related to cyberattacks, litigations or other digital investigations.

Digital forensics and incident (DFIR) services combine two major components:

- ⊙ **Digital forensics:** This investigative branch of forensic science collects, analyzes and presents digital evidence such as user activity and system data. Digital forensics is used to uncover the facts about what happened on a computer system, network devices, phones or tablets and is often employed in litigations, regulatory investigations, internal company investigations, criminal activity and other types of digital investigations.

- ⊙ **Incident response:** Incident response, similar to digital forensics, investigates computer systems by collecting and analyzing data. This is done specifically in the context of responding to a security incident, so while investigation is important, other steps such as containment and recovery are weighed carefully against each other while responding to an incident.

History of Digital Forensics and Incident Response

In the early days of digital forensics and incident response, while the goals of matters pertaining to each may have differed, the tools, process, methodology and technology used were, in many ways, similar or identical. Historically, the method of collecting data for DFIR matters was often to collect forensic images of user's computers and company servers as well as copies of log data, where stored separately. These large sets of data were then analyzed using investigative tools to convert and interpret data on the computer systems into information that could be understood by computer experts, who could then work to identify potentially relevant information.

Digital forensic matters generally still follow the same process as they did historically because of the deep-dive level of scrutiny required to collect and analyze data to then present in court or to a regulator. However, in modern-day incident response matters, the tools and approach have evolved to better meet the differing goals of incident response by leveraging ever-evolving technology.

Today, incident response is often performed using EDR or XDR tools that give responders a view into data on computer systems across a company's environment. This is often accessible immediately or very quickly across dozens, hundreds or even thousands of endpoints. This rapid access to useful investigative information means that in an incident, responders can start getting answers about what is happening very quickly even if they do not already know where in the environment they need to look. Such tools can also be used to remediate and recover by identifying, stopping and removing malware or other tools used by a threat actor in the environment.

Digital forensics generally seeks to collect and investigate data to determine the narrative of what transpired. Incident response generally seeks to investigate, contain and recover from a security incident. They share a history as well as many tools, processes and procedures. In addition, a matter involving responding to an incident today may end up in litigation in the future. Because of the history, the overlap in tools/process, and because an incident response matter may lead into a digital forensics matter or vice versa, these two types of services are commonly still described as one group of services: digital forensics and incident response (DFIR).

Digital forensics

Digital forensics is a branch of forensic science that covers digital technology. Analysts focus on the recovery, investigation, and examination of material found on digital devices.

The end goal of digital forensics is to gather and preserve evidence to aid in prosecuting cybercrime, should the culprits behind an attack face criminal charges.

There are generally four major reasons why an organization engages in digital forensics:

⊙ To confirm whether a cyberattack occurred

⊙ To understand the full impact of a cyber incident

⊙ To identify the cause behind a cyberattack

⊙ To collect evidence proving a cyberattack occurred

Like any forensic investigation, speed is critical, especially if an attack is ongoing. Acting fast can help stop active cyber incidents and reduce the overall damage to a victim organization.

Computers, networks, and devices are continuously producing data that may be crucial to an investigation, even while sitting idle. Over time, the risk that this data is deleted, overwritten, or otherwise altered increases.

Many forensic artifacts are highly dependent on the state of a computer in the immediate aftermath of an incident. Forensic investigators need to move quickly to ensure they capture all this information before it's lost.

Incident response

Incident response (IR) is a set of activities a business engages in during a cybersecurity incident. For the purposes of IR, a cyber incident can be defined as any event that compromises information confidentiality, integrity, and/or availability—core principles of information security that are often referred to as the "CIA triad."

IR activities are typically informed by an IR plan designed to get IT infrastructure back up and running as quickly as possible while mitigating the overall damage of an incident.

First and foremost, these frameworks are designed to support recovery efforts. In a broader sense, they also help organizations build cyber maturity and proficiency. This may help enhance defenses, stopping attacks and incidents from affecting businesses in the first place.

Benefits of DFIR

When digital forensics and incident response are conducted separately, they can interfere with one another. Incident responders can alter or destroy evidence while removing a threat from the network, and forensic investigators may delay threat resolution as they search for evidence. Information may not flow between these teams, making everyone less efficient than they could be.

DFIR fuses these two disciplines into a single process carried out by one team. This yields two important advantages:

Forensic data collection happens alongside threat mitigation. During the DFIR process, incident responders use forensic techniques to collect and preserve digital evidence while they're containing and eradicating a threat. This ensures that the chain of custody is followed and valuable evidence isn't altered or destroyed by incident response efforts.

Post-incident review includes examination of digital evidence. DFIR uses digital evidence to dive deeper into security incidents. DFIR teams examine and analyze the evidence they've gathered to reconstruct the incident from start to finish. The DFIR process ends with a report detailing what happened, how it happened, the full extent of the damage and how similar attacks can be avoided in the future.

Resulting benefits include:

- **More effective threat prevention.** DFIR teams investigate incidents more thoroughly than traditional incident response teams do. DFIR investigations can help security teams better understand cyberthreats, create more effective incident response playbooks and stop more attacks before they happen. DFIR investigations can also help streamline threat hunting by uncovering evidence of unknown active threats.

- **Little or no evidence is lost during threat resolution.** In a standard incident response process, incident responders may err in the rush to contain the threat. For example, if responders shut down an infected device to contain the spread of a threat, any evidence that is left in the device's RAM will be lost. Trained in both digital forensics and incident response, DFIR teams are skilled at preserving evidence while resolving incidents.

- **Improved litigation support.** DFIR teams follow the chain of custody, which means the results of DFIR investigations can be shared with law enforcement and used to prosecute cybercriminals. DFIR investigations can also support insurance claims and post-breach regulatory audits.

- **Faster, more robust threat recovery.** Because forensic investigations are more robust than standard incident response investigations, DFIR teams may uncover hidden malware or system damage that would have otherwise gone overlooked. This helps security teams eradicate threats and recover from attacks more thoroughly.

DEVELOPING AN INCIDENT RESPONSE PLAN

An incident response plan is a set of instructions to detect, respond to and limit the effects of an information security event. Sometimes called an *incident management plan* or *emergency management plan*, an incident response plan provides clear guidelines for responding to several potential scenarios, including data breaches, DoS or DDoS attacks, firewall breaches, malware outbreaks, insider threats, data loss and other security breaches.

Importance of incident response

The Ponemon Institute's Cost of Cyber Crime Study showed that the typical organization experiences an average of 145 security incidents per year and spends $13 million annually year to defend itself. An effective response process can act to significantly reduce these costs. Incident response planning also protects your company's reputation. IDC found that 80% of consumers would take their business elsewhere if directly affected by a data breach. If a security breach is not handled properly, the company risks losing business, as well as investor and shareholder confidence.

Additional benefits of incident response plans include:

- **Data protection** — securing backups, ensuring sufficient identity and access management, and timely patching of vulnerabilities.

- **Reputation reinforcement** — Effective incident response shows a brand's commitment to security and privacy, and can save a company's reputation in the event of a breach.

- **Cost reduction** — According to a study by IBM, the average cost of a breach is $4.35 million. Incident response planning can significantly reduce this cost by limiting the damage caused by an attack.

Incident response steps

According to the SANS Institute's Incident Handlers Handbook, there are six steps that should be taken by the Incident Response Team, to effectively handle security incidents.

- **Preparation** – Perform a risk assessment and prioritize security issues, identify which are the most sensitive assets, and which critical security incidents the team should focus on. Create a communication plan, document roles, responsibilities, and processes, and recruit members to the Cyber Incident Response Team (CIRT).

- **Identification** – The team should be able to effectively detect deviations from normal operations in organizational systems, and when an incident is discovered, collect additional evidence, decide on the severity of the incident, and document the "Who, What, Where, Why, and How".

- **Containment** – Once the team identifies a security incident, the immediate goal is to contain the incident and prevent further damage:

  - **Short-term containment** — for example, isolating network segments or taking down infected production servers and handing failover.

  - **Long-term containment** — applying temporary fixes to affected systems to allow them to be used in production, while rebuilding clean systems.

- **Eradication** – The team must identify the root cause of the attack, remove malware or threats, and prevent similar attacks in the future. For example, if a vulnerability was exploited, it should be immediately patched.

- **Recovery** – The team brings affected production systems back online carefully, to ensure another incident doesn't take place. Important decisions at this stage are from which time and date to restore operations, how to verify that affected systems are back to normal, and monitoring to ensure activity is back to normal.

- **Lessons Learned** – This phase should be performed no later than two weeks from the end of the incident, to ensure the information is fresh in the team's mind. The purpose of this phase is to complete documentation of the incident, investigate further to identify its full scope, understand where the response team was effective, and areas that require improvement.

Incident response planning typically includes:

- The organization's incident response strategy and how it supports business objectives

- Roles and responsibilities involved in incident response

- Procedures for each phase of the incident response process

- Communication procedures within the incident response team, with the rest of the organization, and external stakeholders

- How to learn from previous incidents to improve the organization's security posture

An incident response plan forms the basis of your incident response cycle:

Digital Forensics and Incident Response Challenges

As computer systems have evolved, so too have the challenges involved in DFIR. There are several key obstacles digital forensics and incident response experts face today.

Digital Forensics Challenges

- **Scattered evidence:** Reconstructing digital evidence is no longer reliant upon a single host; it is scattered among different physical or virtual locations. As such, digital forensics requires more expertise, tools and time to thoroughly and correctly gather and investigate threats.

- **Fast pace of technology:** Digital devices, software programs and operating systems are constantly changing, evolving and growing. With this fast pace of change, forensic experts must understand how to manage digital evidence in a large variety of application versions and file formats.

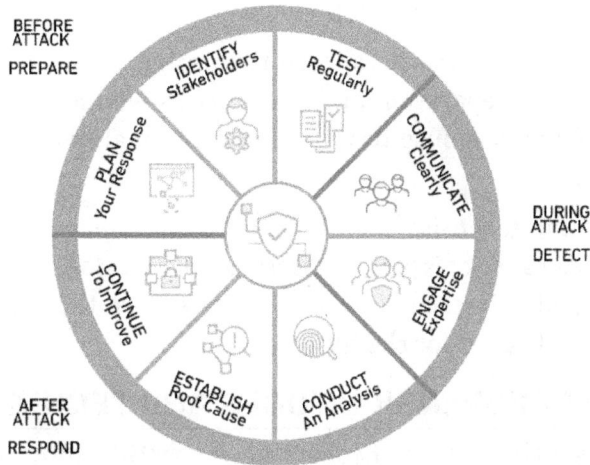

The Elements of an Incident Response Cycle

Incident Response Challenges

- ⦿ **Growing data, dwindling support**: Organizations are facing more and more security alerts but cannot find the cybersecurity talent required to address the volume of information and ultimately the relevant threat data. Increasingly, organizations are turning to DFIR experts on retainer to help bridge the skills gap and retain critical threat support.

- ⦿ **Increased attack surface**: The vast attack surface of today's computing and software systems makes it more difficult to obtain an accurate overview of the network and increases the risk of misconfigurations and user error.

These challenges call for DFIR experts to help support growing alerts and complex datasets and take a unique and flexible approach to threat hunting within modern, ever-evolving systems.

Digital Forensics and Incident Response Best Practices

A robust DFIR service provides an agile response for businesses susceptible to threats. It gives you peace of mind that expert teams with vast knowledge of cyber incidents will respond to attacks quickly and effectively.

Digital Forensics Best Practices

The success of DFIR hinges on rapid and thorough response. It's crucial that digital forensic teams have ample experience and the right DFIR tools and processes in place to provide a swift, practical response to any issue.

Expertise in digital forensics has a number of benefits, including the ability to discover the cause of an incident and accurately identify the scope and impact. Employing the right investigative tools will ensure prompt discovery of the vulnerabilities that led to an attack or unintentional exposure.

Incident Response Best Practices

Incident response services are tailored to manage an incident in real time. IR best practices include preparation and planning as well as timely, accurate and reliable mitigation and response to reduce reputational harm, financial loss and business downtime.

Combined, digital forensics and incident response best practices include determining the root cause of issues, correctly identifying and locating all available evidence/data, and offering ongoing support to ensure that your organization's security posture is bolstered for the future.

CYBERSECURITY FORENSICS TOOLS AND TECHNIQUES

Cyber forensics is the science of collecting, inspecting, interpreting, reporting, and presenting computer-related electronic evidence. Evidence can be found on the hard drive or in deleted files.

It is the process of examining, acquiring, and analyzing data from a system or device so that it can be transcribed into physical documentation and presented in court.

During the inspection, it is critical to create a digital or soft copy of the system's special storage cell. The purpose of carrying out a detailed cyber forensics investigation is to determine who is to blame for a security breach. The entire inquiry is carried out on the software copy while ensuring that the system is not affected.

In the technological age, cyber forensics is an inevitable factor that is incredibly important.

Cybersecurity aims to reduce the risk of cyber-attacks and protect against unauthorized exploitation of systems, networks, and technologies. While digital forensics focuses on the recovery and investigation of artifacts found on a digital device.

Cyber Forensics Scope

As everything becomes digitalized, the scope of cyber forensics expands. It assists us in combating hostile actions by identifying underlying perpetrators. The evidence gathered during inquiries aids cybersecurity specialists in locating the hackers and crackers.

The role of cyber forensic experts is becoming much more crucial nowadays due to the increase in cybercrime. According to NCRB, cybercrime has doubled from 2016 to 2018, and it is predicted to increase as much as four times than the present day. This shows the importance of law enforcement in solving cybercrime and cyber experts facing various cyber forensics challenges.

Cyber forensics enables specialists to remotely examine any crime scene by reviewing the browsing history, email records, or digital trace.

Process Involved in Cyber Forensics

Cyber forensics takes a systematic interpretation, sorting it out concisely.

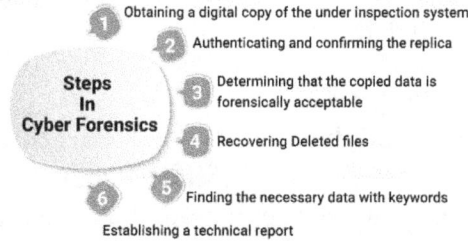

Steps In Cyber Forensics

1. Obtaining a digital copy of the under inspection system
2. Authenticating and confirming the replica
3. Determining that the copied data is forensically acceptable
4. Recovering Deleted files
5. Finding the necessary data with keywords
6. Establishing a technical report

Obtaining a digital copy of the under inspection system

This method entails producing a copy of the system's data to avoid harm from being done to the actual system, which might lead to file confusion with the files already present on the computer. Cloning a hard disc entails replicating the hard drive's files and folders. The duplicate is present on another disc by copying every small piece of data for analysis.

Authenticating and confirming the replica

After copying the files, experts verify that the copied data is consistent and exactly as it exists in the real system.

Determining that the copied data is forensically acceptable

It is possible to change the format of the data while duplicating it from a device, resulting in discrepancies in the operating systems of the investigators and the one from which the data was copied. To avoid this, detectives ensure that the structure stays constant and that the data is forensically acceptable and is written on the hard disk drive in a format that is adequately used in the computer.

Recovering deleted files

Criminals think of innovative ways of deleting the scene and often remove some data that could indicate their misconduct; it is the work of the investigators to recover and reconstruct deleted files with state-of-the-art software.

Forensics specialists can recover files erased by the user from a computer; the files are not permanently wiped from the computer, and forensics specialists can recover them.

Finding the necessary data with keywords

Researchers use specific high-speed tools to get appropriate information by employing buzzwords in the instance document.

The OS perceives vacant space in the hard disc as room for storing new files and directories; however, temporary files and documents that were erased years ago will be stored there until new data is entered. Forensics specialists look for these files using this free space.

Forensics specialists utilize tools that can access and produce pertinent information throughout all data for phrases.

Establishing a technical report

The last phase will be to produce a technical report that is relevant and easily understood regardless of the background of the individual. The result of this report is to state clearly the crime, possible culprits, and innocent individuals.

The technical report must be straightforward for everyone to grasp, irrespective of their background. It should focus mostly on who the culprit is and what techniques they used to commit the crime and how.

Types of active attack -

⊙ Modification of messages

⊙ Masquerading

⊙ Replay

⊙ Denial of Service (DoS)

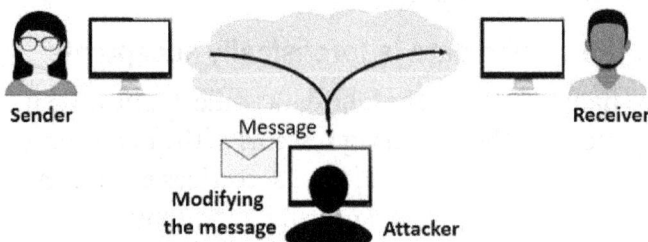

ACTIVE Attacks
Visualization of ACTIVE Attacks

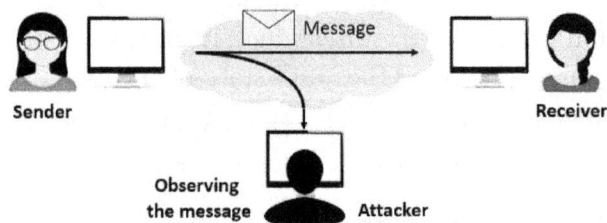

PASSIVE Attacks
Visualization of PASSIVE Attacks

Evolution Of Digital Forensics

The cyber security regime was developed alongwith the evolution of computers & networks. Initially funcoders were involved in breaking the existing security norms. This constant challenge resulted in continuous upgradation of fool-proofing methods & also the branch of 'Computer Forensics' originated from this process to address the violations committed. The first computer forensic technicians were law enforcement officers who were also computer hobbyists. In the USA in 1984 work began in the FBI Computer Analysis and Response Team (CART).

This continued until the late 1990s, after which Digital Forensics became a standalone & fast evolving branch of computer science that collaborate with other sciences to address the specific objective. In 1998 the Association of Chief Police Officers (ACPO) of UK produced the first version of its Good Practice Guide for Digital Evidence (Association of Chief Police Officers, 2012). The ACPO guidelines detail the main principles applicable to all digital forensics for law enforcement in the UK. This further consolidated into Standards accepted by Regulators.

Digital Forensics is the process of using scientific knowledge for collecting, analyzing, and presenting evidence in a manner acceptable to the court of Law.

Digital Forensics perform a vital function in a world where computing technology is witnessing an exponential growth combined with shorter spans of generational change of technology & sharply increasing threat regimes. In a new world, it plays a crucial role to ensure that an individual citizen's identity if undergone a theft or violation is taken care of and the protection mechanisms are progressively set in place.

Types of Computer Forensics

- ⦿ **Disk Forensics:**
  - Disk forensics involves the examination of physical or logical storage media such as hard drives, solid-state drives, and removable storage devices.
  - Investigators analyze these storage media to recover deleted files, discover hidden data, and gather evidence related to digital crimes.

- ⦿ **Network Forensics:**
  - Network forensics focuses on monitoring and analyzing network traffic and log data to investigate security incidents.
  - It helps in identifying the source of cyber attacks, tracking communication between devices, and understanding the extent of network breaches.

- **Memory Forensics:**
  - Memory forensics deals with the analysis of a computer's volatile memory (RAM) to uncover information about running processes, network connections, and malicious activities.
  - It is particularly useful in identifying live cyber threats and rootkits.

- **Mobile Device Forensics:**
  - Mobile device forensics involves the examination of smartphones, tablets, and other mobile devices to retrieve data, messages, call logs, and application usage history.
  - Investigators use specialized tools to access locked or encrypted mobile devices.

- **Database Forensics:**
  - Database forensics focuses on investigating database systems to identify unauthorized access, data breaches, or data manipulation.
  - Investigators analyze database logs and data structures to uncover evidence of wrongdoing.

- **Cloud Forensics:**
  - Cloud forensics deals with the investigation of cloud-based services and data stored in the cloud.
  - It includes examining cloud logs, access controls, and metadata to trace activities and assess security incidents.

- **Malware Forensics:**
  - Malware forensics involves the analysis of malicious software (malware) to understand its behavior, origins, and impact on systems.
  - Investigators study malware code and behavior to determine the scope of an attack.

- **Email Forensics:**
  - Email forensics focuses on the investigation of email communications to gather evidence for legal proceedings.
  - It includes tracking email senders, receivers, timestamps, and content.

- **Live Forensics:**
  - Live forensics involves analyzing a running computer system to identify ongoing malicious activities.
  - Investigators use techniques to preserve system state and extract volatile data without interrupting system operation.

⊙ **Incident Response Forensics:**

- Incident response forensics is conducted as part of a larger incident response process.

- It includes collecting and preserving digital evidence to understand the nature of a security incident and support remediation efforts.

These types of computer forensics play essential roles in investigating cybercrimes, ensuring digital evidence integrity, and strengthening cybersecurity measures in both law enforcement and corporate environments. Each type focuses on a specific aspect of digital investigation, contributing to a comprehensive approach in combating cyber threats.

Techniques of Cyber Forensics

Now discuss the techniques of Cyber Forensics in-depth

⊙ **Evidence Collection:** Cyber forensics experts collect digital evidence from various sources, including computers, servers, mobile devices, and network logs. The process involves preserving the integrity of the evidence to maintain its admissibility in court.

⊙ **Data Recovery:** Deleted or damaged data can often be recovered using specialized tools and techniques. This is crucial for reconstructing events and identifying the perpetrators.

⊙ **Network Analysis:** Analyzing network traffic and logs helps in tracing the origin of cyberattacks, understanding attack patterns, and identifying vulnerabilities.

⊙ **Malware Analysis:** Cyber forensics professionals dissect malware to understand its behavior, propagation methods, and impact on systems. This aids in developing countermeasures and attributing attacks.

⊙ **Memory Analysis:** Examining the volatile memory (RAM) of a compromised system can reveal ongoing malicious activities, such as running processes and network connections.

LEGAL AND ETHICAL CONSIDERATIONS

By the core of definition, Digital forensics is the science of acquiring, preserving, analyzing, and presenting digital evidence in a way that is admissible in a court of law. Hence it involves the collection and examination of data from various digital devices, such as computers, smartphones, and servers, to investigate cybercrime and other digital incidents in ways complying with the legal & ethical frameworks. Today, the digital forensics has become an essential tool for law enforcement agencies and organizations to investigate and prosecute digital crimes.

- *Firstly,* the rules of evidence, which govern the admissibility of evidence in court, apply to digital evidence as well. In many countries, digital evidence must be collected and analyzed in accordance with specific legal procedures, such as search warrants or court orders. Failure to comply with these procedures can result in the evidence being deemed inadmissible in court.

- *Secondly*, the privacy and confidentiality of individuals must be respected during digital forensic investigations. Digital forensic experts must ensure that the collection and analysis of digital evidence do not infringe on the privacy rights of individuals. This means that the collection of data must be conducted in a manner that is proportional to the scope of the investigation and must not involve the collection of irrelevant data.

- *Thirdly,* digital forensic investigations must be conducted by qualified and certified experts who have the necessary skills and knowledge to handle digital evidence. Digital forensic experts must adhere to ethical standards and must not engage in any activities that may compromise the integrity of the evidence.

- *Finally,* the chain of custody of digital evidence must be maintained to ensure that the evidence is admissible in court. The chain of custody refers to the documentation of the custody, control, transfer, analysis, and disposition of digital evidence. It is important to maintain the chain of custody to ensure that the evidence is not tampered with or altered in any way.

Digital Ethics

Digital ethics is the area of ethics that deals with the collection of laws and moral principles that regulate how people interact with one another inside of businesses as well as more widely in markets and society when computer technology is used as a medium. This digital ethics code's goal is to outline the standards of behavior that charities should adhere to when engaging in digital activities including expanding their reach through social media and using donor information to guide fundraising efforts.

How Does Digital Forensics Ethics Work

Ethics plays a crucial role in digital forensics as it involves the analysis of sensitive information. Failure to act ethically in digital forensics investigations can compromise the evidence extracted. It is your duty to carry out a thorough investigation, to tell the truth, and to maintain objectivity. Your baseline behavior is determined by your personal and professional principles.

Digital Forensics professionals have to follow a particular set of codes of ethics to successfully execute investigations. This entails upholding discretion, preventing conflicts of interest, and making sure that their conduct adheres to moral and legal standards.

Analysts of digital forensics must remain neutral and objective throughout the course of the investigation. Any prejudice or biases affecting their examination and interpretation of the evidence must be avoided.

In some circumstances, getting permission to gather and examine digital evidence may be necessary. This is especially true when it comes to communications or personal gadgets when people have a reasonable expectation of privacy.

Digital forensic investigators must abide by all applicable laws and rules, including those governing intellectual property, data privacy, and data protection. Digital forensic investigators should continue their education and training to stay current with the newest methods and tools available.

Legal Issues in Digital Forensics Investigations

To ensure that the data gathered is acceptable in court and does not break any laws, the digital forensics process must follow legal requirements. Here are a few legal concerns for digital forensics.

The US Constitutions Fourth Amendment forbids arbitrary searches and seizures. Before executing a search or seizure, digital forensic investigators are required to follow legal procedures, get a warrant, or have other solid grounds.

The chain of custody records how the evidence was obtained and transported before being presented in court. To maintain the chain of custody and guarantee the integrity and admissibility of the evidence, digital forensic investigators must adhere to tight rules.

The legal requirements for admission of digital evidence must be met, including relevance, authenticity, and dependability. To make sure that the data gathered complies with legal standards, digital forensic investigators must adhere to established norms and processes.

Data privacy and protection laws that are applicable must be complied with by digital forensic investigators. Investigators are required to maintain the confidentiality of personal data and make sure they do not access or divulge any information that is not necessary for the investigation.

Digital forensics investigations may involve multiple jurisdictions, and investigators must comply with the laws of the jurisdictions in which they operate. Jurisdictional issues can complicate digital forensics investigations, and investigators must be aware of the laws that apply to the evidence they collect.

Analyzing intellectual property such as trade secrets, copyrighted content, and other items may be part of digital forensic investigations. To avoid violating any copyright or other intellectual property rights, investigators must adhere to all applicable intellectual property laws.

Legal consideration must be followed throughout digital forensics investigations to guarantee that the evidence gathered is valid for use in court and does not break any rules. Legal problems such as search and seizure, a chain of custody, admissibility of evidence, data privacy and protection, jurisdiction, and intellectual property must be understood by digital forensic investigators.

Future Trends of Digital Forensics

Digital forensics, also known as computer forensics, is a field of investigation that involves the identification, preservation, analysis, and presentation of digital evidence in legal proceedings. With the rapid growth of technology, digital forensics has become an essential part of modern investigations. As we move further into the digital age, there are several future developments that are expected to shape the field of digital forensics.

⦿ **Blockchain Forensics:** Blockchain technology is becoming increasingly popular, with its use extending beyond the cryptocurrency industry. Blockchain is a decentralized and secure method of storing information, and its immutability makes it an ideal tool for recording digital transactions. However, this also makes it difficult to tamper with, which makes blockchain forensics a complex task. Future developments in digital forensics will focus on understanding how to extract digital evidence from blockchain networks.

Digital Forensics

- **Cloud Forensics:** The use of cloud technology is growing, and it is expected to continue to increase in the coming years. Cloud forensics involves the investigation of digital evidence that is stored in the cloud. This can include data stored on cloud servers, virtual machines, and other cloud-based applications. Future developments in digital forensics will focus on understanding how to extract digital evidence from cloud-based systems.

- **IoT Forensics:** The Internet of Things (IoT) is becoming increasingly popular, and it is expected to grow significantly in the coming years. IoT forensics involves the investigation of digital evidence that is generated by connected devices. This can include data from smart homes, wearables, and other IoT devices. Future developments in digital forensics will focus on understanding how to extract digital evidence from IoT devices.

- **Artificial Intelligence in Forensics:** Artificial intelligence (AI) is becoming increasingly popular, and it is expected to have a significant impact on digital forensics. AI can be used to automate tasks, such as data extraction and analysis, which can save time and reduce the risk of errors. Future developments in digital forensics will focus on understanding how to use AI to automate tasks and improve the accuracy of digital evidence analysis.

- **Mobile Forensics:** Mobile devices are becoming increasingly popular, and they are now a primary means of communication and data storage for many people. Mobile forensics involves the investigation of digital evidence that is generated by mobile devices. This can include data stored on smartphones, tablets, and other mobile devices. Future developments in digital forensics will focus on understanding how to extract digital evidence from mobile devices.

CHAPTER-13

EMERGING TECHNOLOGIES IN CYBERSECURITY

INTRODUCTION

A cyber-attack should not be viewed as an isolated event, but rather as a means to achieve various objectives, some of which have significant political, military, criminal, and social implications. It is crucial to understand that a cyber-attack is not a comprehensive strategy, but rather a tactic that can be utilized alongside other cyber and non-cyber tactics to accomplish a broader strategic goal. The ultimate objective of a cyber-attacker can range from personal entertainment, theft of intellectual property, political upheaval, terrorism, or even international warfare.

In any competitive scenario, adversaries strive to gain a competitive edge, and information technology, computer networks, and hacking have emerged as new avenues to achieve this advantage. Computer hardware and software are susceptible to numerous forms of attack, including data theft, data denial, and data manipulation. While hackers possess expertise in exploiting these vulnerabilities, the impact of a cyber attack can be significantly amplified if the hacker is part of a larger network of criminals, soldiers, or spies.

CYBER ESPIONAGE

Espionage takes the spotlight initially, as hackers do not actively manipulate your data, but rather acquire and peruse it. Nevertheless, the quantity of data that hackers can pilfer has already propelled this era into the Golden Age of Espionage. With the increasing prevalence of online activities and the interconnection of previously isolated computers to the Internet, the sensitivity level of the stolen data continues to escalate.

Despite the fragility of the connections, whether through wires or radio waves, every computer on Earth is linked. It falls upon hackers to devise methods of transferring data between any two computers, and professional hackers excel at accomplishing this task. Presently, digitized information is being stolen on a massive scale, and data analysts possess potent tools to swiftly extract valuable insights from that data, separating the valuable from the irrelevant.

CYBER CRIME

Criminals are well-versed in the use of technology. Counterfeiting, for instance, has been around since the days of ancient Greece, making it as old as money itself. In today's digital age, counterfeiters have an even easier time, as both money and intellectual property can be transmitted globally at lightning speed. In 2011, the European Union's carbon trading market experienced a cyber attack, resulting in the theft of over $7 million in credits and the temporary shutdown of the market.

Similarly, in 2012, the European Aeronautic Defence and Space Company (EADS) and German steelmaker ThyssenKrupp were targeted by Chinese hackers, who likely employed cyber attacks for strategic economic gain. This has led to an important trend for businesses to be aware of. They must remain vigilant against advanced persistent threat (APT) cyber attacks, particularly before and during international negotiations.

In 2011, the European Commission reported widespread hacking prior to an EU summit, the French government was compromised before a G-20 meeting, and numerous Norwegian defense and energy companies fell victim to tailored phishing attacks during large-scale contract negotiations.

The U.S.-based International Monetary Fund (IMF) also experienced a significant breach in 2011 due to a phishing attack, which was described as a major security breach.

Cyber crime can simply be the use of IT to facilitate traditional crime such as theft, fraud, or a tactical strike such as hacking an alarm system before unauthorized entry. All of this is possible at the individual, organizational, or nation-state level. In the case of a nation-state attack, there will be no law enforcement agency on the planet capable of completing a successful prosecution; the only recourse would be diplomatic, economic, or military coercion.

Cyber crime encompasses various forms of illegal activities conducted online, including the sharing of illicit images, files, and sensitive information. This category also includes professional hacker groups that offer specialized cyber goods and services, catering to individuals and even governments. These services may involve denial-of-service attacks and the control of previously compromised networks. As our lives increasingly unfold in the digital realm, the prevalence of cyber-only crimes is expected to rise. Consequently, law enforcement agencies will be compelled to delve deeper into cyberspace to combat this evolving threat. The immense power of computers, networks, and computer hacking is not limited to law-abiding individuals; criminals also have access to these tools. Non-state actors, in particular, now possess the means to challenge the authority and dominance of nation-states.

A notable example occurred in 2010 when the "Pakistani Cyber Army" defaced and subsequently disabled the website of India's top police agency, the Central Bureau of Investigation. In another instance in 2011, German Police discovered that servers used to track serious criminals and terrorism suspects had been compromised through a successful phishing attack.

Regrettably, distinguishing between state-sponsored and non-state cyber attacks can be challenging, as some instances involve criminal elements. In fact, researchers at FireEye have observed a nation-state developing and utilizing a sophisticated Trojan, which was later sold to cyber criminals on the black market once their own defenses were in place. This blurring of lines further complicates the landscape of cyber security and necessitates a comprehensive approach to combatting cyber crime.

The rapid evolution of technology has brought immense benefits to our society, but it has also introduced new challenges, particularly in the realm of cybersecurity. As our digital world expands, so does the need for robust security measures to protect sensitive information and critical infrastructure. In this article, we will explore the future of cybersecurity, focusing on the emerging technologies and trends that will shape the landscape of cyber defense.

ARTIFICIAL INTELLIGENCE (AI) AND MACHINE LEARNING (ML)

AI and ML are revolutionizing the field of cybersecurity by enhancing threat detection and response capabilities. These technologies enable security systems to analyze vast amounts of data, identify patterns, and detect anomalies in real-time, thereby improving incident response and reducing false positives. With the ability to adapt and learn from new threats, AI-powered systems offer a proactive approach to cybersecurity.

Internet of Things (IoT) Security

As IoT devices become increasingly interconnected, the security risks associated with them grow exponentially. The future of cybersecurity will witness a focus on developing robust security frameworks for IoT devices. This includes secure device authentication, encryption protocols, and regular security updates to protect against vulnerabilities that can be exploited by cybercriminals.

Blockchain Technology

Blockchain, known for its association with cryptocurrencies, has the potential to transform cybersecurity. Its decentralized and immutable nature makes it an attractive solution for secure transactions and data storage. In the future, we can expect the integration of blockchain technology into various aspects of cybersecurity, such as identity management, secure data sharing, and securing supply chain processes.

Cloud Security

The widespread adoption of cloud computing has given rise to new challenges in securing data stored and processed in the cloud. Future cybersecurity strategies will focus on advanced cloud security solutions, including encryption, access controls, and threat intelligence, to ensure the integrity and confidentiality of cloud-based systems.

Threat Intelligence and Information Sharing

The cyber threat landscape is constantly evolving, requiring organizations to collaborate and share information to stay ahead of sophisticated attacks. The future will witness increased cooperation between public and private sectors, as well as the establishment of threat intelligence platforms, to facilitate timely information sharing and proactive defense against cyber threats.

User Behavior Analytics

Recognizing the significance of human factors in cybersecurity, user behavior analytics will play a crucial role in identifying potential threats. By analyzing user patterns and behaviors, organizations can detect anomalies that may indicate unauthorized access or malicious activities. This approach enhances security awareness and enables early detection of insider threats.

Cyber Activism

You express a desire for a revolution? Hacktivism is the practice of combining hacking and activism, facilitated by groups such as Cult of the Dead Cow and even individuals like Edward Snowden. In today's world, anyone with an Internet-connected computer possesses the equivalent of a historical printing press and radio transmitter.

Cyberspace serves as an ideal platform to advocate for political causes, as long as individuals are willing to eventually take their actions to the streets or the ballot box. Websites can be utilized to sell products or to bring about the downfall of governments, as demonstrated by the case of Hosni Mubarak.

Throughout history, nation-states have held a near-monopoly on the use of violence and the ability to manage international tensions. However, in the age of the Internet, anyone can engage in international affairs, presenting a new challenge for national decision-makers. Ordinary citizens now have the ability to participate in international conflicts, either through the dissemination of propaganda or through computer hacking, without being accountable to any traditional chain of command.

Consequently, one intriguing aspect of conflict in the Internet era is the emergence of "patriotic hackers" who purportedly wage cyber warfare on behalf of their nations, if not their governments.

During the emergence of the World Wide Web in the mid-1990s, Russia found itself embroiled in a prolonged conflict concerning the fate of Chechnya. It was during this time that the Chechens took on the role of pioneers in cyber propaganda, while the Russians became pioneers in the act of shutting down their websites.

In 1998, when NATO launched an attack on Russian ally Serbia over the issue of Kosovo, pro-Serbian hackers joined the battle by launching denial-of-service (DoS) attacks against NATO and infecting their emails with at least twenty-five strains of viruses. The year 2001 witnessed a significant event when a U.S. Navy plane was shot down and its crew detained in China.

This incident led to a patriotic hacker war between pro-U.S. and pro-China hackers, with uncertain consequences for political leadership. In 2007, Russia was suspected of orchestrating the most renowned international cyber activist attack to date, which involved a punitive distributed DoS on Estonia for relocating a Soviet-era statue.

Furthermore, in 2008, during the Russo-Georgian war, analysts observed a close correlation between cyber and conventional operations in all future military campaigns. Finally, in 2010, the "Iranian Cyber Army" disrupted Twitter and the Chinese search engine Baidu, redirecting users to Iranian political messages.

The cyber threat landscape is constantly evolving. The prevalence of Artificial Intelligence (AI) and Machine Learning (ML) tools is leading to a cybersecurity arms race. Both attackers and defenders are realizing the potential of AI and ML to enhance their capabilities. While attackers gear-up to use AI and ML to identify vulnerabilities and launch sophisticated attacks, defenders are leveraging these technologies to detect and prevent these attacks.

AI and ML can also be used to launch targeted and personalized attacks using extremely convincing phishing emails that can trick even the most vigilant users into clicking on malicious links or downloading infected attachments. *In case you missed our previous blog post, we talk a little bit about how ChatGPT could be used to facilitate Phishing for Information.

A Brief History of AI and Machine Learning in Cybersecurity

The history of AI and ML in cybersecurity spans several decades. While early efforts focused on rule-based systems for anomaly detection during the mid to late 1980s, the rise of Big Data after 2000 drove significant changes for AI and ML.

As technology became more sophisticated, machine learning algorithms emerged as a powerful tool for threat detection. In the late 2000s, the application of supervised learning algorithms paved the way for more accurate threat detection and prevention. Unsupervised learning algorithms followed suit, enabling the identification of anomalous patterns and previously unknown threats.

The rise of deep learning in the 2010s revolutionized cybersecurity with its ability to process vast amounts of data and uncover complex patterns. Natural language processing (NLP) techniques also gained prominence, allowing for enhanced analysis of textual data and the detection of social engineering attacks.

Today, AI and machine learning are at the forefront of cybersecurity, continuously evolving to combat ever-evolving threats and shape a more secure digital future. AI and ML techniques leverage the vast amount of data generated by digital systems and networks to identify patterns, anomalies, and potential threats with greater accuracy and efficiency, enabling proactive threat detection and prevention in real-time. This combination of big data and AI/ML has enhanced cybersecurity defenses by empowering organizations to analyze and respond to security incidents more effectively, mitigate risks, and adapt to evolving cyber threats.

Types of AI and Machine Learning

AI plays a pivotal role in cybersecurity so understanding the different types of AI and Machine Learning used in this domain is crucial. This section covers several fundamental types of AI and ML employed in cybersecurity: Supervised Learning, Unsupervised Learning, Reinforcement Learning, Deep Learning, and Natural Language Processing (NLP). These types encompass a range of techniques and methodologies that empower cybersecurity systems to detect, analyze, and respond to threats with increased accuracy and efficiency.

Supervised Machine Learning

Supervised machine learning involves collecting pre-categorized websites (training labels) along with the corresponding html and images for those websites (training features). We then "train" a model to create a mapping from the large number of features to the labels. Feedback is provided to the supervised model in the form of a loss function, where the model is penalized for incorrect answers and rewarded for correct answers. In this way, the machine learning algorithm slowly gets better as more and more labeled data enters the model.

Unsupervised Machine Learning

On the other hand, unsupervised learning involves using only the training features WITHOUT labels to determine useful trends and "clusters" in the data. This method can work well if you have lots and lots of data and need a place to start; however, models will be much less accurate. And yes, it is exhaustive work to analyze and label the amount of websites that is required to achieve a state-of-the-art model.

Human Supervised Machine Learning (HS/ML)

Machine Learning must constantly evaluate models against humans and vice versa to make sure that they are always up to date and accurate. In HS/ML, when a human finds that the algorithm has made a mistake, the data is automatically incorporated back into the system so that the model in question can be retrained to avoid such mistakes in the future. Constant monitoring, flagging, and retraining process is key to building a high degree of accuracy to minimize false positives that can plague many security tools.

Deep Learning

Deep learning is a subset of machine learning methods based on how the human brain is structured to process information. The objective of deep learning algorithms is to deduce comparable insights to those of humans through continuous analysis of data using a predetermined logical framework. To accomplish this, deep learning employs complex arrangements of algorithms referred to as neural networks which are capable of learning complex patterns and representations from data. Deep learning is increasingly being applied to cybersecurity to enhance threat detection, network security, and data protection.

Reinforcement Learning

Reinforcement Learning (RL) is a distinct learning paradigm within machine learning that focuses on decision-making in dynamic environments and draws inspiration from how humans learn through trial and error. This approach involves training an AI system to make decisions and take actions in an environment to maximize a reward or minimize a penalty. In the context of cybersecurity, reinforcement learning can be applied to various scenarios, such as adaptive threat response and dynamic policy enforcement.

By continuously interacting with the environment, the AI system learns optimal strategies and adapts its behavior based on the observed outcomes, enabling it to effectively identify and respond to emerging threats in real-time. RL can be applied to cybersecurity to enhance security measures and decision-making processes. Use case examples include adaptive intrusion detection, automated response and mitigation systems, threat hunting, resource allocation and optimization, and vulnerability assessment and patching.

Reinforcement Learning with Human Feedback

Reinforcement Learning with Human Feedback (RLHF) is a specific form of reinforcement learning that incorporates human feedback into the learning process. In addition to interacting with the environment, the agent also receives guidance or feedback from a human expert in the form of explicit reward signals, demonstrations, or evaluations. Integrating human knowledge into reinforcement learning, helps to improve learning efficiency and achieve better performance. It is often used in applications where human expertise or preferences are valuable.

Natural Language Processing

Natural Language Processing (NLP) is an area within Artificial Intelligence that is specifically focused on interactions between machines and humans, using software that can interact with human language to extract details like sentiment, named people or places, intent, topics, etc. NLP is leveraged for malicious detection to analyze large volumes of data and detect patterns that can be missed by using traditional security tools. The NLP algorithms analyze the language used in email communications, in website content or on social media platforms to look for signs of malicious activity — like botnets, spam, fake accounts, etc. — to identify patterns and trends that may indicate emerging threats or new attack vectors.

Neural Machine Translation

Neural Machine Translation (NMT) is a subfield of NLP that focuses on using artificial neural networks to translate text from one language to another. As the threat landscape is not bound by language or geographical regions, the use of NMT to analyze and translate large volumes of data into multiple languages is critical to malicious detection. Security analysts can leverage NMT to translate communications between attackers, website content, social media posts and other digital content to identify patterns in language that may be indicative of malicious activity.

The applications for AI and Machine Learning in cybersecurity are extensive and can enable organizations to detect and respond to cyber threats in real-time, identify patterns and anomalies in vast amounts of data, and enhance overall cyber risk management. Below are some of the more common security applications for AI and ML.

- ⊙ **Web and DNS Filtering:** AI and ML algorithms play a crucial role in analyzing network traffic, URLs, and DNS requests to identify and block malicious websites, phishing attempts, malware downloads, and other cyber threats. AI and ML can automate web content categorization so that it can be filtered according to an organization's required taxonomy, effectively protecting users from accessing malicious or inappropriate websites, and safeguarding network integrity.

- ⊙ **Vulnerability Management:** ML models can prioritize and assess the severity of vulnerabilities by analyzing factors such as common vulnerabilities and exposures (CVE) data, exploit databases, and patch history. ML algorithms can help security teams efficiently allocate resources for patching or mitigation efforts.

- **Intrusion Detection and Prevention:** AI and ML algorithms can analyze network traffic patterns, system logs, and user behavior to detect anomalies and identify potential cyber threats. ML models can learn from historical data to recognize known attack patterns and flag suspicious activities, aiding in intrusion detection and prevention.

- **Phishing Detection:** ML models can analyze email content, URLs, and other features to identify and block phishing emails and spam. By learning from patterns in large datasets of known phishing attempts, ML algorithms can identify suspicious indicators and help protect users from falling victim to phishing attacks.

- **Fraud Detection:** AI and ML models can be used to detect fraudulent activities in various domains, including financial transactions, online purchases, and identity theft. ML algorithms can learn patterns of fraudulent behavior from historical data and apply that knowledge to identify suspicious transactions or activities in real-time.

- **Malware Detection:** ML algorithms can analyze file characteristics, network traffic, and behavioral patterns to identify and classify malware. ML models can be trained on large datasets of known malware samples to develop accurate malware detection systems.

- **Threat Intelligence:** AI and ML algorithms extract valuable threat intelligence by analyzing vast amounts of data from multiple digital sources including commercial threat feeds, open-source threat intelligence, social media platforms, and dark web forums. ML techniques enable the automated processing, categorization, and correlation of threat data to provide actionable insights for proactive defense.

- **Threat Hunting:** AI and ML techniques can be used to automate data analysis to identify patterns, anomalies, and indicators of compromise. By leveraging these technologies, security teams can proactively detect and mitigate potential threats, reduce false positives, and focus their efforts on investigating high-priority risks, strengthening overall cybersecurity defenses.

- **Network Security and Traffic Analysis:** AI and ML techniques can analyze network traffic logs to detect unusual or malicious activities, such as Distributed Denial of Service (DDoS) attacks or network intrusions. ML models can learn normal traffic patterns and detect anomalies that may indicate potential security incidents.

⊙ **User and Entity Behavior Analytics (UEBA):** AI and ML techniques can be used to identify potential insider threats or abnormal activities by analyzing user behavior, access patterns, and contextual data. By learning typical behavior and detecting deviations, UEBA systems can flag suspicious user actions for further investigation.

Challenges and Considerations

While AI and Machine Learning offer significant cybersecurity benefits, their implementation is not without challenges and considerations. From adversarial attacks and bias in AI systems to explainability and interpretability issues, as well as data privacy and security concerns, navigating these challenges is essential to ensure the effectiveness, reliability, and ethical use of AI and machine learning in cybersecurity.

Adversarial Attacks

As AI and machine learning systems become integral components of cybersecurity, the emergence of adversarial attacks poses a significant challenge. Adversarial attacks exploit vulnerabilities in machine learning models by introducing carefully crafted inputs that deceive the system's decision-making process.

These malicious inputs can cause misclassifications, evasion of detection algorithms, or even compromise the integrity of the entire system. Understanding the nature of adversarial attacks and developing robust defenses against them is paramount to ensuring the resilience and reliability of AI-powered cybersecurity systems.

Bias in AI Systems

Despite the immense potential for enhancing cybersecurity, the presence of bias in the decision-making processes is a critical concern. Bias can arise from various sources, including biased training data, biased algorithms, or biased interpretations of the results. In cybersecurity, biased AI systems can lead to discriminatory outcomes, unequal treatment, or overlooking certain types of threats. Addressing and mitigating bias in AI systems is essential to uphold fairness, equity, and unbiased decision-making, ensuring that cybersecurity solutions serve all users and protect against a wide range of threats without perpetuating existing biases or disparities.

Explainability and Interpretability of Machine Learning Models

As AI systems become more complex and sophisticated, understanding the rationale behind their decisions becomes challenging. This lack of transparency raises concerns about trust, accountability, and the ability to identify potential vulnerabilities or biases within the models. Ensuring explainability and interpretability in machine learning models is crucial for cybersecurity professionals to comprehend the reasoning behind the system's outputs, validate its effectiveness, and address any unintended consequences or errors effectively. By enhancing explainability and interpretability, organizations can build trust in AI systems, improve collaboration between humans and machines, and facilitate better decision-making in the context of cybersecurity.

Data Privacy and Security

The use of sensitive and confidential data to train and deploy AI models can deliver significant benefits although it poses potential risks, including unauthorized access, data breaches, or misuse of personal information. Additionally, there is a need to strike a balance between collecting and utilizing relevant data for effective cybersecurity measures while respecting privacy regulations and ethical considerations. Finding the right balance between safeguarding data privacy and ensuring robust security measures throughout the AI and ML lifecycle are crucial to instill trust and protect individuals' sensitive information, but also a major challenge to overcome.

Future of AI and Machine Learning in Cybersecurity

AI and machine learning continue to push the boundaries of cybersecurity, paving the way for exciting advancements and possibilities. The future holds promise of autonomous cybersecurity systems that evolve and learn, becoming more resilient with each attack. AI and ML will form the backbone of 'Self-Healing' networks, systems capable of identifying, defending against, and repairing damage from cyber attacks without human intervention. Moreover, AI and ML will play a pivotal role in threat hunting, aiding cybersecurity professionals in proactive threat identification. Rather than reacting to breaches, security systems will anticipate and neutralize threats, shaping a proactive cybersecurity environment.

While AI and ML in cybersecurity offer potential for a future of greater threat protection and resilience, this new dawn is certain to expose fresh challenges. In particular, ethical considerations, concerns over automated systems, and the threat of AI-powered malware and increasingly complex cyberattacks demand careful attention. In the end, balancing the power of technology with the wisdom of human oversight will be key. The future of cybersecurity isn't just about building stronger defenses; it's about creating smarter ones.

BLOCKCHAIN FOR SECURE TRANSACTIONS

Blockchain is a kind of a database that stores data digitally on a computer system. This database is a decentralized database that is accessed simultaneously by a big number of users. This requires powerful computers and that offer storage capacity to handle large volume of data. Bitcoin is a good example that can help understand how blockchain technology works as the first cryptocurrency with blockchain technology that was first implemented.

Bitcoin's architecture provides a comprehensive understanding of how blockchain technology operates across various sectors. The emergence of Bitcoin cryptocurrency has offered a transparent, efficient, and secure method for transferring digital assets between two endpoints without the need for central systems.

This solution addresses certain issues associated with our traditional financial system. In some cases, sending money internationally or paying bills can be time-consuming due to banks taking precautions and performing authentication processes to ensure the funds reach the correct recipient. This process becomes even lengthier when different banks are involved, each with their own databases, requiring additional information exchange for user authentication.

As researcher explained, blockchain is a decentralized peer-to-peer system. Security and privacy are crucial aspects that require significant attention. The utilization of hash functions, digital signatures, and public and private keys ensures the validation of transactions before they are added to the blockchain system. The hash function establishes a secure connection between the chains that form the entire blockchain system, as explained in the previous section.

Digital signatures serve as user identities, enabling the identification of activities within the blockchain network, preventing anyone from denying their involvement. Nodes within the network apply a signature to a document, allowing other nodes to recognize it. The private key is used for message signing, while the public key is utilized for signature verification.

Blockchain Technology

Blockchain Technology Definition

The primary objective of blockchain is to serve as a repository for digital information and facilitate its distribution, while ensuring that the information remains unalterable. The concept of blockchain technology was initially introduced in 1991 by Stuart Haber and W. Scott Stornetta in their publication titled "How to time stamp a digital document". Their aim was to establish a system where document timestamps could not be manipulated.

However, it was not until 2009 that the blockchain-based bitcoin project was launched by the pseudonymous Nakamoto Santoshi. Researcher defined bitcoin as an electronic payment system that relies on cryptographic mechanisms instead of central authorities to oversee transactions, enabling direct peer-to-peer transactions without the need for a trusted intermediary like a central bank.

Bitcoin, being the first iteration of blockchain, successfully addressed various issues in the financial sector by enhancing financial services. Subsequently, in 2015, ethereum emerged as the second-largest implemented blockchain, offering improved storage and execution of computer code, thereby enabling the utilization of smart contracts. Although Stuart Haber and W. Scott Stornetta did not explicitly mention the term "blockchain" in their work, their concept of establishing a system where document timestamps could not be modified aligns with the fundamental idea behind blockchain.

Decentralized and centralized network

A decentralized network comprises nodes that function as both clients and servers. This means that each node within the network operates independently and holds an identical copy of the data as other nodes. The decentralized database is designed in a manner that facilitates direct peer-to-peer value transfer, eliminating the need for a trusted central intermediary.

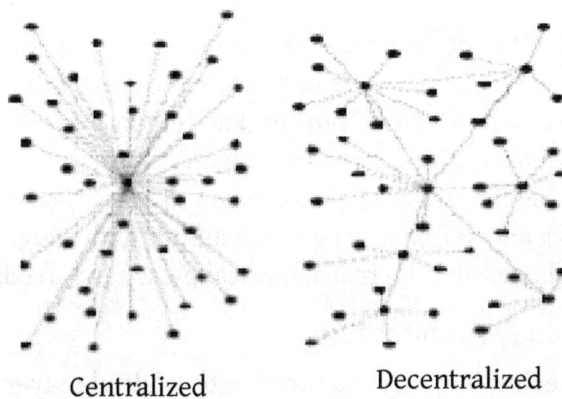

Centralized   Decentralized

Centralized network and Decentralized network

According to researchers, the implementation of a decentralized architecture in blockchain stands in contrast to the client-server model employed in traditional financial systems. In a centralized network, some nodes serve as clients while others act as servers, with clients requesting services from server nodes. The fundamental concept behind decentralization in blockchain is that the majority of nodes participate in decision-making processes. Conversely, in a centralized network, decision-making authority rests solely with a single actor or a small group. In traditional systems, a central database controls transaction flow, whereas in Bitcoin, the authority is distributed among the nodes in the decentralized network. The diagram below depicts both types of networks.

Bitcoin

Bitcoin, the cryptocurrency created by the pseudonymous Santoshi Nakamoto in 2008, is widely recognized as the first successful implementation of blockchain technology. Through Bitcoin, users are able to transfer asset value across a peer-to-peer network without the need for a central authority, such as banks, to oversee or control the transactions. Instead, the technology relies on a consensus protocol mechanism that allows users on the network to verify the transactions, fostering trust and confidence among participants. When a user wishes to send Bitcoin to another recipient, they broadcast a message to all other nodes or computers on the network, indicating the desired amount and recipient. To ensure the validity of these transactions, Bitcoin miners (computers) come into play. These miners work to propose groups of valid new transactions for settlement. Since the Bitcoin network operates on a distributed network where users are pseudonymous and do not have knowledge of each other's identities or contact information, the user includes a private key in the message to identify themselves to the other nodes. As all nodes in the network have the same updated copies, it is easy for them to verify that the user indeed possesses the specified amount of Bitcoin they wish to send. However, to allow for synchronization among the nodes, there is a slight delay in processing the transactions as other nodes update their copies.

Given that multiple nodes may be attempting to make transactions simultaneously, the right to settle the next transaction is determined through a competition to solve a mathematical puzzle. The first node to find the solution is rewarded and this solution also serves as a means of verifying the transactions. These groups of verified transactions are referred to as blocks, and they are added to the Bitcoin network approximately every 10 minutes, although the exact timing depends on the speed at which the mathematical puzzle is solved.

Blockchain Technology Architecture

The blockchain technology is structured with multiple layers, the number of which varies depending on the specific application. Each application has its own unique requirements, resulting in a distinct number of layers.

Generally, researchers agree on six common layers in blockchain technology: application layer, contract layer, incentive layer, consensus layer, network layer, and data layer. However, when it comes to assessing security issues in blockchain technology, most researchers focus on four core layers: application layer, consensus layer, network layer, and data layer. These four layers allow for the identification and isolation of different types of security threats in blockchain.

From a technical standpoint, the analysis of security issues can be conducted and categorized within these four layers, which form the foundation of the bitcoin network. The technical framework of the bitcoin network encompasses various components that fall into these four layers. The network consists of computers/nodes or users who access and utilize the blockchain through the application layer, which provides end-user functionality. The data layer handles transactions and other data stored in blocks, such as timestamps, private and public keys, nonce, hash values, and transactions themselves.

To facilitate the flow of transactions in a peer-to-peer network, the network layer comes into play with communication protocols, peer-to-peer addressing, routing, and naming services. Lastly, the consensus layer employs a consensus mechanism protocol that enables nodes on the peer-to-peer network to make decisions and verify transactions. This thesis will solely focus on these four layers, as they encompass the main components that constitute the technical framework of the bitcoin network. It is worth noting that the remaining two layers, namely the incentive layer and contract layer, have not been discussed from a security perspective in the literature reviewed by this study.

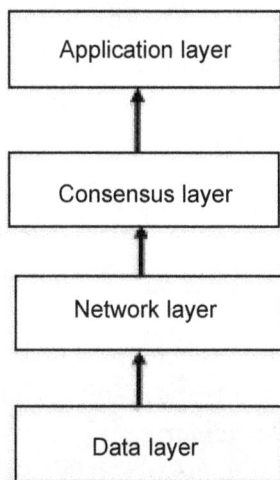

```
┌─────────────────────────┐
│     Application layer    │
└─────────────────────────┘
             ▲
             │
┌─────────────────────────┐
│      Consensus layer     │
└─────────────────────────┘
             ▲
             │
┌─────────────────────────┐
│       Network layer      │
└─────────────────────────┘
             ▲
             │
┌─────────────────────────┐
│        Data layer        │
└─────────────────────────┘
```

Four layers of Blockchain Architecture

The figure below shows four layers following by their explanations.

- ⊙ **Application layer:** Positioned at the top of the blockchain technology architecture, the application layer guarantees the utilization of the technology by end users.

- ⊙ **Network layer:** Also referred to as P2P, the network layer facilitates communication and synchronization among nodes in the network to maintain a valid status of the distributed ledger. Its primary responsibility is to verify the validity of the transmitted transaction.

- ⊙ **Consensus layer:** Within this layer, various consensus algorithms are employed in blockchain to reach decisions. One example is the proof of work algorithm, which will be elaborated on in the subsequent section.

- ⊙ **Data layer:** The data layer encompasses transactions organized in blocks within a decentralized network. These transactions consist of diverse data, such as account information. Furthermore, the components of the blockchain that ensure the distributed ledger's immutability include hash, merkle tree, timestamp, and encryption.

Blockchain Technology Features

Blockchain technologies is composed by different techniques namely, algorithm, cryptography mathematics and peer-to-peer networks. Consensus algorithms are at the core of this technology since they help the active nodes on the network to make decisions. The blockchain technologies composed of six key elements.

Decentralization: In traditional financial system, a centralized entity such as central banks are required to allow and monitor the transactions. In blockchain, a centralized party is not required to perform transactions. Data reliability in blockchain are maintained by consensus algorithm.

Immutable: It is not possible to edit it when it is added on a blockchain system. Each node in the network has a copy of the digital ledger and before adding a transaction to a block, the majority of the nodes in the network need to verify its validity.

Transparency: Since the system is decentralized, all participants have equal right and every participant can view and verify transactions which brings more transparency in the system.

Anonymity: Transactions in blockchain technologies are anonymous. The only thing to know in the transfer of a transaction is the person's blockchain address. This ensure trustiness in the blockchain.

Distributed ledgers: This is one of the important feature that allows ownership of verification. When a participant who wants to add a block on the blockchain, others will have to verify and approve it, thus allow fair participation.

Consensus: This is an algorithm that allows the nodes in the network to make decisions, it allows nodes to come to an agreement quickly. It is a kind of voting system where the majority wins, the minority has to support it. It is one of the important features that allows the network being trustless.

How secure is blockchain technology?

A common misconception is that all blockchain technology is well secured because it relies on cryptography. While it's true that blockchains all use cryptography, there are two major caveats:

- Fundamentally, blockchains are software code, so they're prone to the same kinds of vulnerabilities that affect other software throughout their lifecycles.

- There can be vast differences in the strength of cryptographic algorithms and key lengths as well as their implementations. Effective cryptographic key management is also important in keeping a blockchain secure.

Blockchain technology is not inherently more or less secure than other technologies.

Explaining the different types of blockchain security

At a high level, the types of blockchains are based on their access control models:

- A public blockchain (also called a permissionless blockchain) has no restrictions on who can access it or publish new blocks. Blockchain participants can be anonymous.

- A private blockchain (also known as a permissioned blockchain) restricts who can publish new blocks. It might also restrict who can access the blockchain. Each user of the blockchain must be identified and authenticated. Such a blockchain can be controlled by a group (a consortium blockchain) or an individual.

- A hybrid blockchain refers to having public and private blockchains that are interoperable, essentially forming a blockchain of blockchains.

Because public blockchains are inherently accessible to everyone and don't perform any user authentication, they are much easier for attackers to target and compromise than private blockchains. The rest of this article focuses primarily on public blockchain security.

Common threats to blockchain security

Public blockchains rely on reaching consensus among their participants. There are numerous consensus models for blockchains, and each has security strengths and weaknesses that make it better suited to certain situations. One common consensus model is called proof-of-work. Participants solve difficult problems requiring significant computing power, and producing the correct solution to the problem is proof that a participant has put forth effort and has essentially earned the right to release the new block.

Unfortunately, because public blockchains let anyone participate, attackers have many ways to disrupt consensus. One common threat, a sybil attack, involves an attacker adding a bunch of bogus participants to a blockchain network. This can give the attacker control of most of the participants.

Now the attacker can create fake transactions and have the bogus participants "validate" them. A similar threat, called a 51% attack, involves an attacker or group of attackers banding together to form a mining pool that does more than 50% of the mining for a blockchain.

There are many other threats that generally affect all software:

⊙ Routing attacks, where an attacker tampers with routing configurations so they can intercept unencrypted blockchain network traffic and access or alter it.

⊙ Phishing attacks, where an attacker uses social engineering methods to steal blockchain participants' credentials, such as private keys and passphrases.

⊙ Denial-of-service attacks, such as flooding a blockchain with huge numbers of requests to stop it from functioning.

There are also threats specific to blockchain applications. For example, double spending is when someone tries to spend the same cryptocurrency in two places at the same time. Smart contracts, which are blockchain applications that perform transactions and other processes according to a set of rules defined in their program code, have specific vulnerabilities to guard against.

Best practices to secure blockchain networks

Here are five best practices to secure your blockchain networks:

⊙ Make sure that a blockchain is appropriate for the transactions it would be recording. If records contain personal information or other sensitive information, a blockchain might inadvertently expose it and cause a data breach. Another consideration is whether transactions are truly final once they take place or you need the flexibility to modify or delete previous transactions.

⊙ Remember that blockchains are subject to all the cybersecurity and privacy laws, regulations, and other requirements that any other software must comply with throughout its lifecycle.

⊙ Identity management is important. Even in public blockchain networks, participants still need to know they're communicating with the legitimate network. For private blockchain networks, access management is incredibly important for preventing attackers from gaining unauthorized access to the network.

⊙ Perform regular risk assessments and audits of blockchain technology and related processes, such as key management, and determine how to handle discovered vulnerabilities or other weaknesses.

⊙ Plan for the worst. A major new vulnerability might be found in blockchain code, a private key might be stolen, participants' computers might be compromised — many things can go wrong. Be ready by having response and recovery processes in place ahead of time. There may also be disputes among participants, so be prepared to resolve those as well to prevent your blockchain from being disrupted.

QUANTUM COMPUTING AND ITS IMPLICATIONS

To grasp the significance of quantum computing, let's break it down a bit. Traditional computers, like the one you're using right now, use bits that represent either a 0 or a 1. Quantum computers, on the other hand, leverage quantum bits, or qubits, which can exist in multiple states simultaneously thanks to the principles of superposition and entanglement.

The Power of Quantum Computing

Quantum computing is based on quantum mechanics, which governs how nature works at the smallest scales. The smallest classical computing element is a bit, which can be either 0 or 1. The quantum equivalent is a qubit, which can also be 0 or 1 or in what's called a superposition — any combination of 0 and 1. Performing a calculation on two classical bits (which can be 00, 01, 10 and 11) requires four calculations. A quantum computer can perform calculations on all four states simultaneously. This scales exponentially: 1,000 qubits would, in some respects, be more powerful than the world's most powerful supercomputer. Quantum computing has the potential to revolutionize numerous industries, from healthcare and finance to materials science and artificial intelligence. Its incredible processing power could solve problems that would take classical computers an eternity.

Shattering Cryptography

While quantum computing brings a world of opportunities, it also poses a significant threat to current cryptographic systems. Traditional encryption relies on mathematical problems that are incredibly difficult to solve with classical computers. However, quantum computers could potentially crack these codes using algorithms like Shor's algorithm, putting sensitive data at risk.

Enter Post-Quantum Cryptography (PQC)

The race is on! To stay ahead in this quantum race, the cyber security community is actively working on post-quantum cryptography (PQC). PQC involves developing encryption methods that are resistant to attacks from quantum computers. The transition to PQC is vital to protect sensitive information in the quantum era. PQC algorithms are still under development, and there is no single standard yet. However, there are a number of promising PQC algorithms that could be used to protect data in the quantum era.

Securing Data in a Quantum World

In addition to PQC, other quantum-resistant techniques are emerging, like quantum key distribution (QKD). QKD enables secure communication by using the principles of quantum mechanics to exchange encryption keys without interception. However, QKD is still relatively expensive and complex to implement.

Preparing for the Inevitable

As quantum computing advances, cyber security professionals need to gear up for the quantum revolution. This means enhancing our knowledge, skills, and tools to tackle the evolving threats. Continuous learning and adaptation are crucial in this ever-changing landscape.

Collaboration and Information Sharing

In the face of such a monumental shift, it's essential to foster collaboration and information sharing within the cyber security community. By joining forces, we can collectively address challenges, brainstorm solutions, and keep our networks and data safe from the quantum storm.

Cybersecurity Implications

Quantum computing, and prosaic quantum technology, promise to transform cybersecurity in four areas:

- ⊙ **Quantum random number generation is fundamental to cryptography.** Conventional random number generators typically rely on algorithms known as pseudo-random number generators, which are not truly random and thus potentially open to compromise. Companies such as Quantum Dice and IDQuantique are developing quantum random number generators that utilize quantum optics to generate sources of true randomness. These products are already seeing commercial deployment.

- ⊙ **Quantum-secure communications, specifically quantum key distribution (QKD).** Sharing cryptographic keys between two or more parties to allow them to privately exchange information is at the heart of secure communications. QKD utilizes aspects of quantum mechanics to enable the completely secret exchange of encryption keys and can even alert to the presence of an eavesdropper. QKD is currently limited to fiber transmission over 10s of kilometers, with proofs of concept via satellite over several thousand kilometers. KETS Quantum Security and Toshiba are two pioneers in this field.

- ⊙ **The most controversial application of QC is its potential for breaking public-key cryptography, specifically the RSA algorithm, which is at the heart of the nearly $4 trillion ecommerce industry.** RSA relies on the fact that the product of two prime numbers is computationally challenging to factor. It would take a classical computer trillions of years to break RSA encryption. A quantum computer with around 4,000 error-free qubits could defeat RSA in seconds. However, this would require closer to 1 million of today's noisy qubits. The world's largest quantum computer is currently less than 100 qubits; however, IBM and Google have road maps to achieve

1 million by 2030. A million-qubit quantum computer may still be a decade away, but that time frame could well be compressed. Additionally, highly sensitive financial and national security data is potentially susceptible to being stolen today - only to be decrypted once a sufficiently powerful quantum computer becomes available. The potential threat to public-key cryptography has engendered the development of algorithms that are invulnerable to quantum computers. Companies like PQShield are pioneering this post-quantum cryptography.

⦿ **Machine learning has revolutionized cybersecurity, enabling novel attacks to be detected and blocked.** The cost of training deep models grows exponentially as data volumes and complexity increase. Open AI's GPT-3 used as much carbon as a typical American would use in 17 years. The emerging field of quantum machine learning may enable exponentially faster, more time- and energy-efficient machine learning algorithms. This, in turn, could yield more effective algorithms for identifying and defeating novel cyberattack methods.

Quantum Computing Challenges

Quantum computing promises to transform cybersecurity, but there are substantial challenges to address and fundamental breakthroughs still required to be made. The most immediate challenge is to achieve sufficient numbers of fault-tolerant qubits to unleash quantum computing's computational promise. Companies such as IBM, Google, Honeywell and Amazon are investing in this problem.

Quantum computers are currently programmed from individual quantum logic gates, which may be acceptable for small quantum computers, but it's impractical once we get to thousands of qubits. Companies like IBM and Classiq are developing more abstracted layers in the programming stack, enabling developers to build powerful quantum applications to solve real-world problems.

Arguably, the key bottleneck in the quantum computing industry will be a lack of talent. While universities churn out computer science graduates at an accelerating pace, there is still too little being done to train the next generation of quantum computing professionals.

The United States's National Quantum Initiative Act is a step in the right direction and incorporates funding for educational initiatives. There are also some tremendous open-source communities that have developed around quantum computing — perhaps the most exciting and active being the IBM Qiskit community. It will take efforts from governments, universities, industry and the broader technology ecosystem to enable the level of talent development required to truly capitalize on quantum computing.

AI and Quantum Computing

As technology advances at an exponential rate, we're witnessing a paradigm shift in computing capabilities with the rise of artificial intelligence (AI) and quantum computing. While these technologies promise unparalleled innovations in various fields, they also pose significant cybersecurity threats. In this blog post, we'll explore how AI and quantum computing are poised to create some of the greatest cybersecurity challenges in the coming years and discuss the potential implications for businesses and individuals.

The Rise of AI and Quantum Computing

Artificial Intelligence (AI)

AI is a branch of computer science that seeks to create machines capable of mimicking human intelligence. Machine learning, a subset of AI, enables computers to learn from data and improve their performance over time. In recent years, AI has become increasingly sophisticated, leading to significant advancements in fields such as natural language processing, computer vision, and data analysis.

Quantum Computing

Quantum computing is a revolutionary technology that leverages the principles of quantum mechanics to process information. Unlike classical computers, which use bits to represent data as 0s and 1s, quantum computers use qubits that can exist in multiple states simultaneously. This property, known as superposition, allows quantum computers to perform complex calculations at unprecedented speeds.

Quantum-powered AI could translate into breakthrough solutions for complex problems across a wide range of industries and scientific fields that are beyond the current capabilities of classical computers and traditional AI techniques, said Scott Likens, global AI and innovation technology leader at PwC.

According to Likens, business and IT leaders should have quantum computing and AI developments on their radar today since the pairing offers a number of benefits, including the following:

- ⊙ **Speed.** AI on classical computing is limited by hardware. Training recent large language models — which depend on massive data sets — can take days or weeks, or even longer. AI supported by quantum hardware could shorten the time required to train these models.

- ⊙ **New mechanics.** Machine learning (ML) powers most AI systems. The current ML algorithms work well at predicting — as seen with generative AI — but need help scaling with other types of computational problems. Quantum systems might unlock new patterns of problem-solving since they are based on the principles of quantum mechanics, such as superposition, entanglements and interference, which depend on vastly different processes than current digital computers.

- ◉ **Quantum machine learning algorithms.** There is also significant progress on new quantum-inspired ML algorithms that are exponentially faster than classical computers. These ML algorithms rely on new techniques rooted in quantum mechanics to further enhance the processing ability for machine learning.

- ◉ **Energy efficiency.** Quantum machine learning algorithms that can be trained faster will likely consume less energy than classical computers, as AI and ML training and storing data presently use a massive amount of energy. The process of querying these algorithms in production, called inference, might also require less energy either on classical or quantum computers. Inference occurs when an ML algorithm processes live data points to calculate an output, such as a single numerical score. For organizations striving to achieve environmental, social and governance goals, the combined technologies could potentially help meet net-zero emissions commitments.

- ◉ **Operational improvements.** Quantum computers process information in parallel on the same set of qubits, while existing classical computers need to spread these parallel computations across separate chips. The innate parallel processing of quantum computers promises exponential increases in optimization tasks that could enhance resource allocation, supply chain management and financial modeling.

Organizations hesitant to invest in a single quantum computer should know that there are ways for quantum and classical computing to interact, although combining the processes is still in its early stages.

Businesses will eventually be able to combine quantum and classical approaches for faster computation and analysis for better-optimized solutions, Likens said.

The dangers of quantum-powered AI

For all the excitement around the AI-quantum computing convergence, the potential pairing holds dangers as well. The integration could lead to many new problems and challenges for business and society.

As AI systems become more capable, their complexity might reach a point where people can no longer understand — or control — them, which in turn would lead to ethical and safety issues, Likens said. The complexity of quantum systems might also exacerbate the lack of transparency and interpretability in AI algorithms. These issues also contribute to concerns about bias.

Balancing innovation with ethical and security considerations will be crucial as these technologies evolve.

With the rise of businesses seeking value creation in AI, there's a growing trend that workers fear becoming obsolete. AI powered by quantum computing could be another aspect for employees to worry about soon.

Quantum computing and AI could lead to mass unemployment as the systems become more capable than humans across various domains, said Chirag Dekate, vice president analyst at Gartner.

The quantum-powered AI organization

A widespread convergence of quantum computing and AI might be near term as both areas undergo rapid transformation.

Significant recent developments have occurred in underlying quantum computing hardware, algorithms, software, and the infrastructure for interconnecting quantum and classical computers, Likens said.

Newer quantum-inspired algorithms show promise for enhancing predictions, generating new content and better decision-making, and this could translate into advances in important areas, he said. Quantum simulations in healthcare have the potential to speed up drug discovery and analysis using quantum optimization techniques. In addition, quantum AI can benefit areas such as cybersecurity and finance by handling high-dimensional data.

Preparing for the Quantum Future

The quantum revolution is upon us. Although the profound impact of large-scale fault-tolerant quantum computers may be a decade off, near-term quantum computers will still yield tremendous benefits. We are seeing substantial investment in solving the core problems around scaling qubit count, error correction and algorithms. From a cybersecurity perspective, while quantum computing may render some existing encryption protocols obsolete, it has the promise to enable a substantially enhanced level of communication security and privacy.

CHAPTER-14

CYBERSECURITY TRAINING AND AWARENESS

Security awareness training is a strategy used by IT and security professionals to prevent and mitigate user risk. These programs are designed to help users and employees understand the role they play in helping to combat information security breaches. Effective security awareness training helps employees understand proper cyber hygiene, the security risks associated with their actions and to **identify cyber attacks** they may encounter via email and the web.

Effective security awareness training lets employees practice proper cyber hygiene, recognize the security risks tied to their actions and identify potential cyber attacks that can be encountered through email and web platforms.

Common benefits of security awareness training include the following:

⊙ **Prevents financial loss.** Cyber attacks can financially cripple businesses and harm their brand reputation. "Cost of a Data Breach Report 2023" from IBM Security and the Ponemon Institute put the average cost of a data breach among the 550 surveyed companies at $4.45 million per incident — a 15% increase over the past three years. Security awareness training teaches employees how to protect their organization's assets, data and financial resources. By reducing the likelihood of security incidents and breaches, organizations can minimize their financial losses and maintain a more secure and resilient environment.

⊙ **Minimizes the risk of incidents.** The volume of attacks against organizations is also growing. Verizon's "2023 Data Breach Investigations Report" scrutinized 16,312 security incidents spanning 20 industries around the globe. The report confirmed that 5,199 of these incidents were data breaches and that 74% of breaches — including social engineering, misuse or errors — involved humans and 83% of breaches involved external bad actors. The Federal Bureau of Investigation's "Internet Crime Report 2022" suggested that phishing attacks ranked number one with 300,497 complaints, followed by personal data breaches, resulting in a loss of $52 million. Proper security awareness training can prevent and minimize these types of incidents by empowering employees to be proactive in identifying and addressing potential threats.

◉ **Reduces human error.** Cybersecurity experts generally agree humans tend to be the root cause of most incidents. Security awareness training can equip employees with the knowledge, skills and mindset necessary to reduce human errors, making organizations more resilient against security threats.

◉ **Cultivates a cybersecurity mindset.** Despite the flurry of risks out there, organizations can help prevent incidents or lessen the effect of successful attacks by educating their employees on how to identify cybersecurity risks, avoid potential attacks and properly respond to a cyber event.

◉ **Prevents data loss and damage.** Efficient security awareness training enables employees to understand the significance of safeguarding sensitive data; preventing the leakage of personally identifiable information, intellectual property and financial resources; and upholding the company's brand reputation.

Difference between security awareness and security training

The terms *security awareness* and *security training* are closely intertwined but have noticeable differences:

◉ **Security awareness** is the process of educating and directing an employee's attention to security-related issues inside an organization. Employees who are aware of security concerns are more inclined to feel accountable for maintaining security, understand its importance, and are aware of the consequences and disciplinary actions for noncompliance.

◉ **Security training,** on the other hand, focuses on imparting specialized knowledge and skills to staff members so they can improve their capacity to recognize and effectively address security issues. The main goal of security training is to provide useful advice on security best practices, including how to handle sensitive information appropriately, spot phishing emails and develop secure browsing habits.

In short, security awareness fosters a security culture and mindset within an organization, whereas security training imparts skills required to manage and mitigate security risks.

CYBERSECURITY AWARENESS TRAINING IN ORGANIZATIONS

Cybersecurity awareness training has a critical role to play in minimizing the serious cybersecurity threats posed to end users by phishing attacks and social engineering. Key training topics typically include password protection, management, privacy, email/phishing security, web/internet security, and physical and office security.

There's also a business case to be made for security awareness training, as explored in the Aberdeen Group's report, *Security Awareness Training: Small Investment, Large Reduction in Risk.* The researchers conducted a workshop with enterprise security leaders to find out why they invest in security awareness and training. They found that:

- 91% use security awareness to reduce cybersecurity risk related to user behavior.
- 64% use it to change user behavior.
- 61% use it to address regulatory requirements.
- 55% use it to comply with internal policies.

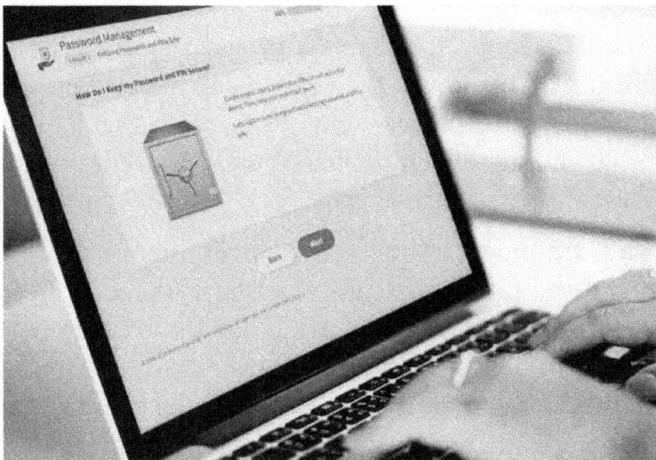

As these statistics suggest, some organizations use security awareness training simply because they must, in order to comply with external or internal requirements. But this training also makes financial sense, according to the report: "an incremental investment in security awareness training results in a median reduction in the annualized risk of phishing attacks of about 50%, and a median annual return on investment of about 5 times."

THE EVOLUTION OF SECURITY AWARENESS TRAINING

While the core concepts of cybersecurity awareness training aren't new, it has reached mainstream consciousness relatively recently. One indication of its emergence was the 2004 launch of National Cyber Security Awareness Month.

The initiative, by the National Cyber Security Alliance and US Department of Homeland Security, was intended to help people stay safer and more secure online, encouraging such practices as the regular updating of antivirus software.

Since then, the annual awareness month has inspired similar events in other countries, expanded its themes and content, and drawn increased participation across industries and government, as well as universities, nonprofits, and the general public.

The focus, methods, and effectiveness of security awareness training have undergone significant changes over the years. Back in 2004, most programs were driven by the need for compliance — simply meeting regulatory requirements. Today, that focus has shifted to seeing cybersecurity awareness training as a means to manage and mitigate organizational risk.

Along the way, training methods themselves have matured. In 2004, the dominant paradigm was for annual presentations, either as in-person training sessions or long-form computer-based training. Unfortunately, these lengthy, infrequent sessions do not result in good knowledge retention. A gradual shift toward short, focused training on individual topics represented an improvement, but these trainings were still presented infrequently, which allows knowledge to dissipate over time.

Around 2014, security awareness training began shifting toward continuous education and improvement, in which a program includes ongoing cycles of assessments and training. The latest developments have been "just-in-time" and in-context training, which adds the ability to launch training in response to an end user exhibiting poor cybersecurity behavior, such as unsafe web browsing.

STRONG SECURITY AWARENESS TRAINING

An effective cybersecurity awareness training program should reach workers who have varying degrees of technical aptitude and cybersecurity knowledge, as well as different learning styles.

The training program should be multifaceted with a collection of lessons and learning opportunities so it engages everyone in the company. In addition, a comprehensive program includes role-based content, delivering instructional material tailored to the needs of an employee's role, as well as third-party stakeholders, such as business partners and contract workers, to ensure those individuals don't put the organization at risk.

Effective programs have the following key components:

- **Educational content.** This should range from written material to interactive online learning to gamification sessions so workers can access information in formats they learn best, whether it's audio, visual or other formats. Content should include lessons and modules with varying degrees of complexity so workers can access the most relevant information according to their roles.

- **Follow-up and ongoing messaging.** This reminds workers of the company's cybersecurity policies. It delivers short refreshers on how to identify and avoid security risks and violations, as well as how to handle possible security problems, and alerts them to any emerging threats.

- **Simulated attack testing.** Using phishing attempts, social engineering tactics, surveys, quizzes and other assessments helps evaluate how well the enterprise workforce adheres to the organization's cybersecurity policies and identifies any individuals who fall short in following cybersecurity best practices.

- **Worker involvement reporting and measurement.** This monitors the effectiveness of the organization's awareness training, helping to identify any weaknesses in the program and areas that require strengthening.

- **Compliance-specific requirements.** These ensure that employees are well informed about the specific compliance requirements and the significance of adhering to them. For instance, compliance standards, such as the Health Insurance Portability and Accountability Act and Payment Card Industry Data Security Standard, have particular elements that end users must be educated on during security awareness training.

A good training program typically has a mix of the following:

- Formal education, such as structured lessons and mandatory instruction.

- Informational learning opportunities, such as weekly emails containing tips, policy updates and cybersecurity news updates.

- Experiential sessions and even gamification, where workers are required to work through phishing simulations and scenarios to test their understanding and reinforce their training so they're better prepared to handle real-world cybersecurity challenges.

Create and implement a successful security awareness training program

Organizations can enhance their security posture by creating a successful security awareness program. Important steps in creating this program include the following:

- ⊙ The chief information security officer (CISO) and the organization's cybersecurity team should be leaders in crafting a cybersecurity awareness training program and should enlist other executives to gain support and to understand the most significant risks the proposed program should address. Those risks should align with the organization's overall cybersecurity strategy the CISO develops in conjunction with other C-suite colleagues.

- ⊙ The CISO should work in conjunction with their human resources (HR) department, which typically leads workplace training and development, to ensure the organization has a well-formed and effective program.

- ⊙ Workers charged with developing the program should incorporate the specific threats facing their industry and their organization when developing a training program since these can vary across verticals.

- ⊙ The security awareness training program should be comprehensive, starting with rudimentary lessons and moving up to advanced materials. It should also include an assessment process to help organizations identify a worker's level of cybersecurity awareness and subsequently create a learning pathway for them.

- ⊙ Organizational leaders need to consider that different roles within the organization face different risks and threats while developing the training program. For example, an entry-level employee with limited access to sensitive data and core IT systems likely encounters fewer risky scenarios than a high-level executive who works with the organization's proprietary information and financial systems or a senior IT employee who is authorized to work on the core technologies that enable the business.

- ⊙ Larger organizations with significant HR departments might be able to develop and deliver their awareness training program or at least supplement it with outside resources. Many organizations choose to outsource most or all the training, however, considering this is the most effective and efficient way to implement necessary education for its employees. Either way, organizational leaders should have mechanisms to measure whether the training is effective at both the enterprise level and the individual employee level.

PROMOTE A WORK CULTURE THAT PRIORITIZES SECURITY AWARENESS

According to *Cybercrime Magazine* forecasts, businesses will lose nearly $10.5 trillion annually by 2025, or $19,977,168 each minute, due to cybercrime. Therefore, a strong cybersecurity culture is vital for any organization to secure its information, assets and reputation.

The following can help businesses promote a security-centric work culture:

- **Inclusiveness.** Employers should ensure that everyone within the organization understands that security belongs to them. Security should be incorporated into the company's vision and mission to emphasize its importance at all levels, from executives to frontline employees.

- **Training and education.** Businesses should establish routine security awareness training initiatives to instruct employees on potential security threats and best practices. These programs can cover subjects such as identifying phishing attempts, maintaining secure passwords and safeguarding data.

- **Regular communication and updates.** Employers should routinely notify staff of security-related updates, incidents, news and reminders using a variety of media, including emails, newsletters, posters and intranet portals.

- **Security development lifecycle (SDL).** Organizations should establish an SDL to guide security practices in software and system development. An SDL is essential for creating a long-lasting security culture and involves security requirements, threat modeling and security testing.

- **Security champions.** Organizations can designate individuals who can educate their peers, push for greater security awareness and act as a point of contact for issues or queries relating to security.

- **Incentives and recognition.** By rewarding and recognizing individuals who excel in security awareness and practices, organizations can recognize success. Small incentives, such as cash rewards, can motivate and foster a positive security culture.

How often should security awareness training occur?

Experts agree that cybersecurity awareness training should be ongoing within the enterprise. Continuous training helps workers build a security mindset so they can stay diligent and gives organizations opportunities to educate workers on updated policies and procedures and alert them to the new and evolving threats and risks they could face.

To achieve ongoing and effective security training, the following points should be considered:

- According to a paper from the Advanced Computing Systems Association titled "An investigation of phishing awareness and education over time: When and how to best remind users," businesses should ideally perform cybersecurity awareness training every four to six months. Research showed that employees can still identify phishing emails effectively four months after initial training, but their retention of the knowledge begins to decline after six months.

- Organizations should establish a schedule to determine what training to deliver to which employees and how frequently training must occur. For example, security awareness training should ideally take place when a new employee joins the company as part of a mandatory onboarding process.

- Many experts also advocate for at least an annual certification process for employees with a combination of formal and informal lessons available throughout the year to keep security best practices fresh in mind for workers.

- When assessments, evaluations or testing indicate a lapse in best practices, organizations should consider mandatory training for the entire enterprise or individual employees.

- Organizations can opt to use a learning management system to make training content easily and readily available to employees.

TOOLS FOR TRAINING END USERS

Today, infosec professionals use a variety of tools to train end users, as can be seen in our *State of the Phish™ Report*. The dominant tool — and one that continues to grow in popularity — is computer-based awareness training.

- 79% use computer-based awareness training.
- 68% use phishing simulation exercises.
- 46% use awareness campaigns (videos and posters).
- 45% use in-person security awareness training.
- 38% use monthly notifications or newsletters.

Well-designed training programs often make use of several of these tools. Equally important is to deploy these tools in a systematic, methodical way that allows you to track and measure progress over time.

Our highly effective training solutions utilize our Continuous Training Methodology, designed with Learning Science Principles to engage the learner and change behavior.

BUILDING A CYBER-AWARE CULTURE

The concept of cyber security culture refers to the attitudes, knowledge, assumptions, norms and values of the workforce of an organisation with respect to cyber security. These are shaped by the goals, structure, policies, processes, and leadership of the organisation.

A good cyber security culture is one in which both the organisational determinants of culture (policy, process, leadership, social norms etc.) and the individual determinants of culture (attitudes, knowledge, assumptions etc.) align with the organisation's approach to cyber security, manifesting in cyber security conscious behaviours.

Core to creating an effective cyber security culture is recognising that people make an organisation secure, not technology. People are both the best response to cyber-attacks and the weakest link in cyber security chains. So, it's critical to foster an environment where employees have the knowledge and instinct to be the first line of defence.

It's useful to look at what we can learn from organisations with dangerous work environments, such as power-stations, oil platforms and railways. They tried training their staff and found the behaviour improvement didn't last long.

Sociologist Barry Turner first started to find the reason for these failings in the 1970s as he postulated culture was key. Several high-profile accidents in the 1980s, such as the sinking of the Herald of Free Enterprise, the Chernobyl explosion and the Challenger Space Shuttle accident, led to greater understanding and acceptance of his theory. This emphasised that organisational structures, culture, policies and management procedures all play a role in the occurrence of industrial accidents and incidents. During the last 30 years, high-hazard industries have worked hard to align their business culture with their safety goals and have seen real reductions in accidents.

Other organisations can now use these lessons to accelerate the adoption of a cyber security culture. This starts with building on existing strengths, connecting with hearts, nudging the right habits and leadership championing adoption. Leaders must simultaneously listen to employees and understand how changes impact the way in which they engage with cyber security, and make adjustments where appropriate.

Cyber security culture needs to reflect organisational and leadership goals

Cyber security culture goals must be strategic, organisationally aligned and risk aligned. You need to understand what the current cyber security culture within your organisation looks like. You need to explore your lived culture, purpose and values, and the way that they impact people's engagement with cyber risk. It's important to know the reality of where you're starting from by understanding mindsets and behaviour, this helps you determine where the significant gaps are and develop a roadmap for change.

Underpinning the success of these initiatives is support from leadership. It's important to emphasise the role leaders play in setting the example. Where they buy into and actively embody and advocate security consciousness, people follow. Conversely, when the tone at the top isn't aligned, awareness campaigns will be undermined.

Finally, it's critical that, as you implement changes to your cyber culture, you listen and adjust. You need to keep listening to your employees and understand how changes impact the way in which they engage with cyber security. Having an objective and honest understanding of how your efforts have landed will help you make the right adjustments to continue moving towards your goal. It also allows you the opportunity to celebrate successes and acknowledge positive shifts.

Strategies for Building a Cybersecurity Culture

Establish Leadership Commitment and Support

The foundation of a strong cybersecurity culture starts with the commitment and support of an organization's leadership. Executives and managers must demonstrate the importance of cybersecurity by setting the tone from the top and actively participating in security initiatives. They should communicate the organization's security goals and objectives, allocate resources to cybersecurity initiatives, and regularly review and assess the effectiveness of the organization's security posture.

Develop a Comprehensive Security Awareness Program

A comprehensive security awareness program is essential for educating employees about the latest threats, best practices for protecting sensitive data, and the importance of maintaining strong security hygiene. This program must comprise consistent instructional meetings, lectures, seminars, and additional learning events customized to meet the requirements of the establishment and its personnel. The program should cover topics such as phishing, social engineering, password management, and safe browsing habits. Utilizing various learning formats, such as e-learning modules, videos, and interactive activities, can help keep employees engaged and reinforce the importance of cybersecurity.

Encourage Continuous Learning and Skill Development

Building a cybersecurity culture requires continuous learning and skill development. Motivating staff members to register for **Cyber Security Courses** can aid them in staying up-to-date with current dangers, technologies, and optimum procedures. These courses can be offered in-house, or employees can be provided with access to external resources, such as online training platforms and cybersecurity conferences. Offering incentives, such as certification reimbursements or recognition for course completion, can also help motivate employees to pursue ongoing cybersecurity education.

Create a Cybersecurity Ambassador Program

A cybersecurity ambassador program can help promote a security-first mindset across the organization. This involves selecting employees from various departments to serve as cybersecurity champions within their respective teams. These ambassadors should be provided with additional training and resources, enabling them to act as a resource for their colleagues and promote security awareness within their teams. They may additionally assist in recognizing possible security hazards, offer input on the efficiency of the company's security endeavors, and act as a mediator between their unit and the IT security crew.

Implement a Security Incident Reporting System

Creating a culture of cybersecurity includes encouraging employees to report security incidents or suspicious activities promptly. Introducing a security incident notification mechanism enables workers to swiftly and confidentially communicate possible hazards, such as phishing endeavors or unapproved entry to confidential information. This mechanism must be intuitive and available to all workers, with transparent instructions on how to report incidents and the kinds of occurrences that necessitate reporting. Regularly communicating the importance of reporting security incidents can help reinforce the idea that cybersecurity is everyone's responsibility.

Regularly Assess and Evaluate Security Awareness and Training Efforts

To ensure that cybersecurity awareness and training efforts are effective, it is essential to regularly assess and evaluate their impact. This can be done through surveys, quizzes, or testing employees' ability to recognize and respond to simulated security threats. Evaluating the effectiveness of security awareness and training initiatives can help identify areas for improvement and inform the development of future programs. By continuously refining and updating training materials, organizations can ensure that their workforce remains prepared to face the evolving cybersecurity threat landscape.

Foster a Culture of Open Communication and Collaboration

Open communication and collaboration are key to building a strong cybersecurity culture. Motivating staff members to communicate their encounters, worries, and suggestions regarding cybersecurity can foster a feeling of possession and accountability for safeguarding the company's digital resources. Regularly discussing security incidents and the lessons learned from them can also help raise awareness and promote a proactive approach to cybersecurity.

Recognize and Reward Security Conscious Behavior

Recognizing and rewarding employees for their security-conscious behavior can help reinforce the importance of cybersecurity and motivate them to maintain a strong security posture. This can include recognizing individuals who complete a Cyber Security Course, report security incidents, or demonstrate exceptional security practices in their daily work. By acknowledging the efforts of employees in promoting a cybersecurity culture, organizations can encourage continued engagement and commitment to protecting the organization from cyber threats.

BENEFITS OF ENROLLING IN CYBER SECURITY COURSES

Staying Informed of the Latest Threats and Technologies

The sector of cyber security is always progressing, and it's crucial to keep abreast of the most recent hazards, advancements, and optimal methodologies to safeguard an establishment's digital properties. Taking part in Cyber Security Courses can aid staff in staying current with the latest advancements and furnish them with the expertise and abilities necessary to counteract emerging hazards.

Developing and Maintaining Essential Cybersecurity Skills

With the ever-changing cyber security threat scenario, it is imperative to keep upskilling to safeguard an organization's digital assets. Enrolling in Cyber Security Courses can aid employees in acquiring and retaining the critical skills necessary to efficiently combat cyber threats, including identifying threats, handling incidents, and managing risks.

Enhancing Career Opportunities and Advancement

Individuals who aspire to pursue a profession in cyber security can enroll themselves in Cyber Security Training programs to augment their professional qualifications and manifest their dedication to unceasing learning and proficiency enhancement. This can pave the way for better job prospects, career progression, and a rise in earning potential.

Promoting a Security-First Mindset and Culture

By encouraging employees to enroll in Cyber Security Course, organizations can promote a security-first mindset and culture. This can help foster a sense of shared responsibility for protecting the organization's digital assets, ultimately leading to a stronger cybersecurity posture.

Tips for building a cybersecurity culture at your company

Building a cybersecurity culture has always been an important element of an organization's cybersecurity strategy. The massive shift to remote work induced by COVID-19 followed by the growth of the hybrid workplace, however, has fundamentally changed the threat landscape.

Cybersecurity policies of the past and even those instituted at the start of the pandemic must be reevaluated in the face of new cybersecurity challenges, said Candy Alexander, president of Information Systems Security Association (ISSA) International, a not-for-profit international organization for security professionals, and CISO at NeuEon Inc.

"We need to identify the new risks, articulate the new risks and make sure that's aligned with the business strategy," Alexander said.

When risk profiles change, so must an organization's cybersecurity culture, she stressed. The behaviors and mindset required to deal with evolving security risks — a company's cybersecurity culture — must be organization-wide.

Indeed, building a culture of cybersecurity is not just important for the organization. "You need to build it for your customers as well. You need to focus on the entire ecosystem," said Aanchal Gupta, corporate vice president of Azure Security and M365 Security at Microsoft.

Best practices

Building a security culture is a matter of tactics and strategy. It is a journey that calls for articulating the goal and figuring out how to reach it. It requires people skills. Taking an empathetic approach, making cybersecurity personal and relevant to your audience, acting as a close partner to the product and engineering teams, and aligning the security culture with the values of the broader corporate culture are all effective tactics for ensuring a successful security culture implementation.

People think of security as boring and are reluctant to care about it, so it is important to create an emotional connection to make it effective.

Here's an overview of five key best practices that are guaranteed to help information security professionals create organization-wide cybersecurity culture.

Start in the C-suite and make security relatable

The first step toward successfully creating a companywide culture of security is for security leaders to begin working with the C-suite. Security pros should understand and align with the business strategy, identify the risks associated with that strategy and appropriately communicate those risks in business terms.

Once the executives understand — in relatable terms — what the risk is and what the ask is, then they're able to follow through ... and support you.

Make it human-centric

Security teams often mistakenly equate having a "human-centric" security program with implementing security awareness training that every employee is required to take.

This means analyzing stakeholders by understanding their behaviors and challenges and figuring out what needs to be changed and how to implement that change. "Then, based on that ... you create your security culture initiatives for each one of those stakeholder communities," Budge said.

Make security awareness training fun and rewarding

Researcher believes building a cybersecurity culture needs to be a team sport. Making security awareness training fun and rewarding and encouraging a "growth mindset" — that is, an openness to learning and trying new things — are imperative to success. Security awareness training that involves role-playing and simulation games modeled after TV shows lands well with employees, she said, and helps improve learning retention.

Phishing awareness training, for example, can be made more effective when it comes with a reward akin to a bounty program, where employees get rewarded for spotting a simulated phish. The bounty program can also be extended to reward an employee who recognizes an actual phishing campaign and promptly reports it, according to Tim Helming, security evangelist at DomainTools.

"Investing in good-quality, well-executed user education is absolutely vital," Helming said. "If users are well trained from a 'if you see something, say something' standpoint in the cyber realm, then they can be an incredibly valuable asset to us."

However, it is important for the culture to be collaborative and positive and to steer away from a culture of blame and fear, he added.

Invest in the right security tools

Security tools are an integral part of a layered defense, but they are not the panacea for cyber attacks. Helming advised having a well-thought-out complement of cybersecurity tools that can augment the "human aspect" of cybersecurity.

Investing in SIEM solutions that use machine learning techniques, for example, can help empower security operations center staff by augmenting their detection and response capabilities, improve the signal-to-noise ratio and enable security analysts to focus on the threats that matter, Microsoft's Gupta said. However, it is important to remember that, as technology evolves and cyber attacks increase, the cybersecurity skills shortage is only getting worse. It is imperative to recruit, train and retain cyber talent from a wide variety of backgrounds in order to maintain advantage, Gupta added.

Have a CISO succession plan in place

An essential, but often overlooked, element in building a successful cybersecurity culture is to have a CISO succession plan in place, according to Jason Fruge, CISO at Rent-A-Center. That's because, while a culture change can take up to five years, the average tenure of a CISO is just over two years. Companies should, therefore, make sure they have a successor within the organization who can continue that vision to implement that security culture change.

EMPLOYEE TRAINING PROGRAMS

Cybersecurity training also referred to as cybersecurity awareness training, is an approach to building organizational security and mitigating user risk of cyber attacks. These solutions educate employees on how they can individually prevent cybersecurity breaches and data hacks by implementing best practices while using email and other web services.

Components of Cybersecurity Training

Comprehensive cybersecurity training must encompass all kinds of security threats:

Responsibility for company & customer data

First and foremost, employees need to be well trained to understand the ins and outs of their responsibilities related to protecting the company and customer data. Team members should receive in-depth training that underscores any legal regulations that affect how they handle information and company-established best practices.

Data incident reporting

Employees should be aware of how to detect and report suspicious activity and phishing attempts when they see them. Individual cases of cybersecurity breaches and even attempts should be communicated to the responsible parties along with sufficient background information so every effort to guard against future attacks can be made.

Passwords

Employees should understand the importance of using strong, unique passwords for company accounts. Businesses must enact policies to ensure employees are updating their passwords regularly and avoiding doubling up on personal passwords.

Unauthorized software installation

Employees should understand the intended use of their work devices and the rules about what can and cannot be installed on them. Team members should not be installing new applications from the internet unless deemed necessary for their role and signed off on by managers or IT team.

Fraud emails

Fraud emails are the primary vehicle for phishing attacks. In these emails, attackers pose as trusted persons or entities to gain some kind of access or information. Employees should be well-versed in scanning emails for signs of fraudulent activity.

Spot suspicious activity

Emails aren't the only source of cybersecurity threats. Successful cybersecurity awareness training should enable employees to spot security threats across the web, in their messages, and from within the organization.

Reinforce confidentiality

Team members well-trained in cybersecurity measures must understand the importance of confidentiality and the measures necessary to protect it. They should receive detailed instructions on how to protect data and in turn, protect their customers, fellow employees, partners, and the company as a whole.

Challenges of Cybersecurity Training in the Workplace

There is no one-and-done solution to workplace cybersecurity training. Because cyber threats are complex and ever-changing, cybersecurity awareness training needs to be robust and adaptive. There are several challenges that security professionals face when designing and implementing training. Let's discuss a few of them.

Training is an investment

There is no one-and-done solution to workplace cybersecurity training. Because cyber threats are complex and ever-changing, cybersecurity awareness training needs to be robust and adaptive. There are several challenges that security professionals face when designing and implementing training. Let's discuss a few of them.

Avoid the blame game

While it is true that employees can be a source of cybersecurity weakness, blaming individuals for their part in security breaches misses the point and causes more harm than good. It is the larger responsibility of an organization's leaders and IT security teams to equip their team members with everything they need to keep the business and its data safe.

Getting leadership on board

Like with most organization-wide projects, it's critical to get upper management on board. In order to keep leadership excited and involved, continue pointing them to the importance of cybersecurity training for employees. Be clear and transparent about how cybersecurity affects the overall success of the company, and highlight the harm security attacks could have. Use analytic and reporting tools to demonstrate the effectiveness of your training program once in place.

Cyber threats are always evolving

Cybersecurity threats evolve and adapt at a pace that is unnerving, to say the least. In order to ensure that employees are well-equipped to handle the newest threats, cybersecurity training needs to be updated along with them. Many cybersecurity awareness training programs are designed to be delivered in small doses over long periods of time. Taking advantage of one of these solutions will give IT the opportunity to deliver up-to-date information about evolving cybersecurity threats as they emerge.

Cybersecurity best practices for security professionals

- **Update security policies.** Businesses often have outdated security policies that don't take into account the latest technologies, cyberthreats and cybersecurity best practices, such as zero-trust architectures. Security policies are the foundation for enterprise security. Make sure to update your policies first, update your security practices and then train your employees so they understand — and, hopefully, comply — with the new policies.

- **Require strong authentication for all users.** Cyberattacks often use compromised user accounts to gain access to a business's internal resources. Requiring MFA, such as a smart card with a PIN or biometric, for every user can be effective at stopping many cyberattacks. If that's not feasible for your business, at least require users to have strong passwords that attackers won't be able to guess, and implement MFA for security professionals, system administrators, and all others with privileged access to systems and networks.

- **Refresh your network security controls.** If it's been a while since your business reviewed its network security controls, consider whether they need a refresh. For example, do your firewalls and VPN gateways offer the functionality your hybrid workforce needs? Maybe it's time to upgrade or replace them. Also, are you able to monitor network traffic for all of your users, or has cloud migration reduced your visibility? Perhaps you need to deploy additional network security software, or consider adopting cloud-based security solutions like Secure Access Service Edge.

- **Prepare for compromises.** Security breaches and other types of security incidents are inevitable. It's incredibly important to be prepared at all times to handle compromises to reduce the amount of damage that's done. Along with that, your business needs to be equipped to detect security incidents as early as possible. That means not only having the security technology in place to detect and analyze suspicious activity, but also educating employees on what the potential signs of an incident are and how to report them. Ideally, your business should foster a culture of honesty, and not punish employees for making innocent mistakes — otherwise people may hide their errors, which can allow compromises to last longer and do more harm.

- **Keep your security knowledge current.** One of the hazards of working in security is that you may be so busy that you don't have time to keep your security knowledge current. You're understandably focused on handling today's emergencies. However, not only should you stay up-to-date with the latest changes in your specialty areas, but also security is a vast field and there are always more things to learn. Cybersecurity topics such as risk assessment, cyberthreats, threat detection and zero-trust architecture apply to so many areas of security. Also, topics such as physical security often get overlooked altogether. Online courses can help you fill in the gaps.

- **Improve employee awareness of security.** All too often, security awareness activities for employees are just an hour a year of sitting through the same presentation, plus an occasional email. Security awareness activities may be perceived as a waste of time, and unfortunately, they often are. What's needed is a broader cultural shift to understanding the importance of security and the need for everyone to do their part. You can help your business change its cybersecurity culture by taking a few minutes to explain to employees why they are being required or asked to do or not do things a certain way. Cultural changes happen gradually, every time an employee buys into the need for a security practice.

Cybersecurity tips for employees

- **Be skeptical.** It's human nature to be trusting, but when you receive an email, phone call, text, social media request or other form of communication, the sender could be an imposter trying to trick you. Always do a sanity check before you open an attachment, click on a link or provide sensitive business or personal data . Does the communication look legitimate? Would this person or company send you this request? If you're not sure, call the sender and confirm that they sent the message in question. This helps you avoid phishing and other attacks intended to take advantage of your trust.

- ⦿ **Be selective.** Internet access is available almost everywhere, but security threats differ from place to place. Whenever possible, use private networks, such as your home network, instead of public networks like the public Wi-Fi at your local coffee shop. On public networks, your computer is directly exposed to attacks from the internet. Private networks use a firewall, internet router or other device to block attackers from directly connecting to your mobile and other devices. Choose private networks to reduce your risk.

- ⦿ **Be organized.** Many data breaches start with an attacker getting a regular user's password. The attacker can build from there to eventually gain access to the business's most valuable information. To help make things harder for attackers, be organized when it comes to your passwords. Use a password manager program that remembers all your passwords for you. This allows you to create a unique strong password for each business and personal website and app, and the only password you need to remember is the one for the password manager itself. But make sure the password manager's password is strong, and if it's an option, use MFA to safeguard your stored passwords.

- ⦿ **Be prepared.** Even with your security team working hard to provide cybersecurity protection, malicious activities may reach your computer. You should be prepared for them by using antimalware software and keeping your operating system and applications fully patched. However, some attacks may succeed, no matter what you do, so you need to be prepared for that too. For example, ransomware attacks can make your data and your computer inaccessible. Make sure your data is backed up in accordance with your business's policies, and verify from time to time that your backups are still working correctly. This helps ensure your information is safeguarded just in case something bad happens.

CONTINUOUS LEARNING IN CYBERSECURITY

Cybersecurity is a rapidly evolving field, with more sophisticated threats, attacks and vulnerabilities emerging on a daily basis. As a result, it's essential for cybersecurity professionals to engage in continuous learning and skill development in order to stay current with the latest trends and technologies. Let's break down why.

Role of Continuous Learning in Retaining Cybersecurity Expert

As businesses, governments, and individuals increasingly rely on interconnected systems and data, the need for robust cybersecurity measures has never been more critical. Yet, amid this era of escalating cyber threats, there is an ongoing struggle that organizations face: the cybersecurity skills gap.

The cybersecurity skills gap is the stark disparity between the demand for skilled cybersecurity professionals and the limited pool of available talent. This challenge has been exacerbated by the current climate, where many organizations find themselves under hiring freezes and shifting their budgets to different priorities. While cybersecurity remains paramount, organizations are grappling with the dilemma of securing their digital assets while minimizing costs.

As organizations strive to bridge this skills gap and navigate constrained budgets, they are discovering that it's not just about hiring new talent but also about retaining the cybersecurity experts they already have. The importance of retaining these experts cannot be overstated.

In this blog post, we will delve into the vital role of continuous learning in retaining cybersecurity experts and exploring how ongoing education and professional development programs can play a critical role.

The importance of retaining cybersecurity experts

Retaining cybersecurity experts takes on new significance in the current climate. These experts possess invaluable institutional knowledge about an organization's systems, vulnerabilities, and specific security challenges. Losing them can be a costly setback, both financially and in terms of security posture.

Moreover, experienced cybersecurity professionals have a deep understanding of an organization's unique security landscape. Their expertise extends beyond technical knowledge; it includes insights into the organization's culture, practices, and risk tolerance. Replacing them with new hires, even when budgets permit, can disrupt this delicate balance.

Continuous learning as a retention strategy

Continuous learning is a retention strategy that can be highly effective in the field of cybersecurity. Here's how it plays a pivotal role:

- **Professional growth**: Cybersecurity professionals are often passionate about their field and eager to learn. By providing opportunities for continuous learning, organizations demonstrate a commitment to their employees' professional growth. This can be achieved through access to training, certifications, workshops, and conferences.

- **Skill enhancement**: Continuous learning allows experts to deepen their expertise in specific areas and stay relevant in the face of evolving threats. This not only benefits the individual but also adds value to the organization.

- **Adaptation to new threats**: The ability to adapt to new threats quickly is critical in cybersecurity. Continuous learning ensures that professionals are aware of emerging threats and can proactively develop strategies to counter them.

- ◉ **Retention of top talent**: When organizations invest in their employees' development, they demonstrate a commitment to their well-being and career advancement. This commitment fosters loyalty and can deter talented professionals from seeking opportunities elsewhere.

- ◉ **Compliance and regulations**: The regulatory landscape in cybersecurity is constantly evolving, with new laws and compliance requirements emerging regularly. Continuous learning helps experts stay ahead of these changes, ensuring that the organization remains compliant and avoids legal pitfalls.

- ◉ **Innovation**: Cybersecurity is not just about defending against known threats; it's also about innovation. Continuous learning encourages professionals to think creatively and come up with novel solutions to security challenges. This innovative spirit can drive an organization's cybersecurity strategy forward.

IMPLEMENTING CONTINUOUS LEARNING INITIATIVES

To effectively retain cybersecurity experts through continuous learning, organizations should consider the following steps:

Create a learning culture

Building a learning culture within your organization is foundational to retaining cybersecurity experts through continuous learning. This entails creating an environment where learning is not only encouraged but deeply ingrained in the company's ethos.

Start by encouraging senior leaders to actively endorse and participate in continuous learning initiatives. When top management visibly embraces learning, it sets a compelling example and underscores the organization's commitment to skill development.

Dedicate both financial and temporal resources to support learning efforts. Budgets for training programs, workshops, and educational materials should be allocated to ensure that cybersecurity professionals have the tools they need to grow.

Additionally, recognize and reward employees who engage proactively in continuous learning. This recognition can take various forms, such as awards, promotions, or public acknowledgment of their achievements in team meetings or company communications.

There should also be a place for platforms or forums that facilitate knowledge sharing among your cybersecurity experts. These spaces foster a sense of community and provide opportunities for experts to share insights, discoveries, and best practices with their peers.

Invest in training

Investing in training programs is a direct and vital means of empowering your cybersecurity experts to enhance their skills and knowledge. Customize training programs to meet the specific needs of your cybersecurity team. Identify skill gaps through regular assessments and provide targeted training to address these gaps effectively.

Provide a range of learning resources to cater to different learning preferences. These resources may include online courses, cyber ranges, webinars, workshops, conferences, and access to cutting-edge cybersecurity tools. Ensuring accessibility to various learning formats accommodates the diverse learning styles of your team.

Allocate a dedicated budget specifically for continuous learning initiatives. This budget should remain flexible enough to adapt to evolving training needs and seize new opportunities as they arise.

Mentorship and knowledge-sharing

Encouraging mentorship and knowledge-sharing practices within your organization can significantly enhance the retention of cybersecurity experts. This step involves encouraging experienced cybersecurity professionals to take on mentoring roles, particularly with junior staff. Pairing less-experienced team members with seasoned experts allows for knowledge transfer, skill development, and the nurturing of a collaborative learning environment.

Create mechanisms for experts to share their insights, experiences, and best practices with their colleagues. This might involve regular team meetings, cross-functional workshops, or dedicated knowledge-sharing sessions.

Stay informed

Staying informed about the latest trends and best practices in cybersecurity is essential to ensure that your organization's learning initiatives remain relevant and effective. To achieve this, consider conducting ongoing assessments of the evolving skills and knowledge required in the cybersecurity field. Stay attuned to emerging threats, technologies, and regulatory changes that impact your organization's security posture.

Encourage your cybersecurity professionals to engage with industry thought leaders, follow cybersecurity news, and actively participate in relevant forums, conferences, and webinars. Sharing these insights within your organization can spark discussions and inspire innovation.

Ensure that your training materials and curriculum are updated to align with the dynamic nature of the cybersecurity landscape. Ensure that your training content reflects the latest industry standards and practices.

Measure and assess

To gauge the effectiveness of your continuous learning initiatives and ensure that they contribute to retaining cybersecurity experts, establish a framework for measurement and assessment, including:

- **Defining Key Performance Indicators (KPIs)**: Identify KPIs that are relevant to your organization's cybersecurity goals, such as reduced security incidents, improved response times, or enhanced employee satisfaction. These metrics will serve as benchmarks for progress.

- **Regular evaluation**: Periodically evaluate the impact of your continuous learning initiatives. Assess whether employees are acquiring new skills and knowledge and whether security incidents are decreasing as a result of these efforts.

- **Feedback loops:** Encourage feedback from cybersecurity professionals about the effectiveness of training programs, mentorship initiatives, and knowledge-sharing platforms. Use this feedback to refine your continuous learning strategies and adapt to evolving needs.

BUILDING A CONTINUOUS SECURITY MONITORING PROGRAM

Continuous monitoring is refining processes that are in perpetual motion. To start, consider risk tolerance when building your program. If an organization doesn't have a stable understanding of the risks to its environment or where its critical assets are, it's going to be particularly difficult to define processes to avoid threats. When creating any security program, the first step is to understand the unique risks to your environment. The same goes for continuous monitoring efforts. Define the alerting process and how threat intelligence will be escalated based on criticality, exposure and risk. This enables organizations to form a game plan when incidents arise. Otherwise, the focus is driven by the tool or analyst with limited context or understanding of the overall strategy being implemented.

All continuous security monitoring programs require tools and technology. Whether an organization standardizes on open source, proprietary software or a combination of the two doesn't matter. What matters is how data is collected from these tools in order to apply it toward your risk profile and then how it is alerted, escalated and reported. Commonly used tools for these data governance processes include SIEM, vulnerability scanners, patch management, asset discovery and network security tools.

The goal is to collect security data from all aspects of the environment for analysts and administrators to manage and monitor. A continuous security monitoring program starts to take shape when automated alerts and incident prioritization create a pool of data within these systems.

Without the ability to make quick decisions for analysts based off a tuned, correlated and orchestrated technology stack that's been refined with your risk posture, decisions are left open to human interpretation and misinterpretation. CSM systems perform the leg work to enable skilled analysts to search, query and hunt through these programs and make educated decisions. A continuous security monitoring program is not a replacement for a trained analyst, but a tool for professionals to better perform their role.

CHAPTER-15

FUTURE TRENDS AND CHALLENGES IN CYBERSECURITY

Cybersecurity has become a critical issue for businesses and individuals alike, as the threat of cyber-attacks continues to grow. The increasing amount of sensitive information being stored and transmitted online has made it more important than ever to protect against cybercrime. Despite the fact that cybersecurity measures have improved significantly in recent years, so too have the techniques of cyber criminals. As a result, the future of cybersecurity looks set to be a constant battle between those who would protect information and those who would steal it.

One of the biggest trends in the future of cybersecurity is the use of artificial intelligence (AI) and machine learning (ML) technologies. AI and ML algorithms are able to analyze large amounts of data and detect patterns and anomalies that may indicate a potential threat. This allows organizations to quickly identify and respond to cyber-attacks, reducing the risk of damage and minimizing the impact of a breach.

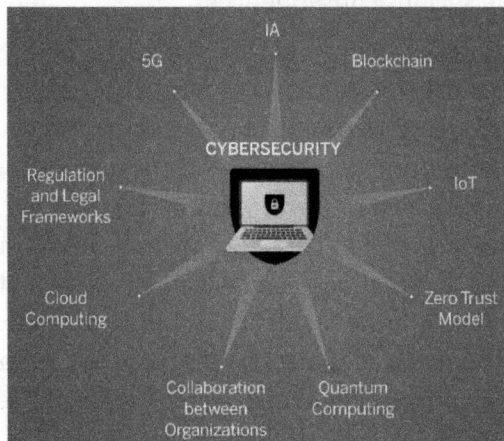

Information security professionals should readjust some widely held views on how to combat cyber risks.

AI-powered cybersecurity solutions can also be used to automate repetitive security tasks, freeing up human resources to focus on more complex issues. AI and ML can also be used to predict future cyber threats, based on historical data and trends. This will allow organizations to proactively defend against potential threats, reducing the risk of successful attacks.

Another trend in the future of cybersecurity is the use of blockchain technology. Blockchain is a decentralized ledger that can be used to securely store and transfer information. Because of its decentralized nature, it is much harder for cyber criminals to compromise a blockchain network, and so it is becoming increasingly popular for applications that require high levels of security. This is particularly true for industries such as finance, healthcare, and government, where the risk of data breaches can have serious consequences.

The rise of the Internet of Things (IoT) is also set to have a major impact on the future of cybersecurity. IoT devices are becoming increasingly common, and are often used to control critical systems and infrastructure. However, many IoT devices have poor security features, and can be easily compromised by cyber criminals. As a result, organizations will need to implement better security measures to protect against IoT-related cyber threats. This may include updating the firmware and software on IoT devices, or replacing them with more secure devices with multiple levels of security like 2FA. Another major trend in cybersecurity is the increasing focus on collaboration between organizations. In the past, organizations have often been reluctant to share information about cyber threats, for fear of revealing their own vulnerabilities. However, this is changing, as organizations recognize that cyber threats are often too complex for any single organization to tackle alone. In response, many organizations are forming partnerships and sharing information to help protect against cyber-attacks. This includes sharing threat intelligence, best practices, and resources, as well as participating in joint cyber security operations.

Cybersecurity also has a major impact on national security, and governments are taking steps to protect their critical infrastructure from cyber-attacks. One example of this is the increasing use of 'zero trust' security models, where access to sensitive information is strictly controlled and monitored. This approach reduces the risk of unauthorized access and helps to prevent cyber-attacks. Governments are also investing in research and development to stay ahead of the latest cyber threats, and to develop new technologies to better protect against these threats. This may include the development of new encryption algorithms, or the use of quantum computing to crack complex codes.

The future of cybersecurity and quantum computing is intertwined, as quantum computing has the potential to revolutionize the way data is protected and processed. Currently, most encryption algorithms used for cybersecurity rely on the fact that certain mathematical problems are difficult to solve with classical computers. However, quantum computers have the ability to solve these problems much more quickly, potentially rendering existing encryption methods obsolete.

On one hand, this means that quantum computers could be used to break existing encryption, posing a significant threat to cybersecurity. On the other hand, it also means that quantum computers could be used to develop new and more secure forms of encryption, offering unprecedented levels of protection for sensitive information.

One potential use of quantum computing in cybersecurity is the development of quantum algorithms to detect and respond to cyber-attacks. These algorithms could be used to analyze large amounts of data and detect patterns that may indicate a potential threat, allowing organizations to quickly identify and respond to cyber-attacks. Additionally, quantum algorithms could be used to predict future cyber threats, based on historical data and trends.

Cybersecurity and cloud computing are closely related, as the increased use of cloud computing has led to new security challenges and concerns. Cloud computing allows organizations to store and process data on remote servers, rather than on local devices, providing many benefits such as increased scalability and cost savings. However, the fact that sensitive data is stored on remote servers makes it more vulnerable to cyber-attacks.

One of the biggest security concerns with cloud computing is the risk of unauthorized access to sensitive information. This can occur if cyber criminals are able to compromise the security of the cloud provider's servers, or if they are able to steal login credentials or other information that allows them to access the cloud-stored data. To mitigate this risk, organizations need to implement strong access controls and encryption, and use trusted cloud providers that implement robust security measures.

Another security concern with cloud computing is the risk of data breaches. This can occur if cyber criminals are able to penetrate the security of the cloud provider's servers and access sensitive information stored on these servers. To minimize this risk, organizations need to ensure that their data is encrypted both in transit and at rest, and that they are using cloud providers that implement strong security measures to protect against data breaches.

In addition to these security concerns, there are also compliance and regulatory considerations that organizations need to be aware of when using cloud computing. For example, organizations that deal with sensitive information such as personal data or financial information, may be subject to strict regulations such as the EU's General Data Protection Regulation (GDPR) or the US' Sarbanes-Oxley Act. These regulations dictate the way that sensitive information can be stored, processed, and transmitted, and organizations need to ensure that they are in compliance with these regulations when using cloud computing. It is expected that large organizations will rely on the quantum internet to safeguard data, but that individual consumers will continue to use the classical internet.

To address these security concerns and regulatory requirements, many cloud providers are offering a range of security features, such as encryption, access controls, and monitoring. Organizations can also implement security measures such as multi-factor authentication, intrusion detection systems, and firewalls, to further enhance the security of their cloud-stored data. The integration of **5G technology** into the world of telecommunications presents both opportunities and challenges for cybersecurity. On one hand, 5G technology offers faster and more reliable communication, as well as increased connectivity, which can be beneficial for various industries and applications. On the other hand, 5G technology also introduces new security risks, as the increased speed and connectivity can be used by cyber criminals to launch more sophisticated and damaging attacks.

One major concern with 5G technology is the risk of cyber-attacks on 5G networks. 5G networks are designed to support millions of devices, which can make them a prime target for cyber criminals. Additionally, 5G networks use software-defined networking (SDN) which makes them more vulnerable to attacks that can take advantage of software vulnerabilities. To minimize this risk, organizations need to implement strong security measures, such as encryption, access controls, and intrusion detection systems, and they need to ensure that they are using trusted 5G network providers that implement robust security measures.

Another security concern with 5G technology is the risk of IoT devices becoming compromised. IoT devices are expected to play a significant role in the 5G ecosystem, and these devices often have limited computing power and security features, making them vulnerable to attacks. To minimize this risk, organizations need to ensure that their IoT devices are properly secured, and that they are using trusted IoT device manufacturers that implement strong security measures.

Furthermore, 5G technology also introduces new privacy concerns. 5G networks are designed to support a wide range of applications and services, which can result in large amounts of sensitive information being transmitted over the network. To minimize this risk, organizations need to ensure that their sensitive information is encrypted both in transit and at rest, and they need to ensure that they are using trusted 5G network providers that implement strong privacy measures. In addition to technology and collaboration, the future of cybersecurity will also be shaped by regulation and legal frameworks. Governments are increasingly passing laws and regulations aimed at protecting sensitive information, and holding organizations accountable for data breaches. This includes laws that require organizations to implement certain security measures, such as encryption and multi-factor authentication, as well as laws that set penalties for data breaches. Organizations will need to stay informed about the latest laws and regulations.

TOP CYBERSECURITY TRENDS

The Emergence of Automotive Cybersecurity Threats

Today's modern vehicles are equipped with sophisticated software, offering seamless connectivity and advanced features such as cruise control, engine timing, and driver assistance systems. However, this reliance on automation and connectivity also exposes vehicles to potential hacking risks. Utilizing technologies like Bluetooth and WiFi for communication, hackers can exploit vulnerabilities to gain control of the vehicle or even eavesdrop on conversations through built-in microphones. With the increasing adoption of automated vehicles, these threats are expected to escalate, necessitating stringent cybersecurity measures, particularly for self-driving or autonomous vehicles.

Harnessing the Power of Artificial Intelligence in Cybersecurity

AI has become a cornerstone in enhancing cybersecurity across various sectors. Through machine learning algorithms, AI has enabled the development of automated security systems capable of tasks like natural language processing, face detection, and threat detection. However, this same technology is also leveraged by malicious actors to devise sophisticated attacks aimed at circumventing security protocols. Despite these challenges, AI-driven threat detection systems offer the ability to respond to emerging threats promptly, providing vital support for cybersecurity professionals.

Mobile Devices: A Growing Target for Cyber Attacks

The proliferation of mobile devices has made them lucrative targets for cybercriminals, with a notable increase in malware and attacks targeting mobile banking and personal data. The extensive use of smartphones for various activities, including financial transactions and communication, amplifies the risks associated with potential breaches. Mobile security becomes a focal point as cybersecurity threats evolve, with anticipated trends indicating a rise in smartphone-specific viruses and malware.

Cloud Security Challenges and Solutions

As organizations rely on cloud services, ensuring robust security measures becomes paramount for data storage and operations. While cloud providers implement robust security protocols, vulnerabilities may still arise due to user-end errors, malicious software, or phishing attacks. Continuous monitoring and updates are essential to mitigate risks and safeguard confidential data stored in the cloud.

Data Breaches: A Persistent Concern

Data breaches remain a significant concern for individuals and organizations worldwide, with even minor software flaws posing potential vulnerabilities. Regulatory frameworks like the GDPR and CCPA aim to enhance data protection and privacy rights, underscoring the importance of stringent security measures. Ensuring compliance with these regulations and implementing proactive security measures are essential to mitigating the risks associated with data breaches.

IoT Security in the Era of 5G

The proliferation of 5G networks ushers in a new era of interconnectedness, particularly with the Internet of Things (IoT). While offering unprecedented connectivity, this also exposes IoT devices to vulnerabilities from external threats and software bugs. The nascent nature of 5G architecture necessitates extensive research to identify and address potential security loopholes. Manufacturers must prioritize the development of robust hardware and software solutions to reduce the risk of data breaches and network attacks.

Embracing Automation for Enhanced Cybersecurity

Automation plays a pivotal role in managing the ever-expanding volume of data and streamlining security processes. In the face of demanding workloads, automation offers valuable support to security professionals, enabling swift and efficient responses to emerging threats. Integrating security measures into agile development processes ensures the creation of more secure software solutions, particularly for large and complex applications.

Targeted Ransomware Attacks

Targeted ransomware attacks pose a significant threat to industries reliant on specific software systems, with potentially devastating consequences. Recent incidents, such as the WannaCry attack on healthcare institutions, underscore the importance of robust cybersecurity measures. Organizations must remain vigilant against ransomware threats and implement proactive strategies to mitigate risks effectively.

Escalating State-Sponsored Cyber Warfare

The escalating tensions between global powers fuel state-sponsored cyber warfare, with cyberattacks increasingly targeting critical infrastructure and sensitive data. High-profile events, including elections, are vulnerable to cyber threats, necessitating heightened security measures. Expectations for 2024 include a surge in data breaches and state-sponsored actors' exploitation of political and industrial secrets.

Mitigating Insider Threats Through Awareness

Mistakes made by individuals continue to play a significant role in data breaches, especially regarding insider threats within organizations. To address this risk, it's vital to enhance awareness and provide thorough training programs for employees. By empowering staff to recognize and address potential vulnerabilities, companies can foster a strong culture of cybersecurity awareness. This approach is essential to safeguard sensitive data and effectively minimize the impact of insider threats.

Addressing Cybersecurity Challenges in Remote Work Environments

The transition to remote work during the pandemic presents fresh cybersecurity hurdles as employees navigate less secure network setups. It's crucial for organizations to emphasize the implementation of strong security protocols, such as multi-factor authentication and secure VPNs, to shield remote workers from cyber threats effectively.

Combating Social Engineering Attacks

Social engineering attacks like phishing and identity theft remain a considerable menace for organizations, leveraging human vulnerabilities to access sensitive information unlawfully. Mitigating the risks linked with social engineering attacks requires a combination of employee training and proactive security measures.

Enhancing Security with Multi-Factor Authentication

MFA provides additional security layers by mandating users to provide diverse authentication forms before accessing accounts or systems. This proactive approach reduces the likelihood of unauthorized access and fortifies the overall cybersecurity posture. It is imperative for organizations to make the adoption of MFA a priority in order to shield against cyber threats effectively.

Defending Against International State-Sponsored Attacks

Sophisticated state-sponsored attackers significantly threaten organizations, targeting critical infrastructure and sensitive data. Proactive security measures, including real-time monitoring and multi-factor authentication, are essential in defending against these advanced threats.

Strengthening Identity and Access Management

Effective identity and access management (IAM) policies help organizations control and monitor access to sensitive data and networks. Implementing robust authentication, authorization, and access control measures is essential in safeguarding against unauthorized access and data breaches.

Real-Time Data Monitoring for Early Threat Detection

Real-time data monitoring enables organizations to detect and respond promptly to suspicious activity, reducing the risk of data breaches and cyber-attacks. Automated alerts and log monitoring are crucial in identifying potential threats and minimizing their impact.

Securing Connected Vehicles Against Cyber Threats

The increasing connectivity of vehicles exposes them to cyber threats, necessitating robust security measures to protect against potential attacks. Encryption, authentication, and real-time monitoring are essential to safeguarding connected vehicles against automotive hacking.

Leveraging AI for Enhanced Security

Artificial intelligence (AI) offers significant potential to revolutionize cybersecurity, enabling real-time threat detection and response. Organizations should leverage AI-driven solutions to strengthen their security posture and mitigate emerging cyber threats effectively.

Ensuring Security for IoT Devices

As the number of Internet of Things (IoT) devices continues to grow, ensuring robust security measures becomes increasingly important. Organizations must prioritize the security of their IoT devices, implementing regular updates and safeguards to protect against potential vulnerabilities.

Strengthening Cloud Security Measures

Cloud computing introduces new security challenges, requiring organizations to implement robust security measures to protect against data breaches and cyber threats. Encryption, authentication, and regular patching are essential components of effective cloud security strategies, ensuring the integrity and confidentiality of cloud-based data and applications.

NEXT UP WITH CYBER SECURITY TRENDS

AI and ML in Cybersecurity

Integrating artificial intelligence (AI) and machine learning (ML) will play a pivotal role in cybersecurity. AI-powered threat detection, anomaly detection, and automated response systems will become more sophisticated in identifying and mitigating cyber threats. Adversarial AI and ML attacks will also challenge cybersecurity professionals to develop robust defenses.

Zero Trust Security Models

Adopting Zero Trust Architecture (ZTA) will expand further as organizations recognize the limitations of traditional perimeter-based security models. ZTA's principles of continuous verification and the principle of "never trust, always verify" will become more widespread to secure sensitive data and resources.

Quantum Computing Resistant Cryptography

The development of quantum computing-resistant cryptography will be essential as quantum computing technology advances. Organizations will need to transition to cryptographic algorithms that can withstand quantum attacks, ensuring the continued security of data and communications.

Cloud Security Evolution

Cloud security is always a priority, with organizations focusing on securing their cloud-native environments and addressing the challenges of misconfigurations and data exposure. Technologies like CASBs and CSPM will gain prominence.

5G Network Security

With the rollout of 5G networks, there will be an increased emphasis on 5G network security. Faster speeds and lower latency will introduce new security challenges, including protecting IoT devices connected to 5G networks and ensuring the integrity of critical infrastructure.

IoT Security

As the IoT ecosystem expands, securing IoT devices will be critical. Enhanced security standards, regulations, and improved IoT device management will be essential to mitigate risks associated with insecure IoT devices.

Supply Chain Security

Organizations will strongly emphasize supply chain security to prevent and detect attacks targeting the software and hardware supply chain. Enhanced visibility into the supply chain and stringent security measures will be implemented to reduce the risk of compromise.

Biometric and Behavioral Authentication

Secure authentication methods, such as facial recognition and fingerprint scanning, will evolve to offer more robust security, with liveness detection and behavioral analytics to prevent spoofing. Multi-modal biometric authentication will become more prevalent.

Privacy Regulations and Data Protection

Privacy regulations will continue evolving, and organizations must adapt to stricter data protection requirements. Consumer data privacy and consent management will become more significant, and businesses must ensure compliance with global data privacy laws.

Cybersecurity Workforce Development

Efforts to address the cybersecurity skills shortage will intensify. More comprehensive training programs, certifications, and partnerships between academic institutions and the private sector will be established to nurture a skilled cybersecurity workforce.

Human-Centric Security

User-centric security awareness and training programs will be expanded to reduce the risk of social engineering attacks. Behavioral analytics and user-focused security tools will help identify unusual user behavior and potential insider threats.

Automated Threat Hunting

Automated threat hunting and threat intelligence platforms will gain prominence in proactively identifying and mitigating emerging threats. These solutions will help organizations stay ahead of threat actors by continuously monitoring for signs of compromise.

International Cybersecurity Collaboration

Collaboration between governments, international organizations, and cybersecurity experts will intensify to address global cyber threats effectively. Cybersecurity information sharing and coordinated responses to cyber incidents will become more common.

Regulatory and Legal Challenges

With new cybersecurity laws, standards, and compliance requirements being introduced, the legal and regulatory landscape will continue to evolve. Organizations must navigate these complex regulations to avoid legal consequences and reputational damage.

Cyber Insurance

The cyber insurance market will grow as organizations recognize the need for financial protection against cyber incidents. Cyber insurance policies will become more tailored to specific industry risks and compliance requirements.

AI-Driven Security Testing

AI-powered penetration testing and vulnerability assessment tools will become more sophisticated in identifying weaknesses in systems and applications, allowing organizations to address security flaws proactively.

Incident Response and Recovery Planning

The development and testing of incident response and recovery plans will be a focus for organizations. The capacity to detect and respond to cyber incidents and recover from them will be critical to minimizing the impact of breaches.

Smart Cities and Critical Infrastructure Security

As smart city initiatives and the digitization of critical infrastructure expand, security measures for these interconnected systems will be paramount. Protecting essential services like power grids and transportation systems will be a top priority.

AI-Powered Cybercriminals

Cybercriminals will increasingly employ AI and ML in their attacks, making them more challenging to detect and mitigate. Adversarial AI will be used to evade security measures and enhance attack strategies.

Ethical Hacking and Bug Bounty Programs

Organizations will continue to embrace ethical hacking and bug bounty programs to detect system vulnerabilities. Crowdsourced security testing will become more common, allowing organizations to proactively fix security issues.

THE EVOLVING THREAT LANDSCAPE

The world of cybersecurity is dynamic, with new threats emerging as quickly as technology evolves. Some of the most significant threats today are ransomware attacks, social engineering attacks, state-sponsored attacks, data breaches, insider threats, AI-driven attacks, and 5G and IoT threats.

- ◉ **Ransomware Attacks:** Ransomware attacks have significantly increased in frequency and sophistication. These attacks involve hackers encrypting a victim's data and demanding a ransom in exchange for the decryption key. In recent years, we have seen an escalation in ransomware attacks, often targeting large organizations and critical infrastructure. Cybercriminals are also adopting "double extortion" tactics, where they threaten to leak the stolen data if the ransom is not paid.

- ◉ **Social Engineering Attacks:** These attacks manipulate people into revealing confidential information, such as passwords or credit card numbers. Phishing is a common type of social engineering attack, where attackers impersonate a trusted entity to trick victims into disclosing sensitive information. Social engineering attacks are particularly challenging to tackle as they exploit human vulnerabilities rather than technical ones.

- ◉ **State-Sponsored Attacks:** These are cyberattacks conducted or sponsored by nation-states, often aimed at causing disruption, stealing sensitive information, or gaining strategic advantage. These attacks are usually sophisticated and hard to trace, posing significant threats to nations and organizations alike.

- ◉ **Data Breaches:** Data breaches involve unauthorized access to sensitive data, often with the intent to steal and sell it on the dark web. These attacks can result in significant financial losses and damage to an organization's reputation.

- ◉ **Insider Threats:** Not all threats originate from outside the organization. Disgruntled employees, contractors, or business partners with access to sensitive information pose significant insider threats. These threats are especially challenging to mitigate due to the trust and access privileges typically given to these individuals.

- ◉ **AI-Driven Attacks:** With the rise of artificial intelligence (AI), cybercriminals are using AI to make their attacks more sophisticated and harder to detect. AI can automate the hacking process, allowing cybercriminals to carry out attacks at scale and speed previously unimaginable.

- ◉ **5G and IoT Threats:** The rapid proliferation of IoT devices and the advent of 5G technology has expanded the attack surface for cybercriminals. These devices often lack adequate security measures, making them easy targets for cyberattacks.

Current and Future Defenses

The escalation of these threats has led to an equal reaction in defense. Cybersecurity professionals are continually developing new strategies and tools to counter these threats. Some notable current defenses include the use of AI for threat detection and response, implementation of robust security protocols, and continuous security awareness training.

The future of cybersecurity lies in a proactive approach, where organizations not only respond to threats but anticipate them. This includes integrating security into the design phase of products, continuously monitoring and analyzing threats, and fostering a culture of security awareness.

It's crucial to remember that while technology plays a significant role in cybersecurity, humans are often the weakest link. Therefore, continuous education and training are critical to ensuring that everyone is equipped with the knowledge and skills to detect and prevent cyber threats.

In light of these threats, it's clear that the role of cybersecurity professionals has never been more critical. As we progress further into the digital age, our defenses must evolve in step with the threats we face. So, how are we meeting these challenges head-on?

One of the key strategies in combating these threats is the deployment of advanced cybersecurity measures. These measures include technologies and practices designed to protect systems, networks, and data from cyber threats.

- **Advanced Threat Protection (ATP):** ATP systems are security solutions that defend against sophisticated malware or hacking-based attacks targeting sensitive data. Advanced threat protection solutions can be available as software or as managed services. They typically include a combination of endpoint protection, network security, malware protection, and threat intelligence.

- **Behavioural Analytics:** To detect malicious activity, many organizations are now implementing behavioral analytics. This involves using machine learning algorithms to analyze patterns of user behavior and identify unusual activity that could signify a cyber threat.

- **Artificial Intelligence and Machine Learning:** AI and machine learning are increasingly being used in cybersecurity. These technologies can learn from past incidents to predict and identify potential threats. They can also automate responses to these threats, reducing the time it takes to resolve them.

- **Cloud Technology:** As businesses increasingly move to the cloud, it's crucial to have robust security measures in place. This includes data encryption, network firewalls, and access control measures.

- **End-User Awareness and Training:** One of the most effective defenses against cyber threats is end-user awareness. This involves training employees on how to identify and respond to potential cyber threats. As a Cybersecurity Tutor, I can attest to the power of knowledge and awareness in combating these threats.

The evolving threat landscape has also reshaped the role of cybersecurity professionals. Today, it's not enough to simply have a strong technical knowledge base. Cybersecurity professionals must also possess a deep understanding of the business landscape and the ability to communicate complex security concepts to non-technical team members. They need to be proactive, constantly staying abreast of the latest trends and threats. They must also be able to think strategically, planning for both current and future threats.

Additionally, cybersecurity professionals need to have a strong ethical grounding. The nature of their work often involves accessing sensitive information and systems, and it's crucial that this access is not misused.

As a Cybersecurity Tutor, I am committed to equipping my students with the skills and knowledge they need to thrive in this challenging and ever-evolving field. This involves not only teaching the technical aspects of cybersecurity but also fostering an understanding of the ethical responsibilities that come with the role.

In conclusion, the modern cybersecurity landscape is complex and rapidly evolving. However, by staying informed, deploying advanced security measures, and fostering a culture of security awareness, we can effectively navigate this challenging landscape. The role of cybersecurity professionals in this journey cannot be understated. As we forge ahead into the digital future, it's clear that the work of cybersecurity professionals will continue to be crucial in safeguarding our information and digital infrastructure.

CYBERSECURITY POLICY AND INTERNATIONAL COOPERATION

The effective combating of Cybercrimes require international cooperation among countries, law enforcement agencies and institutions backed by laws, international relations, conventions, directives and recommendations to fight Cybercrime. Cooperation among countries to the widest extent possible and efficient mutual legal assistance is the need of the day.

The International Telecommunications Union (ITU), a United Nations agency that is considered the "premier global forum through which parties work towards consensus on a wide range of issues affecting the future direction of the ICT industry" (ITU, n.d.), launched the Global Cybersecurity Agenda , which is "a framework for international cooperation aimed at enhancing confidence and security in the information society". The ITU Global Cybersecurity Agenda identifies five strategic pillars: legal, technical, organizational, capacity-building, and cooperation.

The *legal* pillar focuses on harmonized regulations and laws relating to cybersecurity and cyber-dependent and cyber-facilitated crimes. Cases in point are cybercrime laws (see Cybercrime Modules 2 and 3), data protection laws and regulation (see Cybercrime Module 10), cybersecurity laws, and other related laws (e.g., Denmark, Danish Data Protection Act of 2018; Fiji, Crimes Decree 2009: Division 6 - Computer Offences; and United Arab Emirates, Federal Law No. (1) of 2006 on Electronic Commerce and Transactions; and the United Kingdom, Computer Misuse Act of 1990 and Data Protection Act of 2018.

The *technical* pillar covers existing technical institutions, cybersecurity standards and protocols, and the measures needed to deal with cybersecurity threats. An example of a technical institution is a Computer Emergency Response Team (CERT), which is defined as "an organization or team that provides, to a well-defined constituency, services and support for both preventing and responding to computer security incidents" (Wahid, 2016). CERTs vary in capabilities depending on the range and combination of reactive, proactive and/or security quality management services offered (CMU-SEI, 2006). For example, these services can include promptly responding to an incident so that the attack can be quickly contained and investigated, and to facilitate rapid recovery to a pre-incident state (Borodkin, 2001). In addition to incident response, a CERT may engage in other activities, such as conducting vulnerability assessments and providing security briefings; these additional activities depend on the organization. Countries can have national, government, and sector-specific CERTs and Computer Security Incident Response Teams (or CSIRTs), or a combination of some or all of these . CERTs/CSIRTs have also created groups within their regions to share information and coordinate activities, among other things (e.g., Asia-Pacific CERT or APCERT; Africa CERT or AfricaCERT).

A brief history of EU–India Cyber Cooperation

The very nature of a cybercrime makes it difficult to address: it occurs in the borderless realm of cyberspace, and both the criminal and the victim could be located in multiple national jurisdictions. This underscores the need for flexible frameworks of international cooperation to enhance cybersecurity. As the United Nations Office of Drugs and Crime (UNODC) has observed, these mechanisms could include harmonised national cybercrime laws, or bilateral, regional and multilateral cybercrime treaties or arrangements.

The focus of EU-India cyber-cooperation is still primarily on bilateral summits, joint agreements, partnerships, and working groups. Both parties also engage with and through several international cooperation mechanisms for advancing responsible state behaviour in cyberspace. Such initiatives include the India-EU Joint ICT Working Group, India-EU Connectivity Partnership, and the Indian-EU Cyber Dialogue.

India-EU Bilateral Cooperation on Cybersecurity

India and the EU have cooperated on cybersecurity since the early 2000s. They both have, on several occasions, reaffirmed their commitment to "an open, free, secure, stable, peaceful and accessible cyberspace that enables economic growth and innovation." The following table outlines the highlights of EU-India engagements over the years in the cyber domain:

Year	Forum or Platform	Outcome
2003	4th India-EU Summit	India and EU agreed to enhance cooperation in the area of data protection and cybersecurity in the information society sector.
2010	India EU Joint Declaration on International	India and EU agreed to enhance mutual
	Terrorism	assistance in the area of cybersecurity.
2016	13th India-EU Summit	India and EU reaffirmed the need to strengthen
2017	14th India-EU Summit	cyber-cooperation.
2020	15th India-EU Summit	India and EU underlined the need to increase global cyber resilience, including in the health sector.
		Both sides also agreed to increase joint efforts on cybersecurity through the India-EU Connectivity Partnership.
2020	India-EU Connectivity Partnership and the	India and EU agreed to increase joint efforts
	Joint Statement on the India-EU Leaders'	on cybersecurity through the India-EU Con-
	Meeting	nectivity Partnership and the Joint Statement on the India-EU Leaders' Meeting.
2020	India-EU Strategic Partnership: A	India and EU agreed to strengthen coop-
	Roadmap to 2025	eration, work towards tangible outcomes on cybersecurity, and continue to expand existing cooperative efforts.
2020	India-EU Counter-Terrorism Dialogue	The most recent Dialogue where the use of cyberspace by terrorists was discussed.
2020	India-EU Cyber Dialogue	The most recent Dialogue, which was held virtually.
2021	India-EU Joint ICT Working Group	The most recent meeting of the Working Group.

The India-EU Joint ICT Working Group is part of the EU's commitment of working with like-minded partners in "achieving common global objective: a green, digital, just and resilient future for the next generation". The Working Group works on a wide-range of subjects including artificial intelligence, digital platforms, data governance, cybersecurity and networks. Meanwhile, the India-EU Cyber Dialogue focuses on areas of cooperation in cyberspace including internet governance, cyber diplomacy at UN activities, regional cooperation, capacity-building, and emerging cyber-related technologies.

International Mechanisms for Promoting Cybersecurity

Various international cooperation mechanisms exist for advancing responsible state behaviour in cyberspace: the Council of Europe's Convention on Cybercrime, also known as the Budapest Convention; and three UN First Committee state processes, namely, (a) the Group of Governmental Experts (GGE); (b) the Open-Ended Working Group (OEWG); and (c) the recently proposed Programme of Action (PoA) that seeks to end the dual-track discussions (GGE / OEWG) and in their place establish a permanent UN forum on cyberspace. Of these mechanisms, the EU (or individual EU Member States) and India have engaged chiefly on and through the GGE and OEWG. The UN third committee is responsible for the work on the Ad Hoc Committee to Elaborate a Comprehensive International Convention on Countering the Use of Information and Communications Technologies for Criminal Purposes.

The Budapest Convention

The Council of Europe's Convention on Cybercrime, also known as the Budapest Convention was opened for signature in Budapest in November 2001 and came into force in July 2004 as the first international instrument on cybercrime. It is currently the only binding international instrument on cybercrime and seeks to pursue "a common criminal policy aimed at the protection of society against cybercrime, inter alia, by adopting appropriate legislation and fostering international co-operation." Although it is a Council of Europe (COE) instrument, the Convention permits states that are not members of the Council of Europe to accede to the Convention, subject to the unanimous consent of all parties. As of July 2022, there are 66 parties to the Convention.

Overall, the Convention deals with offences such as computer-related fraud, illegal access, misuse of devices, and child pornography. Its principal aims are to: (1) Harmonise domestic laws on cybercrime; (2) Support the investigation and prosecution of cybercrimes; and (3) Facilitate international cooperation on cybercrime. Since 2006, the first Additional Protocol to the Convention that criminalises 'acts of a racist and xenophobic nature committed through computer systems' has been in effect. A recently approved Second Additional Protocol on 'enhanced cooperation and disclosure of electronic evidence' opened for signature by states in May 2022.

EU and Indian positions on the Budapest Convention

The EU continues to support third countries that wish to accede to the Budapest Convention, and to work towards improving international cooperation between law enforcement agencies, judicial authorities, and service providers, in which the European Commission participates in negotiations on the EU's behalf. The EU also engages in multilateral exchanges on cybercrime to ensure the respect of human rights and fundamental freedoms, through inclusiveness, transparency, and by leveraging available expertise, with the goal of delivering value for all.

India has refrained from acceding to the Budapest Convention. While India has not released any official statements regarding the matter, information in the public domain suggests a few possible reasons for its hesitancy. First, as the Convention allows for trans-border access to data, it might be seen as infringing on India's national sovereignty. Second, as India was not involved in the original drafting process, there could be a perception that its priorities are not adequately reflected in the Convention. Finally, the perceived lack of effectiveness of the Convention's Mutual Legal Assistance (MLA) regime could be a disincentive for accession.

In January 2020, the UN General Assembly (UNGA), on the basis of the report of the Third Committee (A/74/401), via a resolution established an open-ended ad hoc intergovernmental committee to draft an international convention on cybercrime (2019-2020). India voted in favour of the resolution.

The UN Group of Governmental Experts (GGE)

The UN First Committee on International Security and Disarmament is where states exchange views on issues related to international peace and security, including those related to cyberspace. These discussions take place through the Group of Governmental Experts (GGE) on advancing responsible state behaviour in cyberspace, and the Open-Ended Working Group (OEWG) on developments in the field of information and telecommunications.

The UNGA established the first GGE in 2004 to explore the impact of developments in ICT on international peace and security. Six GGEs have convened to date, with each Group comprising individual experts representing interested UN Member States, including the five permanent members of the UN Security Council. The mandate of the GGEs has been to examine threats in cyberspace along with possible cooperative measures, and to maintain an open, secure, peaceful and accessible ICT environment. Towards this end, discussions have focused on existing and emerging cyber-threats; cyber norms, rules and principles for states; confidence-building measures (CBMs); the application of international law to the use of ICTs; and international cooperation and cyber capacity building (CCB).

The report of the sixth GGE to the UN General Assembly in 2021 identified a distinct set of norms for promoting responsible behaviour among states; reaffirmed that international law is the basis for preventing conflict and promoting a peaceful ICT environment; reiterated the importance of CBMs to strengthen cybersecurity; and underscored the importance of cooperation related to ICT security. With the completion of the sixth GGE's work in May 2021, no immediate plans have been issued to renew the GGE format. In retrospect, the GGE's two key achievements have been to outline a global cybersecurity agenda; and to introduce the principle that international law applies to cyberspace.

EU and Indian positions on the UN GGE

While the EU itself is not a member of the GGEs, many individual EU member states have held expert positions on past GGEs. It is the EU's position though that it continues to work with international partners to advance and promote an open, stable and secure cyberspace where international law, particularly the UN Charter, is respected, and the voluntary non-binding norms, rules and principles of responsible state behaviour are adhered to. The EU's Cybersecurity Strategy (2020) indicates a clear need for the EU and its member states to take a more proactive stance in discussions at the UN and other relevant international fora. It further states that the EU is best placed to advance, coordinate and consolidate EU member states' positions in international fora, and should develop an EU position on the application of international law in cyberspace.

India was an active member of the fifth (2016-17) and sixth (2019-21) GGEs. While it was not a member of the third GGE for 2014–15, it responded to the Group's deliberations by initiating a national study for examining the norms for cooperation proposed by the GGE and designing a set of national cyber norms. In 2021, India endorsed the long-standing GGE view that the application of international law to cyberspace is critical for building a secure and peaceful ICT environment. India has also expressed its hope that discussions at the UN and other multilateral forums will continue to focus on cooperative measures, CBMs, and cyber norms. In June 2021, India reiterated the importance of a collaborative rules-based approach in cyberspace, and of leveraging the positive momentum generated by the GGE and the OEWG in order to "find further common ground and improve upon the already agreed cyber norms and rules."

The UN Open-Ended Working Group (OEWG)

In 2019, the UNGA set up the Open-Ended Working Group (OEWG) to provide a "democratic, transparent and inclusive platform" for UN member states to participate in the process of determining the rules for ICTs and international security. The OEWG's mandate is to develop rules, norms and principles of responsible behaviour of States; devise ways to implement these rules; identify CBMs and capacity-building measures; and study cyber threats and the application of international law to cyberspace.

The first OEWG of 2019-20 conducted substantive sessions and consultative meetings, allowing UN member states to participate along with other stakeholders such as the academia, industry, and non-government organisations. Its final report, adopted on 12 March 2021, included a set of recommendations on "Rules, Norms and Principles for Responsible State Behaviour, International Law, Confidence-building Measures, Cyber Capacity-building and Regular Institutional Dialogue". The UN General Assembly has since established a new OEWG (2021-25) on security of and in the use of ICTs. The second OEWG aims to build on the work of the GGEs and the previous OEWG and held its first organisational session in June 2021.

EU and Indian positions on the UN OEWG

The EU participated in the first OEWG, contributing interventions and submissions on behalf of EU member states throughout the deliberations. Since the second OEWG began its deliberations, the EU has made submissions to the second OEWG substantive session in 2022 on each of the topics under discussion, namely: organisational matters; existing and potential threats; further developing and implementing the rules, norms and principles of responsible state behaviour; how international law applies to states' use of ICTs; CBMs; capacity-building and regular institutional dialogue.

India actively participated in the first OEWG and contributed substantively towards its final report. In its statement at the June 2019 Organisational Session of the first OEWG, India stated that a *"common understanding on how international law is applicable to State's use of ICTs is important for promoting an open, secure, stable, accessible, interoperable and peaceful ICT environment."* It assured full support to the OEWG, and also provided comments on the initial pre-draft of the OEWG's report and on the zero draft of the OEWG's final substantive report. As mentioned in Section 3.2.1 of this report, in 2021 India lauded the outcomes of the OEWG, and noted the need to build further on its deliberations and the points of consensus achieved.

The Proposed Programme of Action (PoA)

In October 2020, over 40 countries (including EU member states) proposed the establishment of a Programme of Action (PoA) for advancing responsible state behaviour in cyberspace. The PoA seeks to end the dual-track discussions of the GGE and OEWG, and to establish a permanent UN forum to consider the use of ICTs by states in the context of international security. It is envisaged as a single, long-term, inclusive and progress-oriented platforms.

The PoA is expected to offer UN member states newer opportunities to create a framework and political commitment based on recommendations, norms and principles already agreed; have regular, implementation-focused working-level meetings; step up cooperation and capacity building; conduct regular review conferences to ensure the PoA's relevance; and conduct multistakeholder consultations on cyber-related issues.

EU and Indian positions on the PoA

The proposed PoA has met with a mixed response. The EU, through the High Representative together with its member states, aims to take forward their inclusive and consensus-based proposal for a political commitment on the PoA in the UN. The EU's Cybersecurity Strategy specifies that building on the existing acquis as endorsed by the UN General Assembly, the PoA offers a platform for cooperation and exchange of best practices within the UN, and a possible mechanism to implement the norms of responsible state behaviour and promote capacity development.

Some stakeholders believe that the PoA could indeed act as an effective way forward by combining the best of the GGE and OEWG; and eliminating the redundancies and duplications of having two bodies dealing with similar issues and being more inclusive, action-oriented and impactful. India and several other states, however, see a possibility of future discussions on ICTs and cybersecurity continuing within the framework of the OEWG 2021–25. In February 2022, in response to a Parliament Question about the Indian stance on the PoA, the Ministry of External Affairs (MEA) simply noted that "India has been participating in UN-mandated cyber processes and consultations".

Actionable Recommendations

The March 2022 roundtable in New Delhi on enhancing global cybersecurity cooperation served as a curtain-raiser for the ESIWA–ORF roundtable series. Existing cyber efforts between the EU and India were highlighted, and a concise description of international processes for cyber cooperation was provided. The deliberations were guided by three questions:

- ◉ How can EU and Indian diplomatic officials in charge of cyber issues cooperate bilaterally and multilaterally to increase adherence to cyber norms and implementation of cyber confidence-building measures?

- ◉ How can EU and Indian private sector stakeholders be best involved in implementing the normative framework for responsible state behaviour in cyberspace?

- ◉ How can the EU and India jointly address, on a bilateral and multilateral basis, the rise in increasingly lucrative and organised forms of cybercrime such as ransomware?

Based on the roundtable discussions, the authors of this report have drafted seven actionable recommendations. These will be put forward for formal discussions between the EU and India, and eventually will be submitted for consideration during the EU-India Cybersecurity Dialogue meetings.

Recommendation 1: Build upon and expand EU-India cyber interactions

The EU and India could build upon existing cyber interactions by exchanging best practices and lessons learned on the implementation of cyber norms. Both parties could work towards enforcing and promoting responsible behaviour through diplomatic means; engage in discussions on the drafting and implementation of relevant international standards for new technologies such as 5G; and undertake joint efforts to advance global cyber resilience. The Indian government has expressed interest in having points of contact among agencies through which it can share information transnationally. Dedicated EU and Indian points of contact at the policy and technical levels could therefore be appointed to provide guidance for determining cyber roles and responsibilities, coordination functions, and readiness requirements.

Recommendation 2: Promote multistakeholder engagement at various levels

The EU and India agree that multistakeholder initiatives have a valuable contribution to make towards governmental policy positions. However, non-governmental stakeholders sometimes confirm that it is difficult to have their perspectives heard at intergovernmental forums. The EU and India could forge a joint agreement on how they could advance multistakeholder engagement both domestically and internationally, with clearly formulated guidelines for interaction.

Private sector inputs are deemed crucial for international processes, and there is a need to ensure that the latter encourage companies to become involved. As a first step, specialised working groups or bodies in the EU and India that include representatives of both government agencies and industry must be encouraged. These groups could then come together, ideally through regular initiatives of the groups' chairs. Such approaches could be crucial for building public-private consensus and partnerships and could foster a more inclusive ecosystem for cyber cooperation. Relevant subjects for public-private collaboration could include protecting the core stability of the Internet; supply chain security; security-by-design; committing not to hack-back; and commitments not to cyber-attack citizens.

Recommendation 3: Jointly undertake capacity-building exercises and confidence-building measures

The EU and India agree that undertaking joint capacity building exercises and confidence building measures (through training, and the sharing of knowledge and best practices) is necessary, and that private sector and academic stakeholders should be involved, particularly in areas such as promoting cybersecurity, strengthening encryption standards, and developing the capacity of cyber professionals. It is believed that the limited engagement of several Member States with UN processes on cybersecurity could be because of a lack of capacities. The EU and India could therefore cooperate to help close capacity gaps in third countries with respect to cyber diplomacy and cybercrime. European and Indian experiences and mechanisms related to cybersecurity could act as a valuable guide for other nations to bolster their cyber-capabilities. Support to third countries could also be strategic, focusing on issues such as helping eradicate the safe havens for cybercriminals operating out of these countries; or facilitating cooperation among third countries from an enforcement perspective.

The Indo-Pacific region presents a potential new theatre for activities directed at enhancing global cybersecurity. India is already a key actor in the region, and with the EU's adoption of its Indo-Pacific strategy in September 2021, the region could present new opportunities for EU-India-supported capacity development and confidence-building exercises. Strengthening capabilities to counter ransomware in particular could be an important area of intervention. Finally, cybercrime prevention and awareness-raising efforts ought to be a critical component of all capacity-building initiatives as the weakest link is sometimes the person(s) handling the computer. Evolving a joint approach to awareness raising among citizens, bilaterally and multilaterally, would thus be valuable.

Recommendation 4: Explore the implications and possible benefits of the Programme of Action

Supporters of the proposed Programme of Action (PoA), including the EU, see it as a possible action-oriented UN forum that could help further the practical implementation of cyber-tools, promote joint efforts for capacity building, and operationalise cyber norms and principles through multistakeholder engagement. India is closely following developments regarding the PoA and is keen to better understand how it will be shaped, while remaining interested in its possible evolution as a forum for action. It is important therefore that the implications and potential benefits of the PoA are more closely explored, discussed and understood by both sides. The PoA's possible potential for adopting approaches of common interest – such as taking a regional approach to understand and address the needs of individual Member States – could also be examined by the EU and India in greater detail.

Recommendation 5: Work towards crafting new standards for data governance and data sharing

From a non-governmental perspective, the EU and India could work towards showcasing to the world a new approach for creating standards in two areas, namely how data governance can be conducted and how data can be shared swiftly (with or without MLAT requirements). Given that most platforms tend to come from the United States or China, there is a perceived need for a third non-aligned platform. The EU and India could jointly identify (a) what data can be shared and how, and (b) the common standards required for the data and infrastructure layers in question. Both parties could then aim to work towards creating a common joint platform which sets standards in a non-aligned manner. Political dialogue between both parties and a shared normative framework could advance mutual trust and the agenda on data.

Recommendation 6: Work towards developing global standards in selected domains

With a view towards building open, secure public digital infrastructure, the EU and India could work towards developing global standards in domains such as cryptocurrency regulation, anonymity, and counter ransomware. Other immediate areas for cooperation could include setting standards to enhance the security of software and of digital supply chains.

Recommendation 7: Continue to build trust through increased cooperation

The EU and India could achieve much through continued bilateral and multilateral cooperation, and building mutual trust should a key focus of future cyber efforts. Towards this end, sustained interactions should be undertaken at European cybercrime platforms and conferences, and at the new UN Cybercrime Ad Hoc Committee (which is still at a nascent stage of its negotiations and thus presents an opportunity for the EU and India to coordinate on key issues of mutual interest). There is also a need to conduct exchanges on a possible future Convention in the UN Third Committee, and to build upon the deliberations of the existing UN Intergovernmental Expert Group on Cyber Crime. Finally, it is important to ensure that crime does not pay. The EU and India could therefore collaborate to strengthen mechanisms for facilitating cybercrime investigations across borders, along with freezing and confiscations measures directed against perpetrators of cybercrime and cross-border restitution measures for victims.

SHAPING THE FUTURE OF CYBERSECURITY

With the rapid advancement of technology, the cybersecurity landscape is constantly evolving. The interconnectedness of systems, the rise of **cloud computing**, and the proliferation of Internet of Things (IoT) devices have created new avenues for cyber threats.

The following factors highlight the role of technology trends in shaping the future of cybersecurity:

Evolving Threat Landscape

As technology progresses, cyber threats become increasingly sophisticated. Hackers are continuously developing new attack vectors and techniques to breach networks and exploit vulnerabilities. Organizations must stay vigilant and adapt their cybersecurity strategies to mitigate these evolving threats.

Proactive Defense

Latest trends in cybersecurity technology enable organizations to adopt proactive defense mechanisms. This includes advanced threat intelligence platforms, next-generation firewalls, and real-time monitoring systems. By leveraging these technologies, businesses can identify and respond to threats in a timely manner, reducing the potential impact of cyber attacks.

Automation and Orchestration

Automation and orchestration are becoming integral cyber security technology trends. Through the use of machine learning algorithms and artificial intelligence (AI), security systems can automatically detect, analyze, and respond to threats. This helps organizations improve incident response times and minimize the risk of human error. Organizations need to stay vigilant and adapt their security measures to address the ever-changing landscape of trends in information security.

Artificial Intelligence (AI) and Machine Learning: Emerging Technologies in Cyber Security

Threat Detection and Response

AI and machine learning play a crucial role in threat detection and response. These emerging technologies in cyber security can analyze vast amounts of data, identify patterns, and detect anomalies that may indicate a cyber attack. By leveraging AI-driven solutions, organizations can enhance their security analytics and automate incident response processes.

Behavioral Analytics

AI-powered behavioral analytics helps identify suspicious activities and detect insider threats. Machine learning algorithms can analyze user behavior, network traffic, and system logs to establish baseline patterns and identify deviations that may indicate malicious activities.

Predictive Analytics

AI and machine learning models can also be used for predictive analytics in cybersecurity. By analyzing historical data and patterns, these technologies can identify potential vulnerabilities, predict emerging threats, and recommend proactive measures to mitigate risks.

Keeping up with the evolving trends in information security is crucial to safeguarding sensitive data and mitigating potential cyber threats.

Cybersecurity in BFSI: Threats, Challenges, and Key Trends

The banking and financial services industry (BFSI) faces unique cybersecurity challenges due to the sensitivity and value of the data involved. Threats such as phishing attacks, ransomware, and identity theft are prevalent in this sector. Organizations must prioritize robust cybersecurity measures to safeguard customer data, financial transactions, and business operations by making the most of cyber security technology trends.

Secure Banking Platforms

To combat cyber threats, the BFSI sector is adopting secure banking platforms that leverage encryption, multi-factor authentication, and secure communication channels. These technologies provide customers with secure access to their accounts and protect sensitive financial information.

Fraud Detection and Prevention

AI-driven fraud detection systems are gaining prominence in the BFSI industry. These systems can analyze transactional data in real-time, detect suspicious patterns, and flag potential fraudulent activities. By leveraging machine learning algorithms, organizations can minimize financial losses and protect their customers from fraud.

Data Protection and Compliance

Data protection and regulatory compliance are critical in the BFSI sector. Organizations must adhere to strict data privacy regulations, such as the General Data Protection Regulation (GDPR) and Payment Card Industry Data Security Standard (PCI DSS). Implementing robust data protection measures and ensuring compliance is essential for maintaining customer trust and avoiding costly penalties.

Importance of Cybersecurity in Digital Transformation Era

Risks and Vulnerabilities in Digital Transformation

Digital transformation initiatives bring numerous benefits, but they also introduce new risks and vulnerabilities. Increased connectivity, adoption of cloud services, and reliance on third-party vendors create potential entry points for cyber attacks. Organizations must prioritize cybersecurity as they embrace digital transformation to safeguard critical assets and maintain operational continuity.

Cybersecurity by Design

In the digital transformation era, cybersecurity should be embedded in the design and implementation of new technologies and processes. This includes incorporating security measures at every stage of development, performing regular security assessments, and training employees on cybersecurity best practices.

Employee Awareness and Training

Human error is one of the leading causes of cybersecurity incidents. Organizations need to invest in employee awareness and training programs to educate staff about potential threats, phishing attacks, and safe online practices. By fostering a strong cybersecurity culture, businesses can reduce the likelihood of successful cyber attacks.

Emerging Innovations in Technology impacting Cybersecurity

Quantum Computing

Quantum computing has the potential to revolutionize both cryptography and hacking techniques. While it presents opportunities for more secure encryption algorithms, it also poses a threat to traditional cryptographic methods. Cybersecurity professionals need to stay updated on the developments in quantum computing to adapt their security measures accordingly.

Blockchain Technology

Blockchain offers decentralized and immutable data storage, enhancing security and transparency. Its applications in cybersecurity include secure identity management, secure transaction validation, and tamper-proof data storage. Organizations should explore the potential of blockchain technology to strengthen their cybersecurity defenses.

Internet of Things (IoT) Security

As the number of connected devices increases, securing the IoT ecosystem becomes crucial. Robust authentication mechanisms, secure communication protocols, and regular software updates are essential to protect IoT devices from being compromised and used as entry points for cyber attacks.

CHAPTER-16

RESOURCES FOR CYBERSECURITY PROFESSIONALS

Cybersecurity sites and blogs are a wealth of information, news, and ideas. They are provided by news organizations, magazines, websites, and some of the top industry professionals. Here are some of the best top cybersecurity blogs and sites.

Shostack and Friends

Shostack and Friends focuses on economics, privacy, and security in a group blog format.

AFCEA

SIGNAL Media provides news content about communications and information technology in the defense, intelligence, and global security communities. SIGNAL is from AFCEA, the Armed Forces Communications and Electronics Association.

CIO From IDG

CIO offers articles with insight and expertise on business strategy, innovation, and leadership. CIO is published by IDG, International Data Group.

CNET Cybersecurity

CNET Cybersecurity has the latest news on cybersecurity and IT issues. It's hosted by CNET, which is known for delivering the latest on tech, culture, and science.

Computer World Emerging Technology

Emerging Technology features news, how-tos, reviews, and videos from the tech world. It's presented by Computer World magazine, which is for IT and business technology professionals.

CSO From IDG

CSO provides news, analysis, and research on security and risk management for IT security professionals. It is another site presented by IDG.

Daniel Miessler

Daniel Miessler is a cybersecurity professional and writer in San Francisco. Besides a blog, Miessler's site offers a podcast, newsletter, tutorials, and IT projects.

Dark Reading

Dark Reading shares news about new cyberthreats, vulnerabilities, and technology trends. The site is an online community of thought-leading security researchers, chief information security officers, and technology specialists.

Data Insider

Data Insider a blog from Digital Guardian, offers articles on data protection, security, threat research, industry insights, and other cybersecurity issues

Forbes Cybersecurity

Forbes' Cybersecurity blog shares articles about security, hacking, malware, viruses, and other IT issues.

GlobalSign

GlobalSign's blog shares articles about security, IoT, quantum computing, and other IT issues. GlobalSign provides identity and security solutions.

Graham Cluley

Graham Cluley offers computer security news, advice, and opinion on his blog. Cluley is a public speaker and independent cybersecurity analyst who has worked in computer security since the early 1990s.

Infosecurity

Infosecurity shares hot topics and trends, in-depth news analysis, and opinion columns from industry experts. It is presented by Infosecurity Magazine.

ITProPortal

ITProPortal delivers news, reviews, and features about cybersecurity. The British site says it gathers, summarizes, and curates leading enterprise B2B technology stories and trends.

IT Security Guru

IT Security Guru shares articles about security, threat detection, data protection, hacking, and other tech issues. It's a daily digest of breaking IT security news stories.

Krebs On Security

Krebs On Security is a daily blog on cybersecurity and cybercrime. It's written by Brian Krebs, an American journalist and investigative reporter.

Mashable Cybersecurity

Mashable Cybersecurity collects articles that appear on its website. It delivers news on security, hacks, VPNs, and other IT issues.

Naked Security by Sophos

Naked Security provides news, opinion, advice, and research on computer security issues and the latest internet threats. It's provided by Sophos, a British security software and hardware company.

PC Magazine Security Reviews

PC Magazine Security Reviews gathers the latest news, reviews, and how-tos on cybersecurity. It's provided by PC Magazine, a leading authority on technology.

PC World Security

PC World Security gathers current news and reviews in the cybersecurity world. PC World has been an online-only magazine since 2013, after it started as a print magazine in 1983.

Purdue Global Information Technology

Purdue Global Information Technology blog provides career advice, tips for succeeding as an online student, trends in information technology, and guidance on growing your IT career.

SC Media

SC Media has news and reviews of a cybersecurity nature. SC has been sharing news and information about security since 1989.

Schneier On Security

Schneier On Security covers cybersecurity issues. It's written by Bruce Schneier, a fellow and lecturer at Harvard's Kennedy School and a self-described public-interest technologist.

Security Affairs

Security Affairs discusses cybersecurity, hacks, the deep web, malware, hacks, and other security subjects. It is hosted by Pierluigi Paganini, who writes for many security magazines and sites.

Security Bloggers Network

The Security Bloggers Network aggregates a wide range of information security blogs and podcasts that cover a range of topics including data protection, malware, ransomware, and more.

Security Weekly

Security Weekly has information about cybersecurity issues online. Security Weekly is a podcast network for the security community.

Tao Security

Tao Security is a blog on digital security, along with strategic thought and military history. It's written by Richard Bejtlich, a senior fellow in the Center for 21st Century Security and Intelligence.

TechCrunch Security

TechCrunch Security gathers the site's top articles on cybersecurity. TechCrunch reports on technology news, trends, and new tech businesses and products.

The Akamai Blog

The Akamai Blog discusses news, insights, and perspectives on the tech world. Akamai is a global content delivery network, cybersecurity, and cloud service company.

The Hacker News

The Hacker News provides coverage of data breaches, cyberattacks, vulnerabilities, malware, and other security issues. The site says it has over 8 million monthly readers.

The Last Watchdog

The Last Watchdog provides articles about cybersecurity, scams, and other digital issues. It's written by Pulitzer Prize-winning journalist Byron V. Acohido.

The Security Ledger

The Security Ledger explores the impact of cybersecurity on business, commerce, politics, and everyday life.

The State of Security

The State of Security shares articles about ransomware, cyberbullying, hacks, and other security topics. Its own staff and guest writers provide commentary, opinion, and other information.

Threatpost

Threatpost discusses the latest news on cloud security, malware, vulnerabilities, and other IT topics. It is intended for security professionals worldwide.

Troy Hunt

Troy Hunt writes about hacking, browser security, and other security issues. He is a Microsoft regional director and runs the website "Have I Been Pwned."

We Live Security

We Live Security provides articles about malware, scams, security, and other digital issues. It is hosted by ESET, a Slovakia-based company that specializes in malware detection and analysis.

Wired

Wired's Security page collects articles about cybersecurity from the website. Wired focuses on how emerging technologies affect culture, the economy, and politics.

ZDNet Zero Day

ZDNet's Zero Day shares the latest in security research, vulnerabilities, threats, and computer attacks. ZDNet is aimed at IT professionals.

Top Cybersecurity and Tech Podcasts

Cybersecurity and tech podcasts are a great way for IT professionals and students to learn more about their field. Most of the top tech podcasts can be heard on your laptop or on your phone with such software as **Apple Podcasts**, **Google Podcasts**, **Spotify**, **Stitcher**, or other apps.

Accidental Tech

Accidental Tech bills itself as "a tech podcast we accidentally created while trying to do a car show." It features news on tech, security, gaming, and other digital subjects.

Back to Work

Back to Work features talk about online productivity, communication, work, barriers, constraints, and tools. The podcast is presented as a talk show.

Clockwise

Clockwise is a freewheeling discussion of current technology issues. It features two hosts, two guests, and four topics, all under 30 minutes.

CyberWire Daily Podcast

The CyberWire Daily Podcast reviews the top cyber news each day of the week. Host Dave Bittner summarizes the day's stories.

Daring Fireball

Daring Fireball covers a wide range of digital topics. Recent episodes featured discussions about the state of automation on iOS and MacOS, Apple Watches, and USB-C iPhones.

Darknet Diaries

Darknet Diaries bills itself as a podcast about hackers, defenders, threats, malware, botnets, breaches, and privacy. It's run by Jack Rhysider, who ran security for a Fortune 500 company.

Digital Planet

Digital Planet is a weekly program from BBC about technological and digital news from around the world. Among the topics covered are privacy, facial recognition, and digital forensics.

Download This Show

Download This Show is a weekly Australian program about the latest in social media, consumer electronics, digital politics and other issues. Previous shows have discussed Google, Facebook, and streaming platforms.

Mac Power Users

Mac Power Users is about Apple technology and issues with it. Recent shows covered iOS 16, the M2 MacBook Air, iPhones, and the Apple Watch.

Note To Self

Note To Self focuses on the impact that technology has on everyday life. Subjects have included software surveillance, social media, and other issues.

Pivot

Pivot offers insights into the biggest stories in tech, business, and politics. It's hosted by Recode's Kara Swisher and NYU Professor Scott Galloway.

The Privacy, Security, & OSINT Show

The Privacy, Security, & OSINT Show not only provides a roundup of security topics but also interprets daily headlines through the lens of privacy and security.

Risky Business

Risky Business is a long-running podcast about a wide range of information security topics. In-depth analysis of stories and how they impact global security trends provide the backbone of the podcast.

Rocket

Rocket focuses on geek culture, including tech, comics, movies, games, and books.

SC Media Podcasts

SC Media Podcasts cover a variety of topics from several different hosts. Show topics have included end-to-end encryption, cyberspying, bots, and other current issues.

Security Now

Security Now has weekly episodes about the latest breaches, exploits, and other technical cybersecurity developments.

Security Weekly Network

Security Weekly Network features several cybersecurity podcasts. Shows cover enterprise, business, and application security, along with weekly security shows.

Tech Talker

Tech Talker is aimed at both tech professionals and those looking to enter the field. Shows have offered a look at the best iPhone apps, how to rescue a wet device, and other pieces of advice.

TechStuff

TechStuff is about the people, companies, and marketing behind tech, along with its effects on the world. Recent shows have discussed Twitter, whistleblowers, and national security.

The Daily Crunch Spoken Edition

The Daily Crunch Spoken Edition delivers the top startup and technology news from Techcrunch in an audio format.

The Vergecast

The Vergecast is a weekly show that looks at what's happening right now in the world of technology and gadgets.

This Week In Google

This Week In Google discusses the latest Google and cloud computing news. Show topics have included Google debit cards, Zoom security, and Zoom burnout.

This Week In Tech

This Week In Tech features top tech pundits in a roundtable discussion of the latest trends in high tech. Security and privacy issues are typical topics of discussion.

Unsupervised Learning

On Unsupervised Learning, host Daniel Miessler summarizes the top stories in the news related to cybersecurity, technology, and society.

What's New With Wired

What's New With Wired is a daily podcast exploring the ways technology is changing lives. Each day features new stories from Wired.

Wired

Wired features weekly podcasts on a variety of technology topics. Articles have featured discussions of VR, folding phones, and TikTok.

CYBERSECURITY EMPLOYMENT RESOURCES

Employment for cybersecurity professionals usually falls into one of two categories: government and private sector. Here are some of the agencies and companies that provide employment to cybersecurity and IT pros in both sectors.

Government

- **Central Intelligence Agency:** The CIA hires IT and cybersecurity professionals.
- **Department of Homeland Security Cybersecurity:** The DHS has jobs for cybersecurity analysts, among other tech fields.
- **Defense Information Systems Agency:** The DISA employs more than 7,000 civilians in 80 different career series worldwide.
- **Federal Bureau of Investigation:** The FBI is looking for experts in forensic science, computer technology, cybersecurity, and other fields.
- **Federal Reserve:** The central bank of the United States is looking for information technology pros, among other positions.
- **Government Accountability Office (GAO):** The GAO hires information technology management specialists, along with other digital positions.
- **National Security Agency:** Along with jobs for professionals, the NSA offers paid internships, scholarships, and co-op programs for students.
- **Air National Guard:** The Air National Guard is looking for "cyber surety" specialists to ensure the security of computer networks and online communications.

- **U.S. Army:** The Army's Cyber Command is looking for many computer professionals for its positions.

- **U.S. Marine Corps:** The Marines have support staff in IT and other online roles.

- **U.S. Navy:** The Navy is seeking technical computer scientists and computer engineers to become cyber warfare engineers.

- **U.S. Office of Personnel Management:** The federal government is looking to create a cybersecurity workforce.

Private Sector

- **Auth0:** Auth0 provides authentication and authorization for web, mobile, and legacy applications.

- **Duo Security:** Duo provides two-factor authentication and endpoint security for clients.

- **Everbridge:** Everbridge provides communications services for notifications of emergencies.

- **LogRhythm:** LogRhythm designs, develops and delivers cyberthreat solutions.

- **Keeper Security:** Keeper Security prevents password-related data breaches and cyberthreats.

- **MITRE Corporation:** MITRE manages federally funded research and development centers supporting several U.S. government agencies.

- **Ping Identity:** Ping Identity's software provides identity management and identity access management.

- **Rapid7:** Rapid7 provides technology, services and research for client security.

- **SailPoint:** SailPoint provides identity management and governance for unstructured data access.

CYBERSECURITY PROFESSIONAL ASSOCIATIONS

A number of professional associations strive to provide connections and resources for cybersecurity pros. They often provide continuing education and certification. Some also have student memberships. Here is a list of some of the top groups available.

- **(ISC)2:** (ISC)² is an international, nonprofit membership association for information security leaders.

- **Association for Executives in Healthcare Information Security:** AEHiS is an education and networking platform for senior IT security leaders in health care.

- **Center for Internet Security:** CIS is focused on enhancing cyber security in public and private sector entities.

- **Cloud Security Alliance:** The Cloud Security Alliance promotes the use of best practices for providing security assurance within cloud computing.

- **CompTIA:** CompTIA is a non-profit trade association that gives professional certifications for the IT industry. Student memberships are also available.

- **Executive Women's Forum:** The Executive Women's Forum links prominent and influential female executives in information security, risk management, and privacy.

- **ISACA:** ISACA (formerly the Information Systems Audit and Control Association) has been helping information security and IT professionals for 50 years.

- **Information Security Forum:** ISF is an independent, not-for-profit organization with members in many of the world's leading Fortune 500 organizations.

- **Information Security Research Association:** ISRA is one of the leading security research organizations in the information security industry.

- **Information Systems Security Association:** ISSA is an international organization of information security professionals and practitioners.

- **International Association for Cryptologic Research:** IACR is a scientific organization which aims to further research cryptology and related fields.

- **International Association of Security Awareness Professionals:** IASAP members develop and implement security awareness programs in their companies.

- **Internet Security Alliance:** ISA provides cybersecurity expert testimony and thought leadership in government and the media.

- **National Cybersecurity Society:** The NCSS focuses on providing cybersecurity education, awareness, and advocacy to small businesses.

- **Open Web Application Security Project:** OWASP is a nonprofit foundation that works to improve the security of software.

- **The Institute of Internal Auditors:** The IIA says it is the recognized authority, acknowledged leader, global voice, chief advocate, and principal educator in the internal audit profession.

- **Women in CyberSecurity:** WiCyS is dedicated to bringing together women in cybersecurity from academia, research, and industry to share knowledge, experience, networking, and mentoring.

BOT REMOVAL TOOLS

The term Botnet is comprised of the words "Robot" and "Network". A Botnet is a group of Internet connected devices that are affected by malware and connected in a coordinated manner to perform a malicious task. The affected device is called a "Bot" and is controlled by the hackers. Botnets are used to send spam, steal data, gain unauthorized access, and carry out Distributed Denial of Service (DDoS) attacks.

Impact of Botnet infection

The hackers constantly look out for ways to infect maximum number of devices which allows them to create a strong 'Bot Network' or 'Zombie Network'. With the Trojan virus, hackers breach the device security and implement command and control software allowing them to perform malicious activities. Following are the types of botnet attacks:

- DDoS attacks that takes down a machine/network resource temporarily or indefinitely
- Web application attack that allows to steal valuable information
- Credential stuffing attack that allows unauthorized access to user accounts
- Access to a user's device and its Internet connection

These Botnet networks are also made available for sale/rent by original owners on dark web leading to more cybercriminal activities around the world.

How can eScanAV CERT-In Toolkit help you?

As you know botnets can be used to launch different types of large-scale attacks, it is necessary that you protect your network with the perfect tool. To combat and nullify the botnet attacks and other cyberthreats, we are presenting you with the eScanAV CERT-In Toolkit with following capabilities :

- Detect, quarantine and remove latest botnet infection, virus, spyware, adware and malware

- View quarantined files and logs for old and current scan sessions

- Update virus signature database (Manual update)

- No interference with other Anti-Virus softwares or system performance

- Create and maintain detailed logs for all actions

To ensure that this solution reaches mass, we have made it compatible with multiple Windows versions wherein the user only has to download the eScanAV CERT-In Toolkit and run it. That's right. The eScanAV CERT-In toolkit needs no separate installation at all.

How to run the eScanAV CERT-In Toolkit?

Ensure that you have taken a backup of your files/folders to avoid unintentional data loss.

- Download the executable file.

- Free Download

- Right-click the downloaded file and select Run as Administrator. Package extraction process commences and then License Agreement window appears.

- Read the License terms, then select I accept the agreement and then click OK.

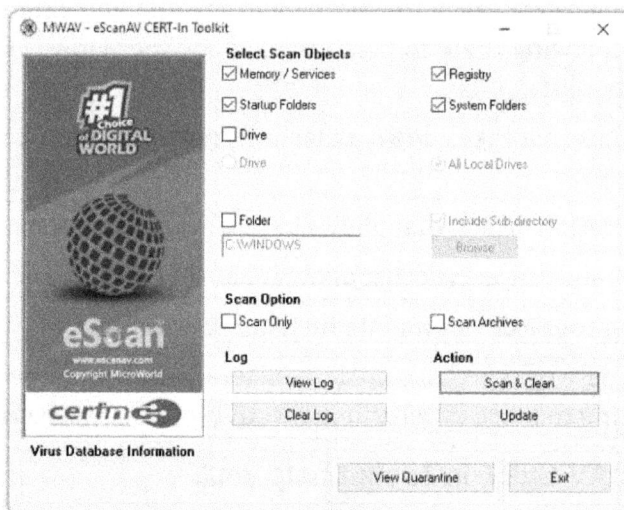

Perform the scan based on following types:

- **Quick Scan**: By default, the options Memory/Services, Registry, Startup folders and System folders are considered as Quick Scan. With Quick Scan, eScanAV CERT-In Toolkit detects if there are any active malicious processes and ends them. If eScanAV CERT-In Toolkit detects any infection, we recommend that you run a Full Scan.

- ◉ **Full Scan**: It lets you scan the computer's entire data by selecting the option by All local drives You can run this scan with and without selecting Quick Scan options.

- ◉ **Custom Scan**: It lets you scan the specific drive/folder and provides option to include subdirectory in scan. You can run this scan with and without selecting Quick Scan options.

GLOSSARY OF CYBERSECURITY TERMS

access control: The means and mechanisms of managing access to and use of resources by users. There are three primary forms of access control: DAC, MAC, and RBAC. DAC (Discretionary Access Control) manages access through the use of on-object ACLs (Access Control Lists), which indicate which users have been granted (or denied) specific privileges or permissions on that object. MAC (Mandatory Access Control) restricts access by assigning each subject and object a classification or clearance level label; resource use is then controlled by limiting access to those subjects with equal or superior labels to that of the object. RBAC (Role Base Access Control) controls access through the use of job labels, which have been assigned the permissions and privilege needed to accomplish the related job tasks. (Also known as authorization.)

Advanced Persistent Threat (APT): An advanced persistent threat, or APT, is a cybersecurity threat that establishes a long-term, unauthorized presence on a network or in a computer system. APTs pursue their objectives repeatedly and through multiple types of cyberattacks.

anti-virus (anti-malware): A security program designed to monitor a system for malicious software. Once malware is detected, the AV program will attempt to remove the offending item from the system or may simply quarantine the file for further analysis by an administrator. It is important to keep AV software detection databases current in order to have the best chance of detecting known forms of malware.

antivirus software: A software program that monitors a computer system or network communications for known examples of malicious code and then attempts to remove or quarantine the offending items. (Also known as Malware Scanner.) Most anti-virus (AV) products use a pattern recognition or signature matching system to detect the presence of known malicious code. Some AV products have adopted technologies to potentially detect new and unknown malware. These technologies include anomaly detection (i.e. watch for programs which violate specific rules), behavioral detection (i.e. watch for programs that have behaviors that are different from the normal baseline of behavior of the system), and heuristic detection (i.e. watch for programs that exhibit actions which are known to be those of confirmed malware; it is a type of technological profiling).

asset: Anything that is used in and is necessary to the completion of a business task. Assets include both tangible and intangible items such as equipment, software code, data, facilities, personnel, market value and public opinion.

attack vector: The term attack vector can be used to describe any technique a hacker uses to gain access to or harm a system.

authentication: The process of proving an individual is a claimed identity. Authentication is the first element of the AAA services concept, which includes Authentication, Authorization, and Accounting. Authentication occurs after the initial step of identification (i.e. claiming an identity). Authentication is accomplished by providing one or more authentication factors—Type 1: something you know (e.g. password, PIN, or combination), Type 2: something you have (e.g. smart card, RSA SecureID FOB, or USB drive), and Type 3: something you are (e.g. biometrics—fingerprint, iris scan, retina scan, hand geometry, signature verification, voice recognition, and keystroke dynamics).

authorization: The security mechanism determining and enforcing what authenticated users are authorized to do within a computer system. The dominant forms of authorization are DAC, MAC and RBAC. DAC (Discretionary Access Control) manages access using ACL (Access Control Lists) on each resource object where users are listed along with the permissions or privileges granted or denied them. MAC (Mandatory Access Control) manages access using labels of classification or clearance on both subjects and objects, and only those subjects with equal or superior clearance are allowed to access resources. RBAC (Role Based Access Control) manages access using labels of a job role that has been granted the permissions and privileges needed to accomplish a specific job or role.

backing up: Creating a duplicate copy of data onto a separate physical storage device or online/cloud storage solution. A backup is the only insurance against data loss. With a backup, damaged or lost data files can be restored. Backups should be created on a regular, periodic basis such as daily. A common strategy is based on the 3-2-1 rule: you should have three copies of your data - the original and 2 backups; you should use 2 different types of media (such as a physical media (such as a hard drive or tape) and a cloud storage solution); and do not store the three copies of data in 1 plane (i.e. backups should be stored offsite). It is important to store backups for disaster recovery at an offsite location in order to insure they are not damaged by the same event that would damage the primary production location. However, additional onsite backups can be retained for resolving minor issues such as accidental file deletion or hard drive failure.

BCP (Business Continuity Planning): A business management plan used to resolve issues that threaten core business tasks. (Also known as Business Continuity Management.) The goal of BCP is to prevent the failure of mission critical processes when they have be harmed by a breach or accident. Once core business tasks have been stabilized, BCP dictates the procedure to return the environment back to normal conditions. BCP is used when the normal security policy has failed to prevent harm from occurring, but before the harm has reached the level of fully interrupting mission critical processes, which would trigger the Disaster Recovery Process (DRP).

behavior monitoring: Recording the events and activities of a system and its users. The recorded events are compared against security policy and behavioral baselines to evaluate compliance and/or discover violations. Behavioral monitoring can include the tracking of trends, setting of thresholds and defining responses. Trend tracking can reveal when errors are increasing requiring technical support services, when abnormal load levels occur indicating the presence of malicious code, or when production work levels increase indicating a need to expand capacity. Thresholds are used to define the levels of activity or events above which are of concern and require a response. The levels below the threshold are recorded but do not trigger a response. Responses can be to resolve conflicts, handle violations, prevent downtime or improve capabilities.

blacklist: A security mechanism prohibiting the execution of those programs on a known malicious or undesired list of software. The blacklist is a list of specific files known to be malicious or otherwise are unwanted. Any program on the list is prohibited from executing while any other program, whether benign or malicious, is allowed to execute by default.

Blockchain: A system in which a record of transactions, especially those made in a cryptocurrency, is maintained across computers that are linked in a peer-to-peer network.

block cipher: A type of symmetric encryption algorithm that divides data into fixed length sections and then performs the encryption or decryption operation on each block. The action of dividing a data set into blocks enables the algorithm to encrypt data of any size.

botnet: A collection of innocent computers which have been compromised by malicious code in order to run a remote control agent granting an attacker the ability to remotely take advantage of the system's resources in order to perform illicit or criminal actions. These actions include DoS flooding attacks, hosting false Web services, spoofing DNS, transmitting SPAM, eavesdropping on network communications, recording VOIP communications and attempting to crack encryption or password hashes. Botnets can be comprised of dozens to over a million individual computers. The term botnet is a shortened form of robotic network.

bug: An error or mistake in software coding or hardware design or construction. A bug represents a flaw or vulnerability in a system discoverable by attackers and used as point of compromise. Attacks often use fuzzing technique (i.e. randomize testing tools) to locate previously unknown bugs in order to craft new exploits.

BYOD (Bring Your Own Device): A company's security policy dictating whether or not workers can bring in their own devices into the work environment, whether or not such devices can be connected to the company network and to what extent that connection allows interaction with company resources. A BYOD policy can range from complete prohibition of personal devices being brought into the facility to allowing any device to be connected to the company network with full access to all company resources. Generally, a BYOD policy puts reasonable security limitations on which devices can be used on company property and severely limits access to sensitive company network resources. BYOD should address concerns such as data ownership, asset tracking, geo location, patching and upgrades, security applications (such as malware scanners, firewalls and IDS), storage segmentation, appropriate vs inappropriate applications, on-boarding, off-boarding, repair/replacement due to damage, legal concerns, internal investigations and law enforcement investigations and forensics.

ciphertext: The unintelligible and seeming random form of data that is produced by the cryptographic function of encryption. Ciphertext is produced by a symmetric algorithm when a data set is transformed by the encryption process using a selected key. Ciphertext can converted back into its original form (i.e. plain text) by performing the decryption process using the same symmetric encryption algorithm and the key used during the encryption process. (Also known as cryptogram.)

clickjacking: A malicious technique by which a victim is tricked into clicking on a URL, button or other screen object other than that intended by or perceived by the user. Clickjacking can be performed in many ways; one of which is to load a web page transparently behind another visible page in such a way that the obvious links and objects to click are facades, so clicking on an obvious link actually causes the hidden page's link to be selected.

cloud computing: A means to offer computing services to the public or for internal use through remote services. Most cloud computing systems are based on remote virtualization where the application or operating environment offered to customers is hosted on the cloud provider's computer hardware. There are a wide range of cloud solutions including software applications (examples include e-mail and document editing), custom code hosting (namely execution platforms and web services) as well as full system replacements (such as remote virtual services to host databases or file storage). (See SaaS, PaaS, and IaaS.) Most forms of cloud computing are considered public cloud as they are provided by a third party. However, private cloud (internally hosted), community cloud (a group of companies' privately hosted cloud), a hosted private cloud (the cloud servers are owned and managed by a third party but hosted in the facility of the customer) and hybrid cloud (a mixture of public and private) are also options.

CND (Computer Network Defense): The establishment of a security perimeter and of internal security requirements with the goal of defending a network against cyberattacks, intrusions and other violations. A CND is defined by a security policy and can be stress tested using vulnerability assessment and penetration testing measures.

cracker: The proper term to refer to an unauthorized attacker of computers, networks and technology instead of the misused term "hacker." However, this term is not as widely used in the media; thus, the term hacker has become more prominent in-spite of the terms misuse. (See hacker.)

critical infrastructure: The physical or virtual systems and assets that are vital to an organization or country. If these systems are compromised, the result would be catastrophic. If an organization's mission critical processes are interrupted, this could result in the organization ceasing to exist. If a country's critical infrastructure is destroyed, it will have severe negative impact on national security, economic stability, citizen safety and health, transportation and communications.

Crypto Currency: A digital currency in which transactions are verified and records maintained by a decentralized system using cryptography, rather than by a centralized authority.

cryptography: The application of mathematical processes on data-at-rest and data-in-transit to provide the security benefits of confidentiality, authentication, integrity and non-repudiation. Cryptography includes three primary components: symmetric encryption, asymmetric encryption and hashing. Symmetric encryption is used to provide confidentiality. Asymmetric encryption is used to provide secure symmetric key generation, secure symmetric key exchange (via digital envelopes created through the use of the recipient's public key) verification of source, verification/control of recipient, digital signature (a combination of hashing and use of the sender's private key) and digital certificates (which provides third-party authentication services). Hashing is the cryptographic operation that produces a representational value from an input data set. A before and after hash can be compared in order to detect protection of or violation of integrity.

CVE (Common Vulnerabilities and Exposures): An online database of attacks, exploits and compromises operated by the MITRE organization for the benefit of the public. It includes any and all attacks and abuses known for any type of computer system or software product. Often new attacks and exploits are documented in a CVE long before a vendor admits to the issue or releases an update or patch to resolve the concern.

cyber ecosystem: The collection of computers, networks, communication pathways, software, data and users that comprise either a local private network or the world-wide Internet. It is the digital environment within which software operates and data is manipulated and exchanged.

cyber teams: Groups of professional or amateur penetration testing specialists who are tasked with evaluating and potentially improving the security stance of an organization. Common cyber teams include the red, blue and purple/white teams. A red team is often used as part of a multi-team penetration test (i.e. security evaluation), which is responsible for attacking the target which is being defended by the blue team. A purple team or white team is either used as a reference between the attack/red and defense/blue teams; or this team can be used as an interpreter of the results and activities of the red and blue teams in order to maximize their effectiveness in the final results.

cyberattack: Any attempt to violate the security perimeter of a logical environment. An attack can focus on gathering information, damaging business processes, exploiting flaws, monitoring targets, interrupting business tasks, extracting value, causing damage to logical or physical assets or using system resources to support attacks against other targets. Cyberattacks can be initiated through exploitation of a vulnerability in a publicly exposed service, through tricking a user into opening an infectious attachment, or even causing automated installation of exploitation tools through innocent website visits. (Also known as drive-by download.)

cyberespionage: The unethical act of violating the privacy and security of an organization in order to leak data or disclose internal/private/confidential information. Cyberespionage can be performed by individuals, organization or governments for the direct purpose of causing harm to the violated entity to benefit individuals, organizations or governments.

cybersecurity: The efforts to design, implement, and maintain security for an organization's network, which is connected to the Internet. It is a combination of logical/technical-, physical- and personnel-focused countermeasures, safeguards and security controls. An organization's cybersecurity should be defined in a security policy, verified through evaluation techniques (such as vulnerability assessment and penetration testing) and revised, updated and improved over time as the organization evolves and as new threats are discovered.

data breach: The occurrence of disclosure of confidential information, access to confidential information, destruction of data assets or abusive use of a private IT environment. Generally, a data breach results in internal data being made accessible to external entities without authorization.

data integrity: A security benefit that verifies data is unmodified and therefore original, complete and intact. Integrity is verified through the use of cryptographic hashing. A hashing algorithm generates a fixed length output known as a hash value, fingerprint or MAC (Message Authenticating Code), which is derived from the input data but which does not contain the input data. This makes hashing a one-way operation. A hash is calculated before an event, and another hash is calculated after the event (an event can be a time frame of storage (i.e. data-at-rest) or an occurrence of transmission (i.e. data-in-transit); the two hashes are then compared using an XOR Boolean operation. If the two hashes exactly match (i.e. the XOR result is zero), then the data has retained its integrity. However, if the two hashes do not match exactly (i.e. the XOR result is a non-zero value), then something about the data changed during the event.

data mining: The activity of analyzing and/or searching through data in order to find items of relevance, significance or value. The results of data mining are known as meta-data. Data mining can be a discovery of individual important data items, a summary or overview of numerous data items or a consolidation or clarification of a collection of data items.

data theft: The act of intentionally stealing data. Data theft can occur via data loss (physical theft) or data leakage (logical theft) event. Data loss occurs when a storage device is lost or stolen. Data leakage occurs when copies of data is possessed by unauthorized entities.

DDoS (Distributed Denial of Service) Attack: An attack which attempts to block access to and use of a resource. It is a violation of availability. DDOS (or DDoS) is a variation of the DoS attack (see DOS) and can include flooding attacks, connection exhaustion, and resource demand. The distinction of DDOS from DOS is that the attack traffic may originate from numerous sources or is reflected or bounced off of numerous intermediary systems. The purpose of a DDoS attack is to significantly amplify the level of the attack beyond that which can be generated by a single attack system in order to overload larger and more protected victims. DDoS attacks are often waged using botnets. (See botnet.)

decentralization: The transfer of control of an activity or organization to several local offices or authorities rather than one single one.

decrypt: The act which transforms ciphertext (i.e. the unintelligible and seeming random form of data that is produced by the cryptographic function of encryption) back into its original plaintext or cleartext form. Ciphertext is produced by a symmetric encryption algorithm when a data set is transformed by the encryption process using a selected key. Ciphertext can converted back into its original form (i.e. plaintext) by performing the decryption process using the same symmetric encryption algorithm and the same key used during the encryption process.

digital certificate: A means by which to prove identity or provide authentication commonly by means of a trusted third-party entity known as a certificate authority. A digital certificate is based on the x.509 v3 standard. It is the public key of a subject signed by the private key of a certificate authority with clarifying text information such as issuer, subject identity, date of creation, date of expiration, algorithms, serial number and thumbprint (i.e. hash value).

digital forensics: The means of gathering digital information to be used as evidence in a legal procedure. Digital forensics focuses on gathering, preserving and analyzing the fragile and volatile data from a computer system and/or network. Computer data that is relevant to a security breach and/or criminal action is often intermixed with standard benign data from business functions and personal activities. Thus, digital forensics can be challenging to properly collect relevant evidence while complying with the rules of evidence in order to ensure that such collected evidence is admissible in court.

DLP (Data Loss Prevention): A collection of security mechanisms which aim at preventing the occurrence of data loss and/or data leakage. Data loss occurs when a storage device is lost or stolen while data leakage occurs when copies of data is possessed by unauthorized entities. In both cases, data is accessible to those who should not have access. DLP aims at preventing such occurrences through various techniques such as strict access controls on resources, blocking the use of email attachments, preventing network file exchange to external systems, blocking cut-and-paste, disabling use of social networks and encrypting stored data.

DMZ (Demilitarized Zone): A segment or subnet of a private network where resources are hosted and accessed by the general public from the Internet. The DMZ is isolated from the private network using a firewall and is protected from obvious abuses and attacks from the Internet using a firewall. A DMZ can be deployed in two main configurations. One method is the screened subnet configuration, which has the structure of I-F-DMZ-F-LAN (i.e. internet, then firewall, then the DMZ, then another firewall, then the private LAN). A second method is the multi-homed firewall configuration, which has the structure of a single firewall with three interfaces, one connecting to the Internet, a second to the DMZ, and a third to the private LAN.

DOS (Denial of Service): An attack that attempts to block access to and use of a resource. It is a violation of availability. DOS (or DoS) attacks include flooding attacks, connection exhaustion and resource demand. A flooding attack sends massive amounts of network traffic to the target overloading the ability of network devices and servers to handle the raw load. Connection exhaustion repeatedly makes connection requests to a target to consume all system resources related to connections, which prevents any other connections from being established or maintained. A resource demand DoS repeatedly requests a resource from a server in order to keep it too busy to respond to other requests.

drive-by download: A type of web-based attack that automatically occurs based on the simple act of visiting a malicious or compromised/poisoned Web site. A drive-by download is accomplished by taking advantage of the default nature of a Web browser to execute mobile code, most often JavaScript, with little to no security restrictions. A drive-by download can install tracking tools, remote access backdoors, botnet agents, keystroke loggers or other forms of malicious utilities. In most cases, the occurrence of the infection based on the drive-by download is unnoticed by the user/victim.

eavesdropping: The act of listening in on a transaction, communication, data transfer or conversation. Eavesdropping can be used to refer to both data packet capture on a network link (also known as sniffing or packet capture) and to audio recording using a microphone (or listening with ears).

encode: The act which transforms plaintext or cleartext (i.e. the original form of normal standard data) into ciphertext (i.e. the unintelligible and seeming random form of data that is produced by the cryptographic function of encryption). Ciphertext is produced by a symmetric encryption algorithm when a data set is transformed by the encryption process using a selected key (i.e. to encrypt or encode). Ciphertext can converted back into its original form (i.e. plaintext) by performing the decryption process using the same symmetric encryption algorithm and the same key used during the encryption process (i.e. decrypt or decode).

Encryption key: The secret number value used by a symmetric encryption algorithm to control the encryption and decryption process. A key is a number defined by its length in binary digits. Generally, the longer the key length, the more security (i.e. defense against confidentiality breaches) it provides. The length of the key also determines the key space, which is the range of values between the binary digits being all zeros and all ones from which the key can be selected.

firewall: A security tool, which may be a hardware or software solution that is used to filter network traffic. A firewall is based on an implicit deny stance where all traffic is blocked by default. Rules, filters or ACLs can be defined to indicate which traffic is allowed to cross the firewall. Advanced firewalls can make allow/deny decisions based on user authentication, protocol, header values and even payload contents.

hacker: A person who has knowledge and skill in analyzing program code or a computer system, modifying its functions or operations and altering its abilities and capabilities. A hacker may be ethical and authorized (the original definition) or may be malicious and unauthorized (the altered but current use of the term). Hackers can range from professionals who are skilled programmers to those who have little to no knowledge of the specifics of a system or exploit but who can follow directions; in this instance, they are called script kiddies.

hacktivism: Attackers who hack for a cause or belief rather than some form of personal gain. Hacktivism is often viewed by attackers as a form of protest or fighting for their perceived "right" or "justice." However, it is still an illegal action in most cases when the victim's technology or data is abused, harmed or destroyed.

hashing: Hashing is the process of transforming any given key or a string of characters into another value.

honeypot: A trap or decoy for attackers. A honeypot is used to distract attackers in order to prevent them from attacking actual production systems. It is a false system that is configured to look and function as a production system and is positioned where it would be encountered by an unauthorized entity who is seeking out a connection or attack point. A honeypot may contain false data in order to trick attackers into spending considerable time and effort attacking and exploiting the false system. A honeypot may also be able to discover new attacks or the identity of the attackers.

IaaS (Infrastructure-as-a-Service): A type of cloud computing service where the provider offers the customer the ability to craft virtual networks within their computing environment. An IaaS solution enables a customer to select which operating systems to install into virtual machines/nodes as well as the structure of the network including use of virtual switches, routers and firewalls. It also provides complete freedom as to the software or custom code run on the virtual machines. An IaaS solution is the most flexible of all the cloud computing services; it allows for significant reduction in hardware by the customer in their own local facility. It is the most expensive form of cloud computing service.

identity cloning: A form of identity theft in which the attacker takes on the identity of a victim and then attempts to live and act as the stolen identity. Identity cloning is often performed in order to hide the birth country or a criminal record of the attacker in order to obtain a job, credit or other secured financial instrument.

identity fraud: A form of identity theft in which a transaction, typically financial, is performed using the stolen identity of another individual. The fraud is due to the attacker impersonating someone else.

IDS (Intrusion Detection System): A security tool that attempts to detect the presence of intruders or the occurrence of security violations in order to notify administrators, enable more detailed or focused logging or even trigger a response such as disconnecting a session or blocking an IP address. An IDS is considered a more passive security tool as it detects compromises after they are already occurring rather than preventing them from becoming successful.

information security policy: A written account of the security strategy and goals of an organization. A security policy is usually comprised of standards, policies (or SOPs – Standard Operating Procedures) and guidelines. All hardware, software, facilities and personnel must abide by the terms of the security policy of an organization. (Also known as security policy.)

insider threat: The likelihood or potential that an employee or another form of internal personnel may pose a risk to the stability or security of an organization. An insider has both physical access and logical access (through their network logon credentials). These are the two types of access that an outside attacker must first gain before launching malicious attacks whereas an insider already has both of these forms of access. Thus, an insider is potentially a bigger risk than an outsider if that insider goes rogue or is tricked into causing harm.

IPS (Intrusion Prevention System): A security tool that attempts to detect the attempt to compromise the security of a target and then prevent that attack from becoming successful. An IPS is considered a more active security tool as it attempts to proactively respond to potential threats. An IPS can block IP addresses, turn off services, block ports and disconnect sessions as well as notify administrators.

ISP (Internet Service Provider): The organization that provides connectivity to the Internet for individuals or companies. Some ISPs offer additional services above that of just connectivity such as e-mail, web hosting and domain registration.

JBOH (JavaScript-Binding-Over-HTTP): A form of Android-focused mobile device attack that enables an attacker to be able to initiate the execution of arbitrary code on a compromised device. A JBOH attack often takes place or is facilitated through compromised or malicious apps.

keylogger: Any means by which the keystrokes of a victim are recorded as they are typed into the physical keyboard. A keylogger can be a software solution or a hardware device used to capture anything that a user might type in including passwords, answers to secret questions or details and information form e-mails, chats and documents.

LAN (Local Area Network): An interconnection of devices (i.e. a network) that is contained within a limited geographic area (typically a single building). For a typical LAN, all of the network cables or interconnection media is owned and controlled by the organization unlike a WAN (Wide Area Network) where the interconnection media is owned by a third party.

link jacking: A potentially unethical practice of redirecting a link to a middle-man or aggregator site or location rather than the original site the link seemed to indicate it was directed towards. For example, a news aggregation service may publish links that seem as if they point to the original source of their posted articles, but when a user discovers those links via search or through social networks, the links redirect back to the aggregation site and not the original source of the article.

malware (malicious software): Any code written for the specific purpose of causing harm, disclosing information or otherwise violating the security or stability of a system. Malware includes a wide range of types of malicious programs including: virus, worm, Trojan horse, logic bomb, backdoor, Remote Access Trojan (RAT), rootkit, ransomware and spyware/adware.

outsider threat: The likelihood or potential that an outside entity, such as an ex-employee, competitor or even an unhappy customer, may pose a risk to the stability or security of an organization. An outsider must often gain logical or physical access to the target before launching malicious attacks.

outsourcing: The action of obtaining services from an external entity. Rather than performing certain tasks and internal functions, outsourcing enables an organization to take advantages of external entities that can provide services for a fee. Outsourcing is often used to obtain best-of-breed level service rather than settling for good-enough internal operations. It can be expensive and increases an organization's security risk due to the exposure of internal information and data to outsiders.

OWASP (Open Web Application Security Project): An Internet community focused on understanding web technologies and exploitations. Their goal is to help anyone with a website improve the security of their site through defensive programming, design and configuration. Their approach includes understanding attacks in order to know how to defend against them. OWASP offers numerous tools and utilities related to website vulnerability evaluation and discovery as well as a significant amount of training and reference material related to all things web security.

PaaS (Platform-as-a-Service): A type of cloud computing service where the provider offers the customer the ability to operate custom code or applications. A PaaS operator determines which operating systems or execution environments are offered. A PaaS system does not allow the customer to change operating systems, patch the OS or alter the virtual network space. A PaaS system allows the customer to reduce hardware deployment in their own local facility and to take advantage of on-demand computing (also known as pay as you go).

packet sniffing: The act of collecting frames or packets off of a data network communication. This activity allows the evaluation of the header contents as well as the payload of network communications. Packet sniffing requires that the network interface card be placed into promiscuous mode in order to disable the MAC (Media Access Control) address filter which would otherwise discard any network communications not intended for the specific local network interface. (Also known as sniffing or eavesdropping.)

patch management: The management activity related to researching, testing, approving and installing updates and patches to computer systems, which includes firmware, operating systems and applications. A patch is an update, correction, improvement or expansion of an existing software product through the application of new code issued by the vendor. Patch management is an essential part of security management in order to prevent downtime, minimize vulnerabilities and prevent new untested updates from interfering with productivity.

patch: An update or change or an operating system or application. A patch is often used to repair flaws or bugs in deployed code as well as introduce new features and capabilities. It is good security practice to test all updates and patches before implementation and attempt to stay current on patches in order to have the latest version of code that has the fewest known flaws and vulnerabilities.

payment card skimmers: A malicious device used to read the contents of an ATM, debit or credit card when inserted into a POS (Point of Sale) payment system. A skimmer may be an internal component or an external addition. An attacker will attempt to use whatever means to imbed their skimmer into a payment system that will have the highest likelihood of not being detected and thus gather the most amount of financial information from victims. (See POS intrusions.)

pen testing: A means of security evaluation where automated tools and manual exploitations are performed by security and attack experts. This is an advanced form of security assessment that should only be used by environments with a mature security infrastructure. A penetration test will use the same tools, techniques and methodologies as criminal hackers, and thus, it can cause downtime and system damage. However, such evaluations can assist with securing a network by discovering flaws that are not visible to automated tools based on human (i.e. social engineering) or physical attack concepts. (Also known as penetration testing or ethical hacking.)

phishing: A social engineering attack that attempts to collect information from victims. Phishing attacks can take place over e-mail, text messages, through social networks or via smart phone apps. The goal of a phishing attack may be to learn logon credentials, credit card information, system configuration details or other company, network, computer or personal identity information. Phishing attacks are often successful because they mimic legitimate communications from trusted entities or groups such as false emails from a bank or a retail website.

PKI (Public Key Infrastructure): A security framework (i.e. a recipe) for using cryptographic concepts in support of secure communications, storage and job tasks. A PKI solution is a combination of symmetric encryption, asymmetric encryption, hashing and digital certificate-based authentication.

POS (Point of Sale) intrusions: An attack that gains access to the POS (Point of Sale) devices at a retail outlet enabling an attacker to learn payment card information as well as other customer details. POS intrusions can occur against a traditional brick-and-mortar retail location as well as any online retail websites. (See payment card skimmers.)

ransomware: A form of malware that holds a victim's data hostage on their computer typically through robust encryption. This is followed by a demand for payment in the form of Bitcoin (an untraceable digital currency) in order to release control of the captured data back to the user.

restore: The process of returning a system back to a state of normalcy. A restore or restoration process may involve formatting the main storage device before re-installing the operating system and applications as well as copying data from backups onto the reconstituted system.

risk assessment: The process of evaluating the state of risk of an organization. Risk assessment is often initiated through taking an inventory of all assets, assigning each asset a value, and then considering any potential threats against each asset. Threats are evaluated for their exposure factor (EF) (i.e. the amount of loss that would be caused by the threat causing harm) and frequency of occurrence (i.e. ARO—Annualized Rate of Occurrence) in order to calculate a relative risk value known as the ALE (Annualized Loss Expectancy). The largest ALE indicates the biggest concern or risk for the organization.

risk management: The process of performing a risk assessment and evaluating the responses to risk in order to mitigate or otherwise handle the identified risks. Countermeasures, safeguards or security controls are to be selected that may eliminate or reduce risk, assign or transfer risk to others (i.e. outsourcing or buying insurance) or avoid and deter risk. The goal is to reduce risk down to an acceptable or tolerable level.

SaaS (Software-as-a-Service): A type of cloud computing service where the provider offers the customer the ability to use a provided application. Examples of a SaaS include online e-mail services or online document editing systems. A user of a SaaS solution is only able to use the offered application and make minor configuration tweaks. The SaaS provider is responsible for maintaining the application.

sandboxing: A means of isolating applications, code or entire operating systems in order to perform testing or evaluation. The sandbox limits the actions and resources available to the constrained item. This allows for the isolated item to be used for evaluation while preventing any harm or damage to be caused to the host system or related data or storage devices.

SCADA (Supervisory Control and Data Acquisition): A complex mechanism used to gather data and physical world metrics as well as perform measurement or management actions of the monitored systems for the purposes of automatic large complex real-world processes such as oil refining, nuclear power generation or water filtration. SCADA can provide automated control over very large complex systems whether concentrated in a single physical location or spread across long distances.

security control: Anything used as part of a security response strategy which addresses a threat in order to reduce risk. (Also known as countermeasure or safeguard.)

security perimeter: The boundary of a network or private environment where specific security policies and rules are enforced. The systems and users within the security boundary are forced into compliance with local security rules while anything outside is not under such restrictions. The security perimeter prevents any interactions between outside entities and internal entities that might violate or threaten the security of the internal systems.

SIEM (Security Information and Event Management): A formal process by which the security of an organization is monitored and evaluated on a constant basis. SIEM helps to automatically identify systems that are out of compliance with the security policy as well as to notify the IRT (Incident Response Team) of any security violating events.

sniffing: See packet sniffing and eavesdropping.

social engineering: An attack focusing on people rather than technology. This type of attack is psychological and aims to either gain access to information or to a logical or physical environment. A social engineering attack may be used to gain access to a facility by tricking a worker into assisting by holding the door when making a delivery, gaining access into a network by tricking a user into revealing their account credentials to the false technical support staff or gaining copies of data files by encouraging a worker to cut-and-paste confidential materials into an e-mail or social networking post.

SPAM: A form of unwanted or unsolicited messages or communications typically received via e-mail but also occurring through text messaging, social networks or VoIP. Most SPAM is advertising, but some may include malicious code, malicious hyperlinks or malicious attachments.

spear phishing: A form of social engineering attack that is targeted to victims who have an existing digital relationship with an online entity such as a bank or retail website. A spear phishing message is often an e-mail although there are also text message and VoIP spear phishing attacks as well, which looks exactly like a legitimate communication from a trusted entity. The attack tricks the victim into clicking on a hyperlink to visit a company website only to be re-directed to a false version of the website operated by attackers. The false website will often look and operate similarly to the legitimate site and focus on having the victim provide their logon credentials and potentially other personal identity information such as answers to their security questions, an account number, their social security number, mailing address, email address and/or phone number. The goal of a spear phishing attack is to steal identity information for the purpose of account takeover or identity theft.

spoof (spoofing): The act of falsifying the identity of the source of a communication or interaction. It is possible to spoof IP address, MAC address and email address.

spyware: A form of malware that monitors user activities and reports them to an external their party. Spyware can be legitimate in that it is operated by an advertising and marketing agency for the purpose of gathering customer demographics. However, spyware can also be operated by attackers using the data gathering tool to steal an identity or learn enough about a victim to harm them in other ways.

supply chain: The path of linked organizations involved in the process of transforming original or raw materials into a finished product that is delivered to a customer. An interruption of the supply chain can cause a termination of the production of the final product immediately or this effect might not be noticed until the materials already in transit across the supply chain are exhausted.

threat assessment: The process of evaluating the actions, events and behaviors that can cause harm to an asset or organization. Threat assessment is an element of risk assessment and management. (Also known as threat modeling and threat inventory.)

Trojan Horse (Trojan): A form of malware where a malicious payload is imbedded inside of a benign host file. The victim is tricked into believing that the only file being retrieved is the viewable benign host. However, when the victim uses the host file, the malicious payload is automatically deposited onto their computer system.

two-factor authentication: The means of proving identity using two authentication factors usually considered stronger than any single factor authentication. A form of multi-factor authentication. Valid factors for authentication include Type 1: Something you know such as passwords and PINs; Type 2: Something you have such as smart cards or OTP (One Time Password) devices; and Type 3: Someone you are such as fingerprints or retina scans (aka biometrics).

two-step authentication: A means of authentication commonly employed on websites as an improvement over single factor authentication but not as robust as two-factor authentication. This form of authentication requires the visitor provide their username (i.e. claim an identity) and password (i.e. the single factor authentication) before performing an additional step. The additional step could be receiving a text message with a code, then typing that code back into the website for confirmation. Alternatives include receiving an e-mail and needing to click on a link in the message for confirmation, or viewing a pre-selected image and statement before typing in another password or PIN. Two-step is not as secure as two-factor because the system provides one of the factors to the user at the time of logon rather than requiring that the user provide both.

unauthorized access: Any access or use of a computer system, network or resource which is in violation of the company security policy or when the person or user was not explicitly granted authorization to access or use the resource or system

virus: A form of malware that often attaches itself to a host file or the MBR (Master Boot Record) as a parasite. When the host file or MBR is accessed, it activates the virus enabling it to infect other objects. Most viruses spread through human activity within and between computers. A virus is typically designed to damage or destroy data, but different viruses implement their attack at different rates, speeds or targets. For example, some viruses attempt to destroy files on a computer as quickly as possible while others may do so slowly over hours or days. Others might only target images or Word documents (.doc/.docx).

vishing: A form of phishing attack which takes place over VoIP. In this attack, the attacker uses VoIP systems to be able to call any phone number with no toll-charge expense. The attacker often falsifies their caller-ID in order to trick the victim into believing they are receiving a phone call from a legitimate or trustworthy source such as a bank, retail outlet, law enforcement or charity. The victims do not need to be using VoIP themselves in order to be attacked over their phone system by a vishing attack. (See phishing.)

VPN (Virtual Private Network): A communication link between systems or networks that is typically encrypted in order to provide a secured, private, isolate pathway of communications.

vulnerability: Any weakness in an asset or security protection which would allow for a threat to cause harm. It may be a flaw in coding, a mistake in configuration, a limitation of scope or capability, an error in architecture, design, or logic or a clever abuse of valid systems and their functions.

whitelist: A security mechanism prohibiting the execution of any program that is not on a pre-approved list of software. The whitelist is often a list of the file name, path, file size and hash value of the approved software. Any code that is not on the list, whether benign or malicious, will not be able to execute on the protected system. (See blacklist.)

Wi-Fi: A means to support network communication using radio waves rather than cables. The current Wi-Fi or wireless networking technologies are based on the IEE 802.11 standard and its numerous amendments, which address speed, frequency, authentication and encryption.

worm: A form of malware that focuses on replication and distribution. A worm is a self-contained malicious program that attempts to duplicate itself and spread to other systems. Generally, the damage caused by a worm is indirect and due to the worm's replication and distribution activities consuming all system resources. A worm can be used to deposit other forms of malware on each system it encounters.

zombie: A term related to the malicious concept of a botnet. The term zombie can be used to refer to the system that is host to the malware agent of the botnet or to the malware agent itself. If the former, the zombie is the system that is blinding performing tasks based on instructions from an external and remote hacker. If the latter, the zombie is the tool that is performing malicious actions such as DoS flooding, SPAM transmission, eavesdropping on VoIP calls or falsifying DNS resolutions as one member of a botnet.

BIBLIOGRAPHY

1. Dasgupta, D., Shrein, J. M., & Gupta, K. D. (2019). A survey of blockchain from security perspective. *Journal of Banking and Financial Technology*, 3(1), 1-17.

2. Dawson, C.W, "The essence of computing projects, a students guide", Prentice Hall, 2000, Great Britain.

3. Goldfeder, S., Gennaro, R., Kalodner, H., Bonneau, J., Kroll, J. A., Felten, E. W., & Narayanan, A. (2015). Securing Bitcoin wallets via a new DSA/ECDSA threshold signature scheme.

4. Gorkhali, A., Li, L., & Shrestha, A. (2020). Blockchain: a literature review. Journal of Management Analytics, 7(3), 321-343.

5. Haber, S., & Stornetta, W. S. (1990, August). How to time-stamp a digital document. In Conference on the Theory and Application of Cryptography (pp. 437-455). Springer, Berlin, Heidelberg.

6. Hasanova, H., Baek, U. J., Shin, M. G., Cho, K., & Kim, M. S. (2019). A survey on blockchain cybersecurity vulnerabilities and possible countermeasures. International Journal of Network Management, 29(2), e2060.

7. Heilman, E., Kendler, A., Zohar, A., & Goldberg, S. (2015). Eclipse attacks on bitcoin's peer-to-peer network. In 24th {USENIX} Security Symposium ({USENIX} Security 15) (pp. 129-144).

8. Homoliak, I., Venugopalan, S., Reijsbergen, D., Hum, Q., Schumi, R., & Szalachowski, P. (2020). The Security Reference Architecture for Blockchains: Toward a Standardized Model for Studying Vulnerabilities, Threats, and Defenses. IEEE Communications Surveys & Tutorials, 23(1), 341-390.

9. Kan, Michael. "Chinese Firm Recalls Camera Products Linked To Massive DDOS Attack". PCWorld. N.p., 2017. Web. 19 Feb. 2017.

10. Lu, Z. (2018). The architecture of blockchain system across the manufacturing supply chain.

11. Minerva, R., Biru, A., & Rotondi, D. (2015). Towards a definition of the Internet of Things (IoT). IEEE Internet Initiative, Torino, Italy.

12. Mitrovic, P, "Handbok i IT-säkerhet" Pagina Förlags AB, Göteborg, Sweden, 2001

13. Mohanta, B. K., Jena, D., Panda, S. S., & Sobhanayak, S. (2019). Blockchain technology: A survey on applications and security privacy challenges. Internet of Things, 8, 100107. Money are challenging the global economic order". New York: St. Martin's Press.

14. Mosakheil, J. H. (2018). Security threats classification in blockchains.

15. Nakamoto, S., & Bitcoin, A. (2008). A peer-to-peer electronic cash system. *Bitcoin. –URL: https://bitcoin. org/bitcoin. pdf*, 4.

16. Natoli, C., & Gramoli, V. (2017, June). The balance attack or why forkable blockchains are ill-suited for consortium. In 2017 47th Annual IEEE/IFIP International Conference on Dependable Systems and Networks (DSN) (pp. 579-590). IEEE.

17. Okoli, C., & Schabram, K. (2010). A guide to conducting a systematic literature review of information systems research.

18. Olsson, F, "Trådlösa nätverk – WLAN i praktiken", Pagina Förlags AB 2002

19. Pfleeger, C P, "Security in computing", 2nd ed, Prentice Hall, New Jersey, USA, 2000

20. Saad, M., Spaulding, J., Njilla, L., Kamhoua, C., Shetty, S., Nyang, D., & Mohaisen, A. (2019). Exploring the attack surface of blockchain: A systematic overview. arXiv preprint arXiv:1904.03487.

21. Sayeed, S., & Marco-Gisbert, H. (2019). Assessing blockchain consensus and security mechanisms against the 51% attack. Applied Sciences, 9(9), 1788.

22. Shah, T., & Jani, S. (2018). Applications of blockchain technology in banking & finance. Parul University, Vadodara, India.

23. SIG Security 2001, "Säkerhet vid trådlös datakommunikation", Studentlitteratur, Lund, Sweden, 2001

24. Stallings, W, "Local and Metropolitan Networks", 6th ed, Prentice Hall, New Jersey, USA, 2000

25. Stallings, W, "Network and internetwork security principles and practice", Prentice-Hall, New Jersey, USA, 1995

26. Stallings, W, "Network security essentials – applications and standards" Prentice-Hall, New Jersey, USA, 2000

27. Stallings, W., & Brown, L. (2017). *Computer security: Principles and practice* (4th ed.). Pearson Education, Inc.

28. Stankovic, J. A. (2014). Research directions for the internet of things. IEEE Internet of Things Journal, 1(1), 3-9.

29. Stratopoulos, T. C., Wang, V. X., & Ye, J. (2020). Blockchain technology adoption. *Available at SSRN 3188470.*

30. Treleaven, P., Brown, R. G., & Yang, D. (2017). Blockchain technology in finance. *Computer*, *50*(9), 14-17.

31. Vigna, P. & Casey, M. (2015). "The age of cryptocurrency : / how bitcoin and digital

32. Vyas, C. A., & Lunagaria, M. (2014). Security concerns and issues for bitcoin. Int. J. Comput. Appl, 10-12.

33. Wadlow, T A, "The process of network security – Designing and managing a safe network", Addison-Wesley, Reading, Massachusetts, USA, 2000.

34. Wani, S., Imthiyas, M., Almohamedh, H., M Alhamed, K., Almotairi, S., & Gulzar, Y. (2021). Distributed Denial of Service (DDoS) Mitigation Using Blockchain—A Comprehensive Insight. Symmetry, 13(2), 227.

35. Webster, J., & Watson, R. T. (2002). Analyzing the past to prepare for the future: Writing a literature review. MIS quarterly, xiii-xxiii.

36. Yassein, M. B., Shatnawi, F., Rawashdeh, S., & Mardin, W. (2019, November). Blockchain Technology: Characteristics, Security and Privacy; Issues and Solutions. In 2019 IEEE/ACS 16th International Conference on Computer Systems and Applications (AICCSA) (pp. 1-8). IEEE.

37. Zhang, R., Xue, R., & Liu, L. (2019). Security and privacy on blockchain. ACM Computing Surveys (CSUR), 52(3), 1-34.

38. Zheng, Z., Xie, S., Dai, H., Chen, X., & Wang, H. (2017, June). An overview of blockchain technology: Architecture, consensus, and future trends. In 2017 IEEE international congress on big data (BigData congress) (pp. 557-564). IEEE.

INDEX